McGraw-Hill's

500 Organic Chemistry Questions

Also in McGraw-Hill's 500 Questions Series

McGraw-Hill's

500

Organic Chemistry Questions

Ace Your College Exams

Estelle Meislich, PhD
Herbert Meislich, PhD
Jacob Sharefkin, PhD

New York Chicago San Francisco Lisbon London Madrid Mexico City
Milan New Delhi San Juan Seoul Singapore Sydney Toronto

Estelle Meislich, PhD, earned her BS degree in chemistry from Brooklyn College and her MA and PhD in organic chemistry from Columbia University. She held a research assistantship in the Department of Neurology at Columbia Medical School, where she designed and synthesized the first antidote for a nerve gas. After teaching at City College of CUNY for many years, she moved to Bergen Community College, where she is now Professor Emeritus. She is the author of a laboratory manual for nurses and other allied health students as well as several papers in the *Journal of Chemical Education*.

Herbert Meislich, PhD, has his BA from Brooklyn College and MA and PhD from Columbia University. He is Professor Emeritus at the City College of CUNY, where he taught organic and general chemistry for 40 years at both the undergraduate and doctoral levels. He received the Outstanding Teacher Award in 1985. He has coauthored eight textbooks, three laboratory manuals in general and organic chemistry, and 15 papers on his research interests.

Jacob Sharefkin, PhD, is Professor Emeritus of Chemistry at Brooklyn College. After receiving his BS from City College of New York, he was awarded an MA from Columbia University and a PhD from New York University. His publications and research interests in qualitative organic analysis and organic boron and iodine compounds have been supported by grants from the American Chemical Society, for which he has also designed national examinations in organic chemistry.

Copyright © 2013 by The McGraw-Hill Companies, Inc. All rights reserved. Printed in the United States of America. Except as permitted under the United States Copyright Act of 1976, no part of this publication may be reproduced or distributed in any form or by any means, or stored in a database or retrieval system, without the prior written permission of the publisher.

1 2 3 4 5 6 7 8 9 10 11 12 13 14   QFR/QFR   1 9 8 7 6 5 4 3 2

ISBN   978-0-07-178965-3
MHID   0-07-178965-0

e-ISBN   978-0-07-178966-0
e-MHID   0-07-178966-9

Library of Congress Control Number: 2012951986

McGraw-Hill products are available at special quantity discounts to use as premiums and sales promotions or for use in corporate training programs. To contact a representative, please e-mail us at bulksales@mcgraw-hill.com.

This book is printed on acid-free paper.

CONTENTS

Introduction   vii

Chapter   1   **Structure and Properties**   1
Questions 1–22

Chapter   2   **Bonding and Molecular Structure**   5
Questions 23–44

Chapter   3   **Chemical Reactivity and Organic Reactions**   9
Questions 45–67

Chapter   4   **Alkanes**   15
Questions 68–89

Chapter   5   **Cycloalkanes**   18
Questions 90–110

Chapter   6   **Stereochemistry**   22
Questions 111–132

Chapter   7   **Alkenes**   26
Questions 133–157

Chapter   8   **Alkyl Halides**   31
Questions 158–178

Chapter   9   **Alkynes, Dienes, and Orbital Symmetry**   36
Questions 179–200

Chapter 10   **Aromaticity and Benzene**   40
Questions 201–221

Chapter 11   **Aromatic Substitution, Arenes**   44
Questions 222–246

Chapter 12   **Spectroscopy and Structure Proof**   49
Questions 247–271

Chapter 13   **Alcohols and Thiols**   59
Questions 272–291

Chapter 14   **Ethers, Epoxides, Glycols, and Thioethers**   63
Questions 292–311

Chapter 15 **Aldehydes and Ketones** **67**
Questions 312–332

Chapter 16 **Carboxylic Acids** **70**
Questions 333–354

Chapter 17 **Acid Derivatives** **76**
Questions 355–375

Chapter 18 **Carbanion-Enolates and Enols** **81**
Questions 376–397

Chapter 19 **Amines** **85**
Questions 398–419

Chapter 20 **Phenols and Their Derivatives** **90**
Questions 420–440

Chapter 21 **Aromatic Heterocyclic Compounds** **95**
Questions 441–460

Chapter 22 **Amino Acids, Peptides, and Proteins** **100**
Questions 461–480

Chapter 23 **Carbohydrates** **105**
Questions 481–500

Answers **109**

INTRODUCTION

You've taken a big step toward success in chemistry by purchasing *McGraw-Hill's 500 Organic Chemistry Questions.* We are here to help you take the next step and score high on your first-year exams!

This book gives you 500 exam-style questions that cover the most essential course material. Each question is clearly explained in the answer key. The questions will give you valuable independent practice to supplement your regular textbook and the ground you have already covered in your class.

This book and the others in the series were written by experienced teachers who know the subject inside and out and who can indentify crucial information as well as the kinds of questions that are most likely to appear on exams.

You might be the kind of student who needs to study extra before the exam for a final review. Or you might be the kind of student who puts off preparing until the last minute before the test. No matter what your preparation style, you will benefit from reviewing these 500 questions, which closely parallel the content and degree of difficulty of the questions on actual exams. These questions and the explanations in the answer key are the ideal last-minute study tool.

If you practice with all the questions and answers in this book, we are certain you will build the skills and confidence needed to excel in your exams.

—Editors of McGraw-Hill Education

McGraw-Hill's

500 Organic Chemistry Questions

CHAPTER 1

Structure and Properties

1. What are the important differences between organic and inorganic compounds?

2. What are the three important classes of organic compounds?

3. Specify the type of chemical bond in the following compounds:
   (A) Li_2O
   (B) PH_3
   (C) N_2O
   (D) CaF_2

4. How does the Lewis–Langmuir octet rule explain the formation of chemical bonds?

5. Identify donor and acceptor species in the formation of coordinate covalent bonds in the following:
   (A) H_3O^+
   (B) $Cu(NH_3)_4^{2+}$
   (C) $AgCl_2^-$
   (D) $H_3N:BF_3$

6. Write *electron-dot* structures for the following covalent compounds:
   (A) F_2O
   (B) H_2O_2
   (C) PCl_3
   (D) CH_3Cl
   (E) N_2H_4 (hydrazine)

7. Determine the positive or negative charge, if any, on the following:

(A)   H—C—Ö:
with H above and below C

(B)   H—C=Ö:
with H above C

(C)   H—C—C·
with H above and below each C

(D)   H—N—Ö—H
with H above and below N

(E)   :C—Cl:
with :Cl: above and :Cl: below C

8. Write structural formulas for the following:
   (A) HOCl
   (B) CH_3Br
   (C) HONO
   (D) ClCN

9. Write two isomeric structures with the molecular formula C_2H_6O.

10. Derive all structural formulas for the isomers of the following:
   (A) C_3H_8
   (B) C_4H_{10}
   (C) C_5H_{12}

11. Write structural formulas for all the C_4H_8 isomers.

12. Give structural formulas for cyclic compounds having the molecular formula C_5H_{10}.

13. Determine the formal charges on each atom in the following:
    (A) H:O:Cl
    (B) NH_4^+
    (C) $H_2O:BF_3$

14. Write Lewis structures with FCs for the following:
    (A) Nitric acid, $HONO_2$
    (B) Sulfuric acid, $HOSO_2OH$

15. With the aid of formal charges, determine which Lewis structure is more likely to be correct for each of the following molecules:
    (A) Cl_2O: $:\ddot{O} - \ddot{C}l - \ddot{C}l:$ *or* $:\ddot{C}l - \ddot{O} - \ddot{C}l:$
    (B) N_2O: $:N \equiv \overset{+}{N} - \ddot{\underset{..}{O}}:^-$ *or* $^-:\ddot{N} = \overset{+2}{O} = \ddot{N}:^-$

16. (A) Define a *functional group*.
    (B) Why are functional groups important in organic chemistry?

17. (A) Write the structure for a 3-C carboxylic acid.
    (B) Show structures for the following derivatives of this acid:
        I. an ester
        II. an acid chloride
        III. an amide

18. Analysis of a compound **A** gives 92.25% C and 7.743% H. Calculate the following:
    (A) its empirical formula
    (B) its molecular formula
    The molecular weight (MW) is determined to be 78.11g/mol.

19. An 11.75-g sample of a hydrocarbon is volatilized at 1-atm pressure and 100°C to a gas that occupies 5.0 L. What is its MW? ($R = 0.0821$ L · atm/ mol · K)

20. Complete combustion of 0.858 g of compound **X** gives 2.63 g of CO_2 and 1.28 g of H_2O.
    (A) Find the % composition of **X**.
    (B) What is the lowest MW it can have?

21. The molal freezing point depression constant for camphor as a solvent is 40°C kg/mol. Pure camphor melts at 179°C. When 0.108 g of compound **A** is dissolved in 0.90 g of camphor, the solution melts at 166°C. Find the molecular weight of **A**.

22. In a nitration of benzene, 10.0 g of benzene gave 13.2 g of nitrobenzene.

(A) What is the *theoretical yield* of nitrobenzene?

(B) What is the *percentage yield*?

CHAPTER 2

Bonding and Molecular Structure

23. Give the relationship between the principal energy level (shell), n, and
    (A) the maximum number of e^-s in a shell
    (B) the number of sublevels (subshells) in a shell
    (C) For the third shell ($n = 3$), give
        I. the maximum number of electrons
        II. the number of subshells

24. (A) Give the shape and draw the cross section of the following:
        I. a $1s$ AO
        II. a $2p$ AO
    (B) How are these shapes determined?
    (C) State whether an electron can ever be in the nucleus of an atom with
        I. an s AO
        II. a p AO
    (D) Respond to the question, "How can an e^- move from one lobe of a p AO to the other lobe without passing through the nucleus?"

25. (A) State the *Aufbau* (German for "building up") *principle* for filling orbitals with electrons.
    (B) State and explain *Hund's rule* for filling orbitals.
    (C) Give the electron distribution for a ground state C atom that
        I. follows Hund's rule
        II. does not follow Hund's rule
    (D) If individual C atoms could be isolated (they cannot be), what different physical properties would separate the two electron distributions given in (C)?
    (E) Which are the valence electrons?

26. Draw an energy diagram showing the relationship between two AOs and the MOs resulting from their combination.

27. Sketch the combination of the needed AOs to form the following MOs:
(A) σ_s (sigma)
(B) σ_{sp}
(C) π_y (pi)

28. Sketch the formation of the following MOs:
(A) σ_s^*
(B) σ_{sp}^*
(C) π_y^*

29. (A) How are electrons distributed in the MOs when two atoms interact to form a bond?
(B) Illustrate (A) with H_2^+, H_2, H_2^-, HHe, and He_2. Give the symbolism for the molecular orbital electronic structure.
(C) How can a MO electronic structure be used to predict whether these (or any species) can exist?
(D) Which, if any, do not exist?
(E) List each substance in decreasing order of stability.

30. (A) Define the term *bond order*.
(B) Give the bond order of C_2, N_2, O_2, NO, CN^-.

31. (A) Account for the observed bond angles of
I. 107° in NH_3
II. 105° in H_2O
(B) Could N and O use ground state AOs to form equivalent bonds?
(C) Why do N and O use HOs for bonding?

32. (A) Give the HO used by N and C.
(B) Predict its shape for each of the following:
I. NH_4^+
II. CH_3NH_2
III. $H_2C{=}O$
IV. $H_2C{=}NH$
V. $HC{\equiv}N$

33. What kinds of hybrid orbitals are predicted for the underlined atom?
    (A) H$_2$$\underline{N}$OH
    (B) H$_2$$\underline{S}$
    (C) $\underline{B}$F$_4^-$
    (D) HO$\underline{C}$≡$\underline{N}$
    (E) O=$\underline{C}$=O
    (F) H$_2$$\underline{C}$=$\underline{C}$=O

34. (A) Arrange the gaseous hydrogen halides in order of decreasing dipole moments and rationalize your order.
    (B) The dipole moments for the methyl halides are: CH$_3$F, 1.82 D; CH$_3$Cl, 1.94 D; CH$_3$Br, 1.79 D; and CH$_3$I, 1.64 D. Explain.

35. *Organometallics* are compounds containing C—metal bonds. Metals typically have low electronegativity values, and the C—metal bond moment is toward the more electronegative C.
    (A) What generalization can be made as to the nature of the C—metal bond and the electronegativity of the metal?
    (B) State the kind of bond you would expect between C and
        I. an alkali metal
        II. a group 2 metal
        Give an example of each.
    (C) Give an example of a C—metal bond that contains little or no ionic character. (Refer to a table of electronegativity values, if necessary.)

36. The usual ONs of the following atoms are given: for H, +1; for O, −2; and for halogens (X), −1. Determine the ON of the underlined atom in each species:
    (A) $\underline{C}$O$_2$
    (B) $\underline{P}$Cl$_3$
    (C) $\underline{N}_2$O$_5$
    (D) $\underline{S}$O$_3^{2-}$
    (E) $\underline{N}$H$_4^+$

37. (A) How does the oxidation number reveal whether a substance has undergone oxidation or reduction?
    (B) Identify the following changes as oxidations, reductions, or neither.
        I. CH$_4$ → CH$_3$OH
        II. H$_2$CCl$_2$ → H$_2$C=O
        III. H$_2$C=CH$_2$ → H$_3$CCH$_3$
        IV. HC≡CH → CH$_3$C=O
                              |
                              H

38. Define the three types of intermolecular forces that can lead to interactions between neutral molecules, in order of decreasing strength.

39. The boiling point of H_2O (100°C) is much higher than that of HF (−83°C), even though they both form H bonds and have similar molecular weights. Explain.

40. The three isomeric pentanes, C_5H_{12}, have boiling points of 9.5, 28, and 36°C. Match each boiling point with the correct structure and give your reasons.

41. (A) Differentiate between structural isomers and *contributing* (*resonance*) structures.

   (B) What is a resonance hybrid?

42. Write resonance structures for the following substances, showing all outer-shell electrons and formal charges when present:

   (A) formate ion, HCO_2^-

   (B) nitrite ion, NO_2^-

   (C) formaldehyde, H_2CO

   (D) nitrate ion, NO_3^-

43. (A) Describe the resonance hybrid of

   I. NO_2^-

   II. NO_3^-

   in terms of overlapping atomic orbitals.

   (B) What is meant by the term *delocalization* (*resonance*) *energy*?

   (C) Compare the delocalization (resonance) energies (*stabilities*) of NO_2^- and NO_3^-.

44. Explain why each of the following structures is not a resonance form.

   (A) $:\ddot{O}{=}\ddot{O}:$ and $:\ddot{O}{-}\ddot{O}:$

   (B) $H_2\ddot{N}{-}O{-}H$ and $H_2\ddot{N}{=}O{-}H$

   (C) $CH_3{-}\underset{\underset{OH}{|}}{C}{=}CH_2$ and $CH_3{-}\underset{\overset{\|}{O}}{C}{-}CH_3$

CHAPTER 3

Chemical Reactivity and Organic Reactions

45. Classify each of the following carbon intermediates:

(A) $C_2H_5\overset{..}{C}$ — H

(B) $(CH_3)_3C\cdot$

(C) $CH_3\overset{..}{C}HCH_3$

(D) $H_2C = CH$ — CH_2^+

46. Supply the structure and type for the intermediate species designated by:

(A) $CH_3CH(OH)CH_3 + H^+ \xrightarrow{\text{heat}} ? + H:\overset{..}{\underset{..}{O}}:H$

(B) CH_3 — $CH = CH$ — $CH_3 + H:\overset{..}{\underset{..}{I}}: \longrightarrow ? + :\overset{..}{\underset{..}{I}}:^-$

(C) CH_3CH_2 — $N = N$ — $CH_2CH_3 \xrightarrow{\text{heat}} ? + :N:::N:$

(D) $CH_3CHI_2 + Zn \longrightarrow ? + ZnI_2$

(E) $CH_3CH_2Cl + AlCl_3 \longrightarrow ? + [AlCl_4]^-$

(F) CH_3 — $C \equiv C:H + Na^+:\overset{..}{N}H_2^- \longrightarrow ? Na^+ + H:\overset{..}{N}H_2$

(G) CH_3 — $\overset{+}{N} \equiv N: \longrightarrow ? + :N:::N:$

47. (A) What is the major factor that influences the relative stabilities of carbanions, radicals, and carbocations?

(B) Define the term *inductive effect*.

(C) How does the inductive effect of alkyl group affect the stability of these three intermediates?

48. Give the type of each of the following reactions. (A reaction may belong to more than one type.)

(A) $H_2C=CH_2 + Br_2 \longrightarrow H_2CBr-CH_2Br$

(B) $HO:^- + CH_3Cl \longrightarrow CH_3OH + Cl^-$

(C) $Me_2NH_2^+ + CH_3O^- \longrightarrow Me_2NH + CH_3OH$

(D) $CHCl_3 + OH^- \longrightarrow :CCl_2 + H_2O + Cl^-$

(E) 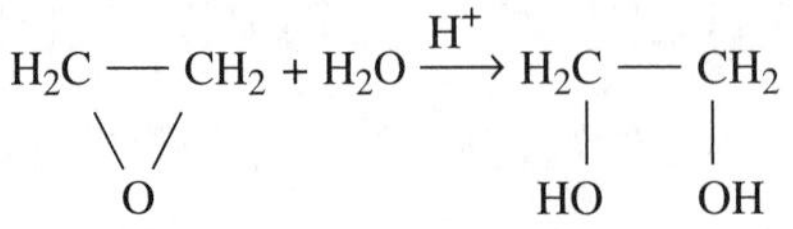 $H_2C-CH_2 + H_2O \xrightarrow{H^+} H_2C-CH_2$

      $\backslash / $ | |

        O   HO   OH

(F) $CH_3CHBrCHBrCH_3 + Zn \longrightarrow CH_3CH=CHCH_3 + ZnBr_2$

(G) $(NH_4)^+ (NCO)^- \longrightarrow O=C(NH_2)_2$

(H) $C_6H_6 + Cl_2 \xrightarrow{Fe} C_6H_5Cl + HCl$

(I) 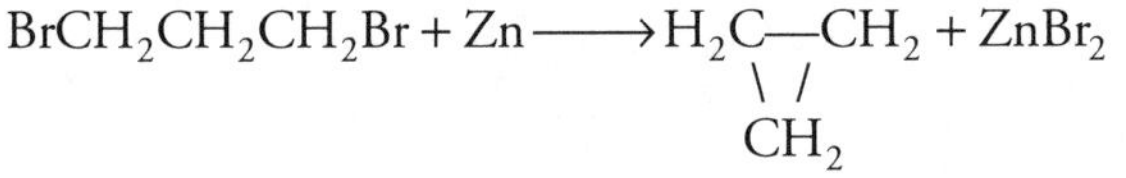 $BrCH_2CH_2CH_2Br + Zn \longrightarrow H_2C-CH_2 + ZnBr_2$

                                        $\backslash / $

                                     CH_2

(J) $H_3C-N=N-CH_3 \xrightarrow{heat} H_3CCH_3 + N_2$

(K) 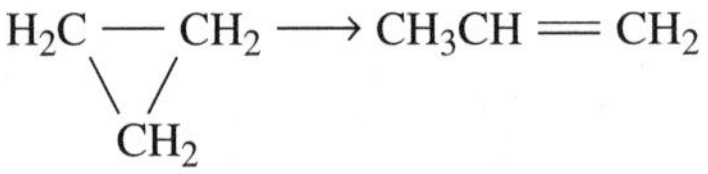 $H_2C-CH_2 \longrightarrow CH_3CH=CH_2$

       $\backslash / $

        CH_2

49. The following equation represents the mechanistic steps for chlorination of methane:

Initiation step: 1. $:\ddot{C}l:\ddot{C}l: \xrightarrow{energy} :\ddot{C}l\cdot + \cdot\ddot{C}l:$

Propagation steps: 2. $H_3C:H + \cdot\ddot{C}l: \longrightarrow H_3C\cdot + H:\ddot{C}l:$

                         3. $H_3C\cdot + :\ddot{C}l:\ddot{C}l: \longrightarrow H_3C:\ddot{C}l: + \cdot\ddot{C}l:$

(A) Write the equation for the overall reaction obtained from the sum of the propagation steps 2 and 3, and give its classification.

(B) List the intermediates in all the steps.

(C) Which steps are homolytic?

(D) Classify step 1.

(E) List the displacement steps.

(F) Are any of the steps additions?

(G) Which step follows step 3?

(H) Name the reactions whose steps keep repeating themselves.

(I) Write an equation for the formation of a by-product from the collision of intermediates. Classify this reaction.

50. Identify the species I and II as electrophiles (E) or nucleophiles (Nu) in the following reactions:

Species I	Species II	
(A) $(CH_3)_2\overset{..}{O}:$	$+ BMe_3$	$\longrightarrow (CH_3)_2 \overset{+}{\underset{..}{O}}\!-\!\overset{-}{B}Me_3$
(B) $:CN:^-$	$+ CH_3Br$	$\longrightarrow H_3C{:}CN+{:}\overset{..}{\underset{..}{Br}}{:}^-$
(C) $H{:}C{\equiv}C{:}H$	$+ :\overset{..}{N}H_2^-$	$\longrightarrow H{:}C{\equiv}C{:}^- + H{:}\overset{..}{N}H_2$
(D) C_2H_5Br	$+ AlBr_3$	$\longrightarrow [C_2H_5]^+ [AlBr_4]^-$
(E) $CH_3CH{=}O + :SO_3H^-$ (bisulfite anion)		$\longrightarrow CH_3CH{-}SO_3H$

$$CH_3CH\!\!\underset{\displaystyle O^-}{\overset{\displaystyle |}{}}\!\!SO_3H$$

51. (A) Identify the acids and bases and the conjugate acid-base pairs when

   I. CH_3COOH

   II. CH_3NH_2

   dissociate in water.

   (B) What generalization can be made about the net direction of the acid-base equilibrium?

   (C) Draw a conclusion about the acid-base behavior of H_2O.

52. Identify reactants I and II as a Lewis acid A or Lewis base B in the following:

Reactant I	Reactant II	
(A) $CH_3CH{=}O + H^+$ (from a Brönsted acid)		$\longrightarrow CH_3CH{=}OH^+$
(B) $H_2C{=}O$	$+ :NH_3$	$\longrightarrow H_2C{-}O^-$

$$\overset{\displaystyle H_2C-O^-}{\underset{\displaystyle \overset{+}{N}H_3}{|}}$$

| (C) $O{=}C{=}O$ | $+ OH^-$ | $\longrightarrow O{=}C{-}O^-$ |

$$\overset{\displaystyle O=C-O^-}{\underset{\displaystyle OH}{|}}$$

(D) SiF_4	$+ 2:\overset{..}{\underset{..}{F}}:^-$	$\longrightarrow [SiF_6]^{2-}$
(E) Ag^+	$+ 2:\overset{..}{N}H_3$	$\longrightarrow [Ag(NH_3)_2]^+$
(F) $(CH_3)_3N:$	$+ BF_3$	$\longrightarrow (CH_3)_3 \overset{+}{N}\!-\!\overset{-}{B}F_3$

53. Discuss how

   (A) acid strength is related to K_a, the acid ionization constant, and to pK_a

   (B) base strength is related to K_b, the base ionization constant, and to pK_b

   The values of pK_a and pK_b are defined as $-\log K_a$ and $-\log K_b$, respectively.

54. Account for the greater acidity of acetic acid, CH_3COOH (abbreviated HOAc), in water than in methanol, MeOH.

55. Compare the following:
   (A) the acid strengths of CH_3COOH, $ClCH_2COOH$, $Cl_2CHCOOH$, and Cl_3CCOOH
   (B) the base strengths of their conjugate bases

56. Account for the fact that, unlike other amines (RNH_2), guanidine, $H_2\ddot{N}$—C—$\ddot{N}H_2$, is a strong base.

$\quad\quad\quad\quad\quad\quad\quad\parallel$

$\quad\quad\quad\quad\quad\quad$:NH

57. (A) Which thermodynamic function is most often used in organic chemistry to express the heat of a reaction?
   (B) Give the sign of ΔH for an
    I. exothermic
    II. endothermic reaction
   (C) Give the algebraic sign of ΔH for a reaction involving
    I. breaking
    II. formation of covalent bonds
   (D) Give the symbol used for change in enthalpy for reactions whose participating compounds are in their standard state.

58. (A) Define bond-dissociation energy.
   (B) Find the algebraic sign of the ΔH values used for
    I. bond-dissociation energies, ΔH_d
    II. bond formation
   (C) What is the difference between bond-dissociation energy and bond energy?
   (D) Which value is found in most tables?
   (E) How are bond strengths and ΔH values related?

59. (A) Use the bond-dissociation energy values, given in kcal/mol in parentheses, to calculate the heat of reaction, ΔH_r, for monobromination of methane:

$$H_3C - H\,(102) + Br - Br\,(46) \longrightarrow H_3C - Br\,(70) + H - Br\,(88)$$

   (B) Is this reaction endothermic or exothermic?

60. Find ΔH_r for the following reaction, and decide whether it is exothermic or endothermic. The values in parentheses are, as usual, in kJ/mol.

$$H_2C{=}CH_2(590)+H{-}H(435)\longrightarrow H_3C{-}CH_3\,(\text{for C}{-}\text{C}, 368; \text{ for C}{-}\text{H}, 410)$$

61. (A) Define standard heat of formation, ΔH_f°.

(B) Write the equation for the ΔH_f° formation of acetylene, C_2H_2.

(C) Calculate ΔH_f° for C_2H_2 from the following thermochemical combustion equations (complete oxidations with O_2), where (g) and (l) are for gas and liquid, respectively.

I. $C_2H_2(g)+2.5O_2(g)\longrightarrow 2CO_2(g)+H_2O(l)$ $\Delta H^\circ=-1300$ kJ/mol

II. $C(\text{graphite})+O_2(g)\longrightarrow CO_2(g)$ $\Delta H^\circ=-394$ kJ/mol

III. $H_2(g)+0.5O_2(g)\longrightarrow H_2O(l)$ $\Delta H^\circ=286$ kJ/mol

Note that fractional numbers of moles of O_2 are used in these equations in order to have 1 mol of the compound oxidized. This is done because the ΔH°'s are given per mole of reactant oxidized.

(D) What can be said about the chemical stability of acetylene?

62. Calculate ΔG° for monochlorination of methane ($K_e = 4.8\times10^{18}$ at standard conditions and 25°C).

63. From the signs of ΔH and $T\Delta S$ tabulated below for reactions (A)–(D) predict the sign of ΔG, the direction in which the reaction proceeds, and whether K_e is more or less than 1.

	ΔH	$T\Delta S$
(A)	–	+
(B)	+	–
(C)	–	–
(D)	+	+

64. (A) Use the experimentally determined effect of changes in concentration on reaction rates to find the rate equation for each of the following two reactions of alkyl bromides with OH^-, carried out in an acetone-H_2O mixture as solvent.

Reaction 1:

$$CH_3Br + OH^- \longrightarrow Br^- + CH_3OH$$

Doubling the molar concentration of either CH_3Br or OH^- doubles the reaction rate; doubling both quadruples the rate.

Reaction 2:

$$(CH_3)_3CBr + OH^- \longrightarrow Br^- + (CH_3)_3COH$$

The reaction rate is doubled when $[(CH_3)_3CBr]$ is doubled but is unaffected by changes in $[OH^-]$.

(B) Explain the difference in reaction orders of the two reactions since both are conversions of alkyl bromide to alcohol.

65. Write an equation showing the TS in the abstraction of an H · from CH_4 by Cl · to form H_3C · and HCl.

66. (A) Draw an enthalpy (energy) diagram for a reversible one-step exothermic reaction: $A + B \rightarrow C + D$.

   (B) Compare the relative values of $\Delta H^{\ddagger}_{forward} (\Delta H^{\ddagger}_{for})$ and $\Delta H^{\ddagger}_{reverse} (\Delta H^{\ddagger}_{rev})$.

   (C) Are $\Delta H^{\ddagger}$ and ΔH_r related?

67. Suggest a mechanism involving only unimolecular or bimolecular steps for the following reaction:

$$2A + 2B \longrightarrow C + D; \qquad \text{rate} = k[A]^2[B]$$

CHAPTER 4

Alkanes

68. (A) What is the general formula for an alkane?

    (B) Give the molecular formulas for alkanes with

        I. four Cs

        II. seven Cs

        III. 10 Cs

        IV. 22 Cs

    (C) Give the names of the alkanes having from 1 to 7 carbon atoms in a continuous chain.

69. (A) Provide a structural formula for $CH_3CH_2C(CH_3)_2CH_2CH(CH_3)_2$, and define and identify all the *primary* (1°), *secondary* (2°), *tertiary* (3°), and *quaternary* (4°) Cs.

    (B) Identity all the 1°, 2°, and 3° Hs.

    (C) Give the number of H atoms bonded to a 1°, 2°, 3°, and 4° carbon atom in an alkane.

    (D) Give the number of C atoms bonded to a 1°, 2°, 3°, and 4° carbon atom in an alkane.

70. Write the structural formulas for each of the following compounds:

    (A) 3-Chloro-2-methylhexane

    (B) 2, 3, 4-Trimethylpentane

    (C) 1, 4-Dibromo-2-methylbutane

    (D) 2, 2-Dimethylpentane

    (E) 4-Isopropylheptane

71. Provide the IUPAC names for each of the following:
    (A) $(CH_3)_3CCH_2C(CH_3)_3$
    (B) $C(CH_3)_4$
    (C) $CH_3C(Cl)_2CH(CH_3)_2$
    (D) $(CH_3CH_2)_2CHCH(CH_3)CH_2CH_3$

72. Write structural formulas for the five isomeric hexanes, and name them by the IUPAC system.

73. Derive the structural formulas and give the IUPAC names for all dibromo derivatives of propane.

74. Place each of the following alkanes in order of corresponding increasing boiling point (bp°C), and give your reason for the order: pentane, hexane, and 2,3-dimethylbutane.

75. (A) Predict which compound in each of the following pairs has the higher bp and give your reason:
    I. Pentane and 1-chloropentane
    II. 2-Methylhexane and 2,2-dimethylpentane
    (B) Both CF_4 and hexane are nonpolar and have approximately the same molecular weight, yet CF_4 has a much lower bp (−129°C) than hexane (68°C). Explain.

76. The energy barrier (ΔH) to rotation about the C—C bond in ethane is about 3 kcal/mol at room temperature.
    (A) Draw a diagram showing the variation in energy with the rotation through 180° about the C—C bond of ethane.
    (B) Assuming the contribution to ΔG of the entropy is negligible, calculate the distribution of staggered and eclipsed conformations at 25°C.

77. Draw the conformational isomers of methanol, CH_3OH, an organic alcohol.

78. (A) Define the dihedral angle.
    (B) What are the values of the dihedral angles in the staggered and the eclipsed conformations in ethane?
    (C) Draw *Newman-projection* structures of both conformations.

79. Draw the staggered conformations of 2, 3-dimethylbutane in order of increasing energy.

80. Draw the eclipsed conformations of 2, 3-dimethylbutane in order of increasing energy.

81. From the following average bond energies, given in kcal/mol at 25°C, calculate the ΔH_c° (enthalpy of combustion) of propane: $O=O, 119; C-C, 83; C-H, 99; O-H, 111; C=O$ from CO_2, 192.

82. Indicate the different ways that an alkyl halide can be converted to an alkane with the same skeleton.

83. Write the reaction of CH_3CH_2MgBr with methanol, CH_3OH, and identity the conjugate acid-base pair.

84. (A) Write the equation for the reaction of an alkyllithium compound, RLi, with an amine, $R'NH_2$.

    (B) Explain why Grignard or lithium reagents do not react with alkanes.

85. Prepare butane from chloroethane using the Wurtz synthesis.

86. Laboratory chlorination of alkanes is often done with sulfuryl chloride, SO_2Cl_2, instead of Cl_2 because of its convenience. What is the Lewis structure of SO_2Cl_2?

87. When sulfuryl chloride is used to chlorinate an alkane, an organic peroxide, ROOR, is used as an *initiator*. SO_2 is also a product. Write a mechanism for the chlorination, including the role of the peroxide.

88. Synthesize $(CH_3)_3CCH(CH_3)_2$

    (A) from an alkene

    (B) by a Corey-House synthesis using alkyl halides with more than one carbon

    Show steps and catalysts.

89. Using 1-bromo-3-methylbutane (B) and any other one-or two-carbon compounds, if needed, synthesize

    (A) 2-methylbutane

    (B) 2,7-dimethyloctane

    (C) 2-methylhexane

CHAPTER 5

Cycloalkanes

90. (A) Define cycloalkanes.

(B) Write the following formulas for the first four members of this homologous series with only one ring and no substituent groups:

I. Molecular

II. Structural

III. Line

91. Name each of the following:

(A) 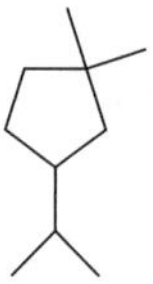

(B) 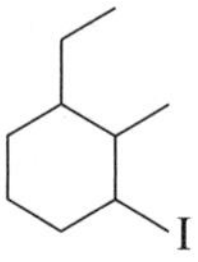

(C) 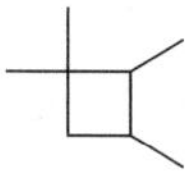

(D) 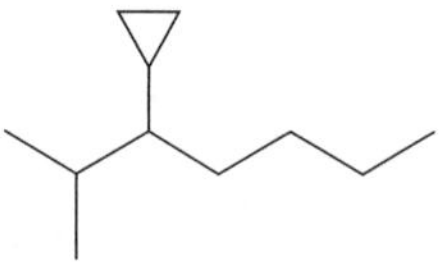

(E) 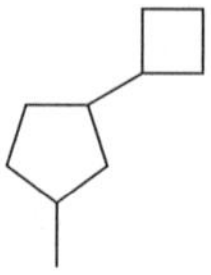

92. Draw line formulas and give the IUPAC name for each of the following fused bicyclics:

    (A) Bicyclobutane

    (B) Two isomers of bicycloheptane

    (C) Three isomers of bicyclooctane

93. Draw line structures and show ring numbering for the following:

    (A) 2-Ethyl-7-iodobicyclo[2.2.1]heptane

    (B) 3-Bromo-6-methylbicyclo[3.2.0]heptane

    (C) 1,3,9-Trimethyldecalin

94. (A) Draw the basic fused *steroid* ring system present in many important naturally occurring compounds such as cholesterol, and designate the rings with letters. Show the location of the angular Me's.

    (B) Classify this polycyclic system.

95. Give the structural formulas and names of the three isomers of dimethylcyclopropane.

96. (A) Is geometric isomerism observed in 3,4-dimethylhexane, $CH_3CH_2CHMeCHMeCH_2CH_3$?

    (B) What structural features must be present in order for stereoisomers to exist?

97. Draw the structures for geometric isomers, if any, of the following:

    (A) 1,1,2-Trimethyl cyclopropane

    (B) 1,2-Dimethylcyclobutane

    (C) 1,3,5-Trimethylcyclohexane

98. Classify cycloalkanes by size and ring strain.

99. Which factors influence the ring strain of cycloalkanes?

100. (A) In terms of hybridization, what assumptions are made to rationalize the observed H—C—H bond angle of 114° in cyclopropane?

    (B) Compare the relative C—H bond lengths in cyclopropane and CH_2 in propane.

101. Draw two conformations of cyclobutane that overcome the eclipsing strain.

102. (A) Based on their special orientation, label the two types of Hs of cyclohexane.

   (B) What happens to these Hs when one cyclohexane chair conformer converts to the other?

103. (A) Draw the following:

   I. The *boat* conformation of cyclohexane

   II. Its Newman projection

   (B) How does the chair conformation of Figure 5-1 convert to the boat conformation?

   (C) Why is the boat conformation less stable than the chair conformation?

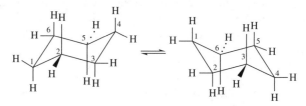

Figure 5-1 Equilibrating Chair Conformations

104. (A) Draw structures for the two conformations of *trans-* and *cis-*1,3-dimethylcyclohexane.

   (B) Label the more stable conformer for each diastereomer, and explain your choices.

   (C) Compare the stabilities of the more stable conformer of each diastereomer.

   (D) Before the advent of conformation theory (mid-1940s), the greater stability of the *cis-*isomer was called an anomaly. Explain why it was so called and how conformation theory explained the problem.

105. Give the product of the electrocyclic reaction of the following:

   (A) 1,3-Pentadiene

   (B) 1,3,5-Hexatriene

106. (A) Identify **A**, a cycloaddition product, and **B** in the following reaction:

$$H_2C=CH-CH=CH_2 + H_2C=CH_2 \longrightarrow A \xrightarrow{H_2/Pd} B$$

   (B) Name this very important cycloaddition.

   (C) What size ring is always prepared by this type of synthesis?

107. Generate the following cyclopropanes in one step from any needed precursor:

(A) 1,1-Dimethylcyclopropane

(B) 1,2-Dimethylcyclopropane (ignore *cis-trans* isomerism)

108. (A) From any monocyclic compound, prepare

     I. cyclobutane (**A**) from any open chain compound

     II. norbornane (**B**) from any monocyclic compound

(B) Classify the cyclizations in (I) and (II).

109. (A) Give the possible products with their names from monobromination of methylcyclohexane.

(B) Predict the major product and explain your choice.

(C) Discuss the distribution of monochlorination products.

110. Give the structures of the products of the following reactions:

(A) 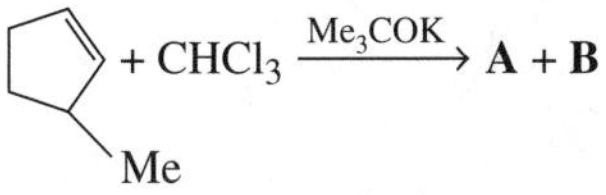 $+ CHCl_3 \xrightarrow{\text{Me}_3\text{COK}} \textbf{A} + \textbf{B}$

(B) $+ CHClBr_3 \xrightarrow{\text{Me}_3\text{COK}} \textbf{C} + \textbf{D}$

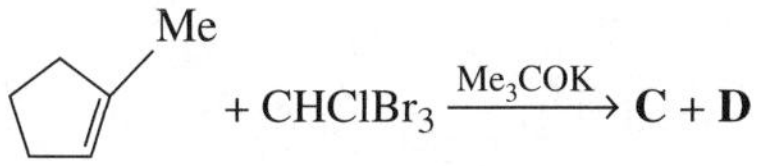

CHAPTER 6

Stereochemistry

111. (A) How do structural (constitutional) isomers differ from stereoisomers?

(B) What is meant by configuration?

112. Define the following terms:

(A) Enantiomer

(B) Diastereomer

113. (A) What is a chiral molecule?

(B) How does it differ from an achiral molecule?

114. Identify which of the following objects possess at least one plane of symmetry:

(A) A tree

(B) A glove

(C) An ear

(D) A nail

(F) A cup

(F) A filled spool of thread

(G) An empty spool

Draw a mirror plane in all such symmetrical objects.

115. Identify the chiral center in each of the following compounds:

(A) 2-Chlorobutane

(B) 1,2-Dichloropropane

(C) 3-Bromo-1-pentene

(D) Ethylmethylpropylchlorosilane

116. Can a tertiary amine ($R^1R^2R^3N:$) or a carbanion ($R^1R^2R^3C:^-$) exist as a pair of enantiomers?

117. How is plane-polarized light used in the analysis of enantiomers?

118. (A) Define the absolute configuration of an enantiomer.

 (B) What are the rules for designating an enantiomer as R (from *rectus*, Latin for "right") or S (from *sinister*, Latin for "left")?

 (C) Illustrate with 1-chloro-1-bromoethane, $ClBrCHCH_3$.

119. Assign R and S designations to the following compounds:

(A)

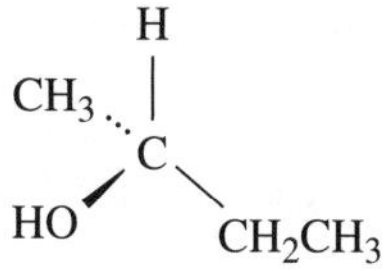

(B)

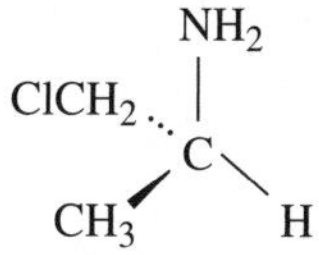

(C)

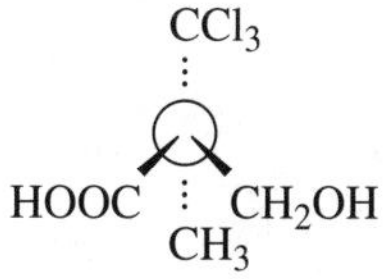

(D)

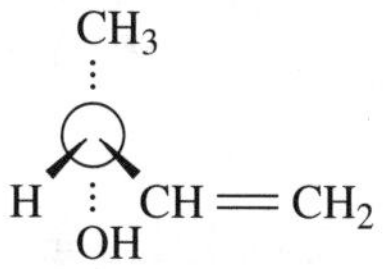

120. Identify each of the following as R or S:

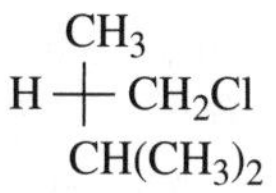

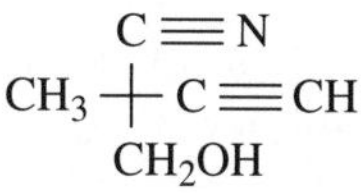

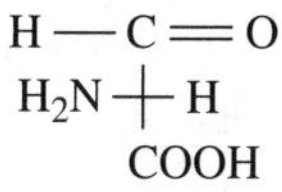

121. Draw a Fischer projection for the naturally occurring amino acid, proline, and give its R/S designation.

122. Give the R/S designation for each of the stereoisomers of 1,3-dibromo-2-methylbutane.

123. Compare the physical and chemical properties of diastereomers.

124. What is the *R/S* designation for *meso*-2,3-butanediol?

125. Why are the following stereoisomers *meso*?

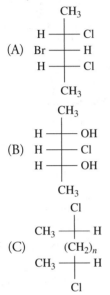

126. Draw all the stereoisomers of 1,2- and 1,3-dimethylcyclopentanes.

127. Draw the enantiomers of 3-bromocyclohexene, and give the *R/S* designation for each.

128. (A) Identify all of the products possible from the radical monochlorination of (*S*)-2-chlorobutane.

    (B) Give their stereoidentity.

129. Predict whether the following reactions occur with racemization, retention, or inversion of configuration, and give your reason.

    (A) $CH_3CH_2CH(OH)CH_2Br + OH^- \longrightarrow CH_3CH_2CH(OH)CH_2OH + Br^-$

    (B) $CH_3CH_2CH=CH_2 + D_2 \xrightarrow{\text{catalyst}} CH_3CH_2CH(D)CH_2D$

    (C) $CH_3CH_2CH(OH)CH(CH_3)_2 + CH_3COCl \longrightarrow CH_3CH_2$
    $CH(OCOCH_3)CH(CH_3)_2 + HCl$

    (D) $CH_3CH(NH_2)COOH + NaOH \longrightarrow CH_3CH(NH_2)COO^-Na^+ + H_2O$

    (E) $CH_3CH_2CH_2CH(Cl)CH_3 + OH^- \longrightarrow CH_3CH_2CH_2CH(OH)CH_3 + Cl^-$

130. State whether the following statements are true or false. Give your reason.

(A) A compound with the S configuration is the (−) enantiomer.

(B) An achiral compound can have chiral centers.

(C) An optically inactive substance must be achiral.

(D) In chemical reactions the change from an S reactant to an R product always signals an inversion of configuration.

(E) When an achiral molecule reacts to give a chiral molecule, the product is always racemic.

131. Two optically active alkenes, **B** and **C**, have the same molecular formula, C_5H_9Cl. After addition of one mole of H_2 to each, **B** is converted to **D** (achiral), and **C** forms **E** (optically active). Give the structures of **B**, **C**, **D**, and **E**.

132. Answer true or false to each of the following statements and explain your choice.

(A) A reaction catalyzed by an enzyme always gives an optically active product.

(B) Racemization of an enantiomer can only occur by breaking of at least one bond to the chiral center.

(C) A racemate can be distinguished from a *meso* or an achiral compound by an attempted resolution.

(D) Conversion of an *erythro* to a *threo* stereoisomer always occurs by inversion at one chiral C.

(E) A D enantiomer rotates the plane of polarized light to the right and an L enantiomer to the left.

CHAPTER 7

Alkenes

133. (A) Define degrees (or element) of unsaturation.

(B) Find the degrees of unsaturation for

    I. C_6H_{14}

    II. C_4H_6

    III. C_6H_6

(C) What structural features induce degrees or unsaturation?

134. Supply IUPAC names for

(A) $CH_3CH = CHCH_2CH_3$

(B) $CH_3CHCH = CHCH_3$
        |
        CH_3

(C) $CH_3CH_2CH_2CHCH_2CH_2CH_3$
                   |
                   $CH = CH_2$

135. Supply IUPAC names for

(A) $CH_3CH = C(NO_2)CH_2CH_3$

(B) $Me_2C = C(Me)CH(Me)_2$

(C) $(Me)_2CHCH = CHCHCH = CH_2$
                        |
                        Me

(D) $H_2C = CHCHCHClCH = CHCHMe_2$
               |
               $CH(Me)CH_2CH_3$
               CH_3

(E)

  C_2H_5

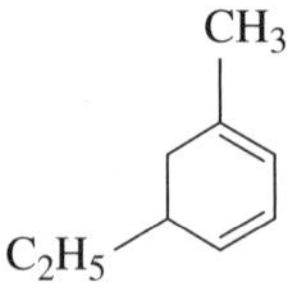

(F) $(H_2C = CH)_2CHCH_2CH = CHCH_3$

136. Assign E or Z configurations to each of the following alkenes:

(A) 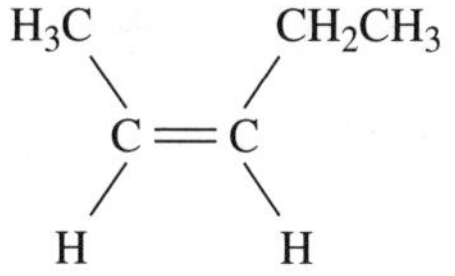
$$\begin{array}{ccc} H_3C & & CH_2CH_3 \\ & \diagdown \quad \diagup & \\ & C = C & \\ & \diagup \quad \diagdown & \\ H & & H \end{array}$$

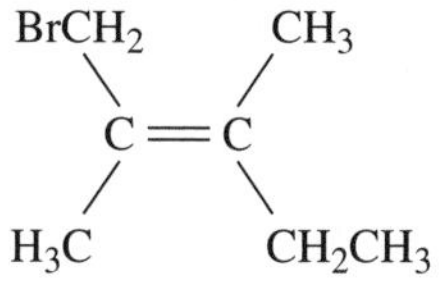

(B)
$$\begin{array}{ccc} BrCH_2 & & CH_3 \\ & \diagdown \quad \diagup & \\ & C = C & \\ & \diagup \quad \diagdown & \\ H_3C & & CH_2CH_3 \end{array}$$

(C)
$$\begin{array}{ccc} Br & & CH(CH_3)_2 \\ & \diagdown \quad \diagup & \\ & C = C & \\ & \diagup \quad \diagdown & \\ HOCH_2 & & CH_2CH_2CH_3 \end{array}$$

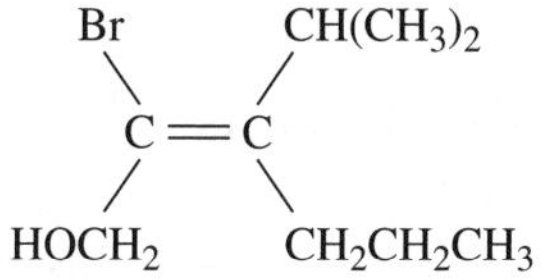

(D) 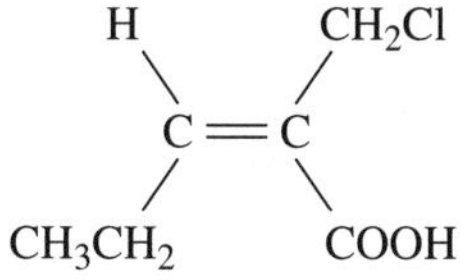
$$\begin{array}{ccc} H & & CH_2Cl \\ & \diagdown \quad \diagup & \\ & C = C & \\ & \diagup \quad \diagdown & \\ CH_3CH_2 & & COOH \end{array}$$

137. Write the structural formulas for:
(A) $(E)(S)$-5-bromo-2, 7-dimethyl-4-nonene
(B) (R)-3-chloro-1-butene
(C) $(E)(S)$-6-fluoro-3, 7-dimethyl-3-octene

138. What is the major method for preparing alkenes by forming the double bond?

139. (A) Use the values $\Delta S = +28\,\text{cal/mol} \cdot \text{K}$ and $\Delta H = +27.6\,\text{kcal/mol}$ to determine the most favorable of the following temperatures for dehydrogenation of butane to *trans*-2-butene:

    I. 25°C

    II. 500°C

    III. 1000°C

(B) Why can a reaction occur even with the unfavorable ΔH?

(C) Find the temperature at which $\Delta G = 0$ and discuss its significance. It is reasonable to assume that in the given temperature range ΔH, the difference in enthalpy between reactant and products remains fairly constant.

140. (A) Write a generalized equation for preparing alkenes from alkyl halides, $C_nH_{2n+1}X$, by *dehydrohalogenation*(−HX) using a base and heat.

    (B) Classify this reaction.

    (C) What is a commonly used base?

141. List the possible products, in order of decreasing yield, from the reaction of 3-bromo-2, 3-dimethylpentane with alc. KOH.

142. Synthesize the following:

    (A) Cyclohexene from cyclohexane

    (B) Propene from propane

143. The rate expression for the acid-catalyzed dehydration of an alcohol is: rate = $k_1[ROH][H^+]$.

    (A) Write a three-step mechanism that is consistent with this expression, using $CH_3CHOHCH_3$ for ROH.

    (B) Identify the slow step and explain your choice.

    (C) Show how this rate expression is consistent with your mechanism.

    (D) Classify this elimination reaction.

144. Give the alkenes formed from acid-catalyzed dehydration of the following:

    (A) $CH_3CH_2CH(OH)CH_2CH_3$

    (B)

    (C) $(CH_3)_3CCH_2OH$

145. Predict the product of the reaction between $Me_2C{=}CH_2$ and ICl.

146. Isobutylene gas dissolves in 63% H_2SO_4 to yield a deliquescent white solid, **A**. When heated in water, the solid changes to a liquid, **B**, bp 83°C. Give the structures of **A** and **B**.

147. Contrast

    (A) H^+-catalyzed hydration

    (B) hydroboration-oxidation

    (C) oxymercuration-demercuration in terms of

        I. regiospecificity

        II. mode of addition

        III. susceptibility to rearrangement

148. (A) Give the products from catalytic hydrogenation of the following:
   I. *cis*-2,3-Dibromo-2-butene
   II. *trans*-2,3-Dibromo-2-butene
   III. 1,2-Dimethylcyclohexene
(B) Classify the mode of addition.

149. Give the structural formulas for **A** and **B** in the following sequence:

$$CH_3CH=CH_2 \xrightarrow{BH_3/THF} A \xrightarrow{CH_3COOH} B$$

150. (A) Give the product of the reaction of a peroxyacid such as peroxybenzoic

acid, $\overset{\overset{\displaystyle O}{\displaystyle \|}}{PhCOOH}$, with

   I. cyclopentene
   II. *cis*-2-butene
   III. *trans*-2-butene
(B) Consider the reaction as an electrophilic addition.

151. Write structural formulas for the compounds that yield the following products on reductive ozonolysis:
(A) 2 mol of $O=C(CH_3)CH_2CH_3$
(B) $H_2C=O + O=CHCH(CH_3)CH(CH_3)_2$
(C) $O=CHCH_2CH_2CH_2CH=O$
(D) $(C_2H_5)_2C=O + O=CHCH=O+O=CHCH_2CH_3$
(E) 2 mol $O=CHCH_2CH=O$

152. Account for the anti-Markovnikov radical addition of HBr to $CH_3CH=CH_2$.

153. The reaction of $Me_2C=CH_2$ with H_2SO_4 or HF gives two isomers, C_8H_{16}.
(A) Give their structural formulas and designate the major isomer.
(B) What is the general name for this reaction?
(C) Account for the unexpected product ratio.
(D) Provide a mechanism.
(E) Why cannot HCl, HBr, or HI be used as acid catalysts?

154. Describe

(A) *radical-induced* polymerization of alkenes

(B) *anion-induced* polymerization of alkenes

(C) What kinds of alkenes undergo anion-induced polymerization?

155. Give the products of the reactions of cyclohexene in CCl_4 with

(A) sulfuryl chloride, Cl_2SO_2

(B) *t*-butyl hypochlorite, Me_3COCl

(C) *N*-bromosuccinimide (NBS)

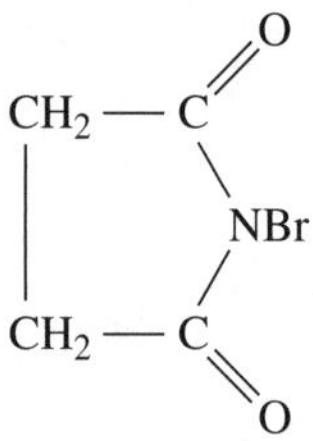

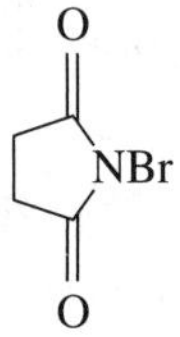

N-Bromosuccinimide

156. From PrOH, prepare

(A) 1,2,3-trichloropropane

(B) 1,3-dibromo-2-chloropropane

(C) 1-bromo-2-chloro-3-iodopropane

(D) 1,1,2-tribromopropane

(E) $BrCH_2CHOHCH_2C$

157. Deduce the structure of a compound $C_{10}H_{14}$ that is hydrogenated with 3 eq of H_2/Pd to give 1-isopropyl-4-methylcyclohexane, and, on reductive ozonolysis, gives the following products:

(A) $H_2C{=}O$

(B) $H-\overset{\|}{\underset{O}{C}}-CH_2-\overset{\|}{\underset{O}{C}}-\overset{\|}{\underset{O}{C}}Me$

(C) $MeC\overset{\|}{\underset{O}{}}-CH_2-CH\overset{\|}{\underset{O}{}}$

CHAPTER 8

Alkyl Halides

158. (A) Classify alkyl halides on the basis of the bonding environment of the C of C—X. Illustrate with general formulas.

(B) Use $C_2H_4Br_2$ to classify dihalides.

159. Write structural formulas and give IUPAC names for and classify the isomers of:

(A) $C_5H_{11}Cl$

(B) $C_4H_8F_2$

160. (A) Write structural formulas and IUPAC names for:

I. methylene bromide

II. chloroform

III. allyl bromide

IV. *t*-amyl chloride

V. neopentylbromide

(B) Illustrate the use of the suffix "form" in naming trihalogen and trinitromethanes.

161. Give the structure of each of the following compounds:

(A) 2, 3-Dibromo-3-ethylheptane

(B) *cis*-2-Bromochloromethylcyclohexane

(C) 1-Bromo-2-iodocyclobutene

(D) *trans*-9-Chlorodecalin

(E) 2-Exo-3-endodichlorobicyclo[2.2.2] octane

162. (A) What two factors influence the boiling points of alkyl halides (as well as other compounds)?

(B) Explain the trends in the following boiling points (in °C):

I. MeI (42.4) > MeBr (3.56) > MeCl (−24.2) > MeF (−78.4) > CH_4 (−161.7)

II. PrBr (71.0) > i-PrBr (59.4)

III. CCl_4(76.8) > $HCCl_3$ (61.3) > H_2CCl_2 (40.1) > H_3CCl (−24.2)

IV. C_2F_6 (−79) > C_2H_6 (−89)

163. Suggest alkene addition reactions to prepare the dihalogen compounds:

(A) 2, 3-Dimethyl-2, 3-dibromobutane

(B) *trans*-1, 2-Dibromocyclopentane

(C) 1-Iodo-2-bromo-2-methylpentane

(D) 2, 2-Dibromobutane

(E) 1, 1-Dichloro-*cis*-2, 3-dimethylcyclopropane

(F) 1, 3-Dibromopropane

164. Alkyl halides are most often prepared from alcohols, rarely by direct halogenation. Supply structural formulas for the alkyl halides synthesized in the reactions:

(A) $CH_3CH_2CH_2CH_2OH \xrightarrow[\Delta]{NaBr, H_2SO_4}$

(B) $(CH_3)_3COH \xrightarrow[\text{room temp.}]{\text{conc. HCl}}$

(C) $CH_3CH(OH)CH_2CH_2CH_3 \xrightarrow{PBr_3}$

(D) $CH_3CH_2CH_2OH \xrightarrow{PI_3 \text{(from P+I}_2)}$

(E) $Me_2CHCH_2OH \xrightarrow{SOCl_2}$

165. (A) Give the product from the reaction of Mg/Et_2O with

I. $BrCH_2CH_2Br$

II. $BrCH_2CH_2CH_2Br$

III. $BrCH_2CH_2CH_2CH_2Br$

(B) Discuss the difference in behavior of (II) and (III) in part (A).

(C) Give the product of the reaction of CBr_4 + MeLi + cyclohexene.

166. Supply formulas for the organic products from the reaction of:

(A) $CH_3C\equiv C:^- K^+ + CH_3CH_2CH_2Cl$

(B) $(CH_3)_2CHO^- Na^+ + CH_3CH_2CH_2Cl$

(C) $CH_3CHClCH_2CH_3 +$ aq. $NaOH$

(D) bromocyclopentane + NaI (acetone)

(E) $Me_2CHBr + Et\ddot{S}:^- Na^+$

(F) $MeI + EtNH_2$

(G) $MeI + Et_2NH$

(H) $CH_3CH_2CH_2Br + Me_2S$

167. Give the organic products of the following reactions:

(A) $n\text{-PrBr} + :N - \ddot{O}: \longrightarrow$ (with $:O:$ double-bonded to N above)

(B) $i\text{-PrBr} + \left[:\ddot{S}C\equiv N:\right]^-$ (isocyanate) $\longrightarrow$

(C) $EtBr + \left[:\ddot{S}SO_3\right]^{2-}$ (thiosulfate) $\longrightarrow$

(D) $ClCH_2CH_2CH_2I + CN^-$ (1 mol each) $\rightarrow$

(E) $H_2NCH_2CH_2CH_2CH_2Br \xrightarrow{-H^+}$

168. (A) Analyze the following generalized rate data, and write the rate expression for the reaction: $RX + Nu:^- \rightarrow NuR + :X^-$ where R is 1° or 2°.

	[RX]	[Nu:⁻]	Rate
I.	0.10	0.10	1.2×10^{-4}
II.	0.20	0.10	2.4×10^{-4}
III.	0.10	0.20	2.4×10^{-4}
IV.	0.20	0.20	4.8×10^{-4}

(B) What are the order and molecularity of the reaction?

(C) Suggest two experimental methods for studying the kinetics if the reactants are $RCl + OH^-$.

169. Give the products of the following displacement reactions:

(A) (R)-$CH_3CHBrCH_2CH_3 + MeO^-$

(B) (S)-$CH_3CHBrCH_2CH_3 + MeO^-$

(C) *rac, cis*-4-Iodoethylcyclohexane $+ OH^-$

(D) 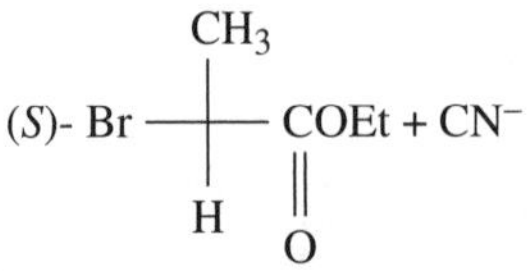 (S)- $Br\underset{H}{\overset{CH_3}{\underset{|}{\overset{|}{-}}}}COEt + CN^-$

         (with C=O below COEt)

170. Give the structural features of RX that most influence the relative S_N1 rates.

171. (A) Explain how the stereochemistry of S_N1 and S_N2 reactions differs.

(B) Account for the detection of about 60% inverted and 40% racemic product from a typical S_N1 reaction.

(C) What is the actual distribution of product from inversion and retention in the typical S_N1 reaction?

172. Hydrolysis of 2-bromo-3-methylbutane (2°) yields only 2-methyl-2-bulanol (3°). Explain.

173. Compare S_N1 and S_N2 reactions of RL with respect to the following mechanistic factors: number of steps; rate and order; molecularity; TS of slow step; stereochemistry; nucleophile.

174. (A) Give the order of decreasing reactivity for eliminations with strong bases of RX, when X = F, Cl, Br, I.

(B) Explain how this information is necessary to decide between E2 and $E1_{cb}$.

175. Compare E1 and E2 reactions of RX with respect to the following mechanistic factors: steps (number and kind); TS; kinetics; driving force, stereospecificity; effect of R; rearrangements; the H/D isotope effect; competing reactions; orientation.

176. From $CH_3CHOHCH_2CH_3$ prepare

(A) $ICH_2CH_2CH_2CH_2I$

(B) $CH_3CH_2CH_2CH_2SMe$

(C) $H_2CBrCHBrCHBrCH_3$ (How many stereoisomers are formed?)

177. Give the symbol S_N1, S_N2, E1, E2 most consistent with each of the following statements. More than one symbol may be used.

(A) MeX cannot react.

(B) 2° RCI reacts with I^- acetone.

(C) 2° RC1 reacts in formic acid that has a high dielectric constant.

(D) 2° RCI reacts with NaOEt/EtOH.

(E) *t*-BuBr reacts in EtOH.

(F) *t*-BuBr reacts with CN^-.

(G) *t*-BuBr reacts with CH_3COOH and some $CH_3COO^-Na^+$.

(H) Unhindered 1° RX reacts with NaOEt/EtOH.

(I) Reactions are concerted.

(J) Reactions are stereospecific.

(K) With saturated Rs, a Saytzeff product is always formed.

(L) R^+s are intermediates.

(M) RI reacts faster than RCI.

(N) Rearrangement of the R skeleton may occur.

(O) With a given substrate some pairs of these may be concurrent.

(P) Electrophilic catalysis is possible.

(Q) Rates are the same.

178. (A) Give a preparation of hexachlorocyclopentadiene (**A**) from cyclopentane.

(B) From **A**, ethylene and cyclopentadiene, prepare the insecticides

   I. Chlordane (**B**)

   II. Aldrin (**C**)

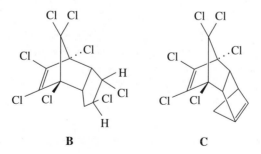

| **B** | **C** |

CHAPTER 9

Alkynes, Dienes, and Orbital Symmetry

179. Give the relative bond lengths and bond strengths of $-C\equiv C-$ and $>C=C<$ and rationalize your answer.

180. Name the structures below by the IUPAC system:

(A) $CH_3C\equiv CCH_3$

(B) $CH_3C\equiv CCH_2CH_3$

(C)

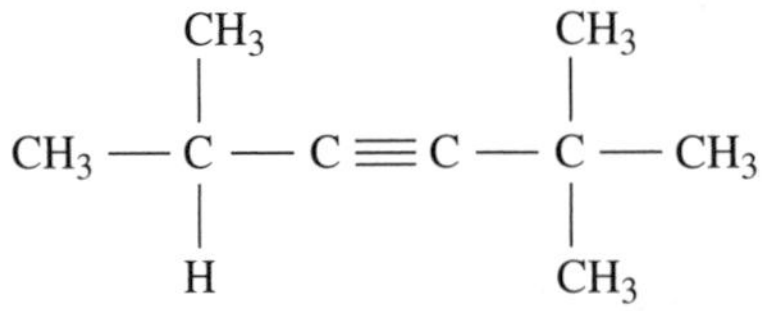

$$CH_3 - \underset{\underset{H}{|}}{\overset{\overset{CH_3}{|}}{C}} - C\equiv C - \underset{\underset{CH_3}{|}}{\overset{\overset{CH_3}{|}}{C}} - CH_3$$

(D) $HC\equiv C-CH_2CH=CH_2$

(E) $HC\equiv C-CH_2CH_2Cl$

181. Give the structural formulas for each of the following compounds:

(A) 1,3-butadiyne

(B) 4-methyl-1-nitro-2-pentyne

(C) (E)-3-penten-1-yne (not 2-penten-4-yne; numbers as low as possible are given to double and triple bonds although this may give the yne a lower number than the ene)

(D) (Z)-5-hepten-1,3-diyne

182. Give the IUPAC names for each of the following:

(A) 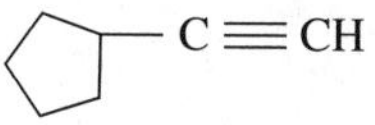 C≡CH

(B) 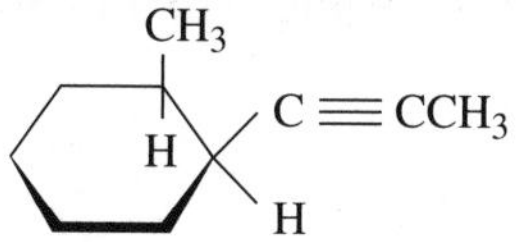 C≡CCH$_3$

(C) C≡C

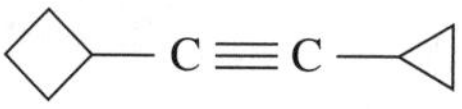

(D) 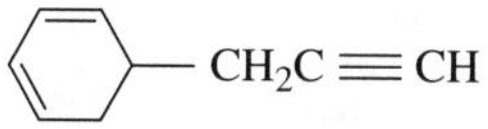 CH$_2$C≡CH

183. List alkanes, alkenes, and terminal alkynes in order of decreasing acidity of their terminal C—H.

184. Write equations for the preparation of

(A) HC≡CD

(B) DC≡CD

185. (A) Write the reactions for the industrial preparation of acetylene from CaO (lime), C (coke), and water, writing the Lewis structure for CaC$_2$.

(B) Formulate the reaction of CaC$_2$ and water as a Brönsted acid-base reaction.

186. From 1,1-dibromopentane synthesize

(A) 2-pentyne

(B) 1-pentyne

187. Starting with any alkyne, prepare ethylcyclohexylacetylene.

188. Write equations for the stepwise reaction of 2-butyne with two moles of H$_2$/Pt.

189. List the products formed when 1-butyne reacts with one equ of

(A) HBr

(B) HBr with peroxides

(C) Br$_2$

Characterize each reaction.

190. Write an equation for the reaction of propyne with water in the presence of H_2SO_4 and $HgSO_4$. Show the intermediate.

191. List the alkynes needed to synthesize the following ketones in the best possible yields:

(A) $(CH_3)_2CHCCH_3$
          $\overset{\displaystyle \|}{O}$

(B) $CH_3CH_2CCH_2CH_2CH_3$
          $\overset{\displaystyle \|}{O}$

(C) 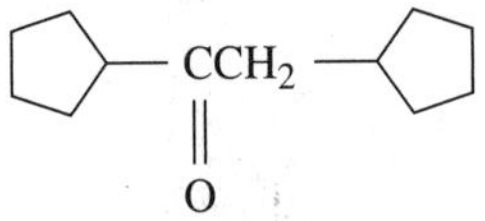 $\langle pentagon \rangle -\ CCH_2\ -\langle pentagon \rangle$
                    $\overset{\displaystyle \|}{O}$

192. Complete the following reactions and name the products:

(A) $2HC{\equiv}CH \xrightarrow[NH_4Cl]{CuCl}$

(B) $2HC{\equiv}CH \xrightarrow[O_2]{Cu^{2+}}$

193. From 2-bromobutane prepare the following:

(A)   (*E*)-2-butene

(B)   (*Z*)-2-butene

194. Give a method of preparation of (*S*)-(*E*)-4-deutero-2-hexene from an alkyne and a chiral halide.

195. Give the structural formulas and IUPAC names of the unbranched isomeric dienes, C_5H_8.

196. Synthesize 1,3-butadiene from acetylene.

197. Prepare 1,3-cyclohexadiene from cyclohexane.

198. A hydrocarbon (**D**) C_7H_{10} is catalytically hydrogenated to C_7H_{14} but does not react with H_2, Ni/B. Vigorous oxidation with $KMnO_4$ affords $HOOC^1C^2H_2C^3H_2C^4C^5H_2C^6OOH$ (**E**). Deduce all the possible
              $\overset{\displaystyle \|}{O}$
structures of **D** and explain your answer.

199. (A) Name the product formed when 1,3-butadiene undergoes an intra-molecular ring closure.

(B) Classify this type of pericylic reaction.

(C) Give the net bonding change for this cyclization.

(D) According to the orbital symmetry concept, describe how the terminal p AOs must rotate toward each other in order to get the proper symmetry if the ring closure goes

    I. thermally

    II. photochemically

200. (A) Give all the possible products from 1,4-addition of HBr to 3-methylenecyclohexene at 45°C.

(B) Which intermediate carbocation (R^+) is more stable?

(C) Predict the major product.

CHAPTER 10

Aromaticity and Benzene

201. The experimentally determined enthalpy of combustion, (ΔH_c), of C_6H_6 is -789.1 kcal/mol. Theoretical values for the "combustion" contribution of each bond are: $C=C$, -117.7; $C—C$, -49.3; and $C—H$, -54.0 kcal/mol.

   (A) Write a balanced equation for the combustion of one mole of benzene.

   (B) From these data, calculate the ΔH for C_6H_6 and explain the difference.

202. Give an orbital picture of benzene. How does it account for benzene's extraordinary stability?

203. Use the molecular orbital theory to account for the greater stability of benzene.

204. Write the structure of all the

   (A) dibrominated derivatives of C_6H_6

   (B) tribrominated derivatives of C_6H_6

205. Compare the stabilities of phenyl (C_6H_5) and cyclohexyl

   (A) cations

   (B) anions

206. (A) What kind of substituent on the benzene ring

   I. destabilizes

   II. stabilizes

   the phenyl carbocation and where is it most effective?

   (B) Write the resonance structures of the carbocation, and evaluate their contribution to the hybrid if there is a substituent with an unshared pair of e⁻s (e.g., —F :) on the adjacent atom.

207. (A) Draw resonance structures for

        I. C_6H_5F

        II. $C_6H_5NO_2$

showing which Cs of the ring bear the partial charges induced in the ring by extended π bonding.

  (B) Use electrostatic theory to rationalize this same charge distribution.

208. Name the following substances:

(A)

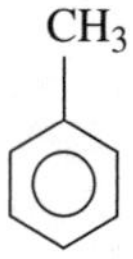

CH_3

(B)

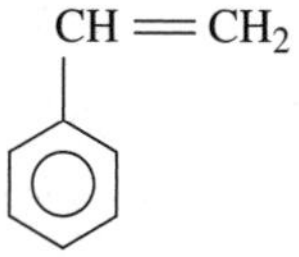

$CH = CH_2$

(C)

CH_3

CH_3

(D)

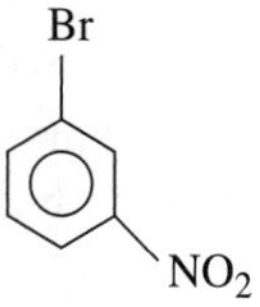

Br

NO_2

(E)

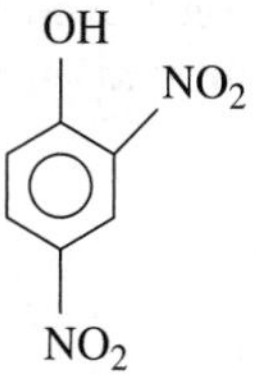

OH

NO_2

NO_2

(F)

NH_2

Cl

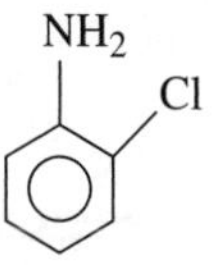

209. Draw the structural formulas of the following:

(A) Benzaldehyde

(B) Mesitylene

(C) Cumene

(D) 2-Chloro-4-ethylbenzoic acid

(E) Acetophenone

(F) Phthalic acid

(G) *p*-Toluenesulfonic acid

210. Give the structure and name of each of the following substances:

(A) "TNT"

(B) "DDT"

(C) "DES", diethylstilbestrol

(D) "PABA"

211. State Hückel's rule for determining whether a molecule is aromatic.

212. List aromatic, antiaromatic, and nonaromatic compounds in decreasing order of resonance energies (stabilities).

213. (A) Write Kekulé-type resonance structures for cyclooctatetrene, C_8H_8 **(A)**.

(B) On the basis of these contributing structures, predict its stability.

(C) The ΔH_h for hydrogenating **A** to cyclooctane is about four times the value for the addition of H_2 to cyclooctene. What does this tell you about the structure of **A**?

(D) Is the ability to write equivalent contributing resonance structures always reliable for predicting aromaticity of conjugated carbocylic polyenes?

214. Give a synthesis of benzene from

(A) acetylene

(B) hexane

215. Synthesize benzene using a Diels–Alder reaction.

216. Give the product of the reduction of benzene by Li or Na in liquid NH_3 and EtOH.

217. Draw structures for the following:

    (A) β-Nitronaphthalene

    (B) α-Naphthol

    (C) 1,5-Dichloro-naphthalene

    (D) 1-Naphthalenesulfonic acid

    (E) 2-Naphthoic acid

218. Use a Diels–Alder reaction to synthesize the following:

    (A) Tetralin

    (B) Naphthalene

219. Give the products of the reaction of

    (A) anthracene with Na in alcohol

    (B) phenanthrene with Na in alcohol

220. Indene, C_9H_8, isolated from coal tar, reacts with $KMnO_4$ and decolorizes Br_2 in CCl_4. It is catalytically hydrogenated under mild conditions to indane, C_9H_{10} (**E**), and under vigorous conditions to C_9H_{16} (**F**). Oxidation of indene yields phthalic acid. What are the structures of indene, Indane, and **F**?

221. Give simple chemical tests to distinguish cyclohexane, cyclohexene, and benzene.

CHAPTER 11

Aromatic Substitution, Arenes

222. (A) What types of reagents effect characteristic benzene substitution?

    (B) Why is it called *electrophilic aromatic substitution*?

223. (A) Write

        I. the contributing resonance structures

        II. the delocalized hybrid structure to account for the relative stability of the benzenonium ion

    (B) Describe the orbital hybridization of the Cs in the benzenonium intermediate.

224. Which is the rate-determining step in electrophilic aromatic substitution?

225. Discuss the essential role of the catalysts used for aromatic electrophilic substitutions.

226. Write an equation for each of following reactions and identify the electophile (E) and base (B) for each:

    (A) $HOCl + H^+$

    (B) HNO_3

    (C) $ICl + ZnCl_2$

    (D) $HONO + H^+$

227. (A) Give the product of the reaction of benzene and $AlCl_3$ with

    I. $CH_3CH_2CH_2COCl$, an acyl chloride

    II. $(CH_3CH_2CH_2CO)_2O$, an acid anhydride

(B) What is the electrophile? Show contributing resonance structures.

(C) Why is the product in (A) *not* rearranged?

(D) How can we use the acylation to synthesize unrearranged alkyl side chains on an aromatic ring? Illustrate by preparing $Ph(CH_2)_3CH_3$.

228. Compare the Friedel–Crafts alkylation with RX and acylation with RCOX as to the

(A) mechanism

(B) kind and amount of catalyst

229. Supply structures for the products of the reaction of benzene with

(A) $CH_3CH=CH_2$ (HF, 0°C)

(B) cyclohexanol (BF_3, 60°C)

(C) $[Me_2CHCO]_2O$ ($AlCl_3$)

(D) $CH_2=CHCH_2Cl$ ($ZnCl_2$)

230. (A) How do substituent groups (G) on an aromatic ring influence the course of electrophilic aromatic substitution?

(B) Classify them by their effects.

231. Explain that halogens are *o-*, *p*-directors, but are deactivating.

232. Compare the activating effects of the following *o*, *p*-directors and explain your order.

(A) $-\ddot{\text{O}}\text{H}$, $\ -\ddot{\underset{..}{\text{O}}}\!:^{-}$, and $\ -\ddot{\text{O}}\text{C}-\text{CH}_3$
$$\underset{\text{O}}{\overset{\|}{}}$$

(B) $-\ddot{\text{N}}\text{H}_2$ and $-\ddot{\text{N}}\text{H}-\text{C}-\text{CH}_3$
$$\underset{\text{O}}{\overset{\|}{}}$$

233. Give the principal monosubstitution products from the following reactions, and indicate whether each reaction is faster (F) or slower (S) than with benzene:

(A) Nitration of PhNHCOMe

(B) Bromination of $PhCBr_3$

(C) Chlorination of $PhCMe_3$

(D) Nitration of Ph—Ph

(E) Nitration of PhCOOMe

(F) Sulfonation of $PhCHMe_2$

(G) Nitration of $PhC\equiv N$

(H) Bromination of PhI

234. Indicate by an arrow the position(s) most likely to react in each of the following three isomeric nitrotoluenes. Explain your choices.

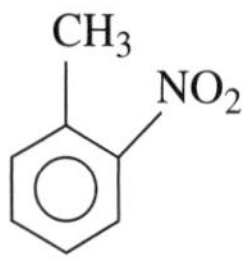

E (*ortho*) 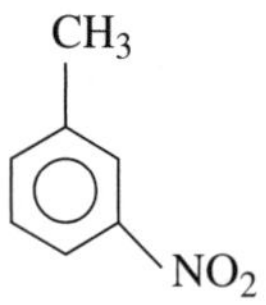   F (*meta*)    G (*para*)

235. (A) Which position in naphthalene preferentially reacts with E^+?

(B) Account for this preference mechanistically.

236. State the rules for deciding which ring reacts with E^+ in naphthyl-G under kinetically controlled conditions.

237. Write the structures for the product(s) of

(A) nitration of 1-methoxynaphthalene

(B) bromination of 2-methylnaphthalene

238. (A) Why is Friedel–Crafts acylation but not alkylation of naphthalene practical?

(B) Give the product of acylation of naphthalene with CH_3COCl and $AlCl_3$ in the solvent

  I. CS_2

  II. $PhNO_2$

(C) Explain the different products in (B).

239. (A) Give the product when PhCl is treated with

  I. $K^+NH_2^-$ in liquid NH_3 at $-33°C$

  II. aq. NaOH at $340°C$

(B) What products are formed when *p*-chlorotoluene is reacted with aq. NaOH at $340°C$?

(C) Explain why the reactions in (A) and (B) are not considered to be addition-elimination reactions.

240. Prepare the following from benzene:

(A) *meta*-chloronitrobenzene

(B) *para*-chloronitrobenzene

(C) *ortho*-chloronitrobenzene

241. Use benzene and any inorganic or aliphatic reagents to synthesize in good yield each of the following:

(A) *p*-Bromobenzoic acid

(B) *o*-Bromobenzoic acid

(C) *m*-Bromobenzoic acid

242. Use benzene or toluene and any inorganic reagents to prepare

(A) 3-nitro-4-bromobenzoic acid (**A**)

(B) 2-nitro-4-bromobenzoic acid (**B**)

(C) 4-nitro-2-bromo-benzoic acid (**C**)

(D) 3, 5-dinitrobenzoic acid (**D**)

243. Give three methods for introducing an alkyl side chain into the benzene nucleus, and illustrate each method by preparing ethylbenzene.

244. Give the products of the Friedel–Crafts reaction of benzene with
(A) CH_2Cl_2
(B) $CHCl_3$
(C) CCl_4

245. The reaction of Ph_3CCl with Ag or Zn gives a dimer, $(Ph_3C)_2$, originally incorrectly believed to be Ph_3CCPh_3. The dimer gives a yellow solution in benzene, which is decolorized by O_2 and X_2.
(A) What structure is responsible for the color?
(B) Why does the color disappear in the following:
   I. O_2
   II. I_2
(C) What is the structure of the dimer?
(D) Account for the failure to synthesize hexaphenylethane.

246. Deduce the structure of compound **A**, C_9H_8, from the following experimental data: **A** decolorizes Br_2 in CCl_4, and adds one eq. of H_2 under mild conditions, forming **B**, C_9H_{10}. At high temperature and pressure, **A** adds four eq. of H_2. Vigorous oxidation of **A** yields phthalic acid, $1,2\text{-}C_6H_4(COOH)_2$.

CHAPTER 12

Spectroscopy and Structure Proof

Tables 12-1 and 12-2 may be useful in answering some of the questions in this chapter.

Table 12-1   Infrared Absorption Frequencies of Some Common Structural Units

Stretching Frequencies (cm^{-1})			
Single Bonds		**Double Bonds**	
Structural Unit	**Frequency**	**Structural Unit**	**Frequency**
—O—H (alcohols)	3200–3600	$\diagdown \atop \diagup$ C $=$ C $\diagup \atop \diagdown$	1620–1680
—O—D	2100		
—O—H (carboxylic acids)	2500–3600	$\diagdown \atop \diagup$ C $=$ O	
$\diagdown \atop \diagup$ N $-$ H	3350–3500	Aldehydes and ketones	1710–1750
C_{sp}—H	3310–3320	Carboxylic acids	1700–1725
C_{sp^2}—H	3000–3100	Acid anhydrides	1800–1850 and 1740–1790
O=C—H	2715, 2820		
C_{sp^3}—H	2850–2950	Acyl halides	1770–1815
		Esters	1730–1750
C_{sp^2}—O	1200	Amides	1680–1700
C_{sp^3}—O	1025–1200		
		Triple Bonds	
—S—H	2500	—C≡C—	2100–2200
		—C≡N	2240–2280

Table 12-1 Infrared Absorption Frequencies of Some Common Structural Units (*Continued*)

Bending Frequencies (cm^{-1}) of Hydrocarbons				
Alkanes	**CH$_3$** 1420–1470 1375	**=CH$_2$** 1430–1470	**CH(CH$_3$)$_2$** Doublet of Equal Intensities at 1370, 1385 (Also 1170)	**C(CH$_3$)$_3$ Doublet at 1370 (Strong)** 1395 (Moderate)
Alkenes Out-of-Plane	RCH=CH$_2$ 910–920 990–1000	R$_2$C=CH$_2$ 880–1900	RCH=CHR *cis* 675–730 (variable) *trans* 965–975	
Aromatic C—H Out-of-Plane	Monosubstituted 690–710 730–770		Disubstituted *ortho* *meta* *para* 735–770 690–710 810–840 750–810	

Table 12-2 Proton Chemical Shifts

δ, ppm	Character of Underlined Proton	δ, ppm	Character of Underlined Proton
0.2	Cyclopropane:  ▷<H	4–2.5	Bromide: α H Br—C—H
0.9	Primary: R—CH₃	4–3	Chloride: α H Cl—C—H
1.3	Secondary: R₂CH₂	4–3.4	Alcohol: α H HO—C—H
1.5	Tertiary: R₃—CH	4–4.5	Fluoride: α H F—C—H
1.7	Allylic: —C=C—CH₃	4.1–3.7	Ester(I): α H to alkyl O R—C=O O—C<H

δ, ppm	Character of Underlined Proton	δ, ppm	Character of Underlined Proton
2.0–4.0	Iodide: α H $I-\underset{\mid}{\overset{\mid}{C}}-\underline{H}$	5.0–1.0	Amine: $R-N\underline{H}_2$
2.2–2.0	Ester (II): α H to C=O $\underline{H}-\underset{\underset{OR}{\mid}}{\overset{\mid}{C}}-C=O$	5.5–1.0	Hydroxyl: $RO-\underline{H}$
2.6–2.0	Carboxylic acid: α H $\underline{H}-\underset{\underset{OH}{\mid}}{\overset{\mid}{C}}-C=O$	5.9–4.6	Vinylic: $-\underset{\mid}{\overset{\mid}{C}}=\underset{\mid}{\overset{\mid}{C}}-\underline{H}$
2.7–2.0	Carbonyl: α H $-\overset{\mid}{C}=O$ $-\underset{\mid}{C}-\underline{H}$	8.5–6.0	Aromatic: 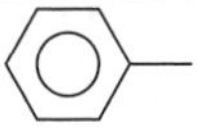 ⬡— $\underline{H}$ $(Ar — \underline{H})$
3–2	Acetylenic: $-C-C\equiv\underline{H}$	10.0–9.0	Aldehyde: $-\overset{\mid}{C}=O$ $\underset{H}{\mid}$
3–2.2	Benzylic: 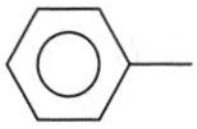 ⬡— $\overset{\mid}{\underset{\mid}{C}}—\underline{H}$	12.0–10.5	Carboxyl: $R-C=O$ $\overset{\mid}{O}-\underline{H}$
3.3–4.0	Ether: α H $R-O-\overset{\mid}{\underset{\mid}{C}}-\underline{H}$	12.0–4.0	Phenolic: ⬡— $O — \underline{H}$
		15.0–17.0	Enolic: $-C=C-O-\underline{H}$

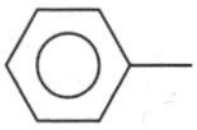

247. (A) For a wave define
   I. the period
   II. the frequency.

   (B) Give the mathematical relationship between frequency and wavelength.

248. (A) Give the relationship between frequency and energy (E) of a wave.

   (B) How are its wavelength and energy related?

249. Calculate the frequencies of violet and red light if their wavelengths are 400 and 750 nm, respectively.

250. List all the electronic transitions possible for

   (A) CCl_4

   (B) $H_2C=O$

   (C) cyclopentene

   (D) CH_3OH

251. (A) What is λ_{max}?

   (B) Give the Beer–Lambert law.

   (C) What is the meaning of $\in_{max}$, the molar extinction coefficient?

   (D) Define *transmittance*.

252. Describe the general procedure used in taking a UV or visible spectrum.

253. Acetone absorbs light at 154, 190, and 280 nm.

   (A) Identify the chromophore responsible for the absorption, and indicate what kind of transition causes each absorption.

   (B) Which transition(s) is (are) not observed in UV spectroscopy?

254. Suggest structures for possible isomers with molecular formula C_4H_6O whose UV spectra show a high-intensity peak at $\lambda_{max} = 187$ nm and a very low-intensity peak at $\lambda_{max} = 280$ nm

255. Select the reactions that might be used in a UV rate study. What would you measure?

(A) $CH_3CH_2COCH_3 \xrightarrow[\text{cat.}]{H_2} CH_3CH_2CH(OH)CH_3$

(B) $CH_3CH_2CH_2Cl + NH_3 \longrightarrow CH_3CH_2CH_2NH_3^+ + Cl^-$

(C) $CH_3CH_2CH(OH)CH_2CH_3 \xrightarrow[\Delta]{H^+} CH_3CH_2CH{=}CHCH_3$

(D) $CH_3CH_2C{\equiv}CH \xrightarrow[H_2O]{H_2SO_4, HgSO_4} CH_3CH_2COCH_3$

(E) $H_2C{=}CHCH{=}CH_2 + HC{\equiv}CH \longrightarrow 1,4\text{-cyclohexadiene}$

(F)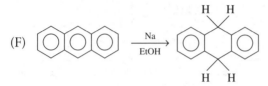

256. (A) Why are water and ethanol not commonly used as solvents in IR spectroscopy?

(B) List the most commonly used solvents.

257. Describe the molecular processes that occur when IR radiation is absorbed by a molecule.

258. (A) Compare the relative wave numbers for stretching and bending vibrations.

(B) Define the "fingerprint" region.

259. Identify the peaks **A–D** in Figure 12-1, the spectrum of ethyl acetate,

$$CH_3\overset{\displaystyle O}{\overset{\displaystyle \|}{C}} - O - CH_2CH_3.$$

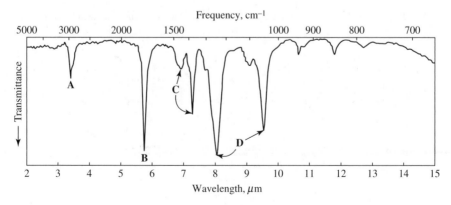

Figure 12-1

260. Match the compounds CH_3CH_2CHO, CH_3COCH_3, and CH_3CH_2COOH with the three IR spectra in Figure 12-2(A), (B), and (C). Give your reasons.

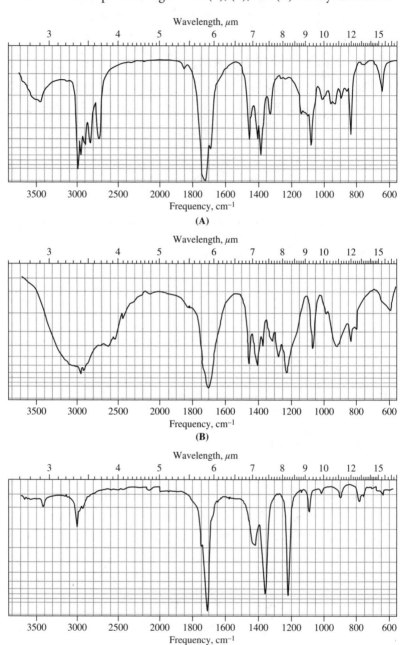

Figure 12-2

261. Explain how the IR spectra of neat samples of phenol, C_6H_5OH, and cyclohexanol would differ.

262. Write a structure for each of the following compounds. Given: the corresponding number of different Hs.

  (A) $C_2H_4Cl_2$, one H
  (B) C_8H_{18}, one H
  (C) C_9H_{12}, two Hs
  (D) noncyclic C_6H_{12}, one H
  (E) C_3H_7Cl, three Hs

263. Explain the splitting pattern for the $-CH^a-CH_3^b$ unit.

264. In which of the following molecules does spin-spin coupling occur? When splitting is observed, give the multiplicity of each kind of H.

  (A) $ClCH_2CH_2Cl$
  (B) $ClCH_2CH_2I$

  (C) 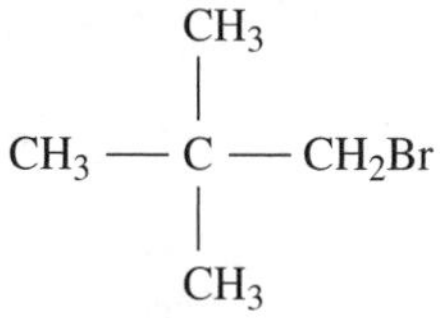 $CH_3 \!-\! \underset{\underset{CH_3}{|}}{\overset{\overset{CH_3}{|}}{C}} \!-\! CH_2Br$

  (D) 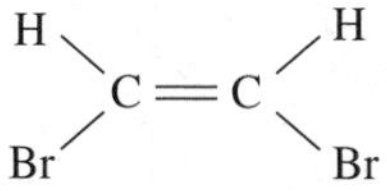
$$\underset{Br}{\overset{H}{}}C=C\underset{Br}{\overset{H}{}}$$

  (E) 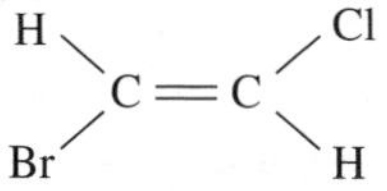
$$\underset{Br}{\overset{H}{}}C=C\underset{H}{\overset{Cl}{}}$$

  (F) 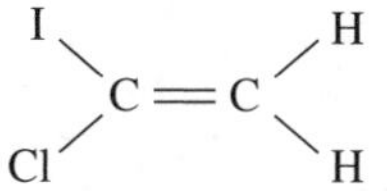
$$\underset{Cl}{\overset{I}{}}C=C\underset{H}{\overset{H}{}}$$

  (G) 
$$CH_2CH_3 \quad \bigcirc \quad CH_2CH_3$$

265. Assign the NMR spectra shown in Figure 12-3 to the appropriate mono-chlorination products of 2,4-dimethylpentane, and justify your assignment. Note the integrations drawn by the spectrometer on the spectra.

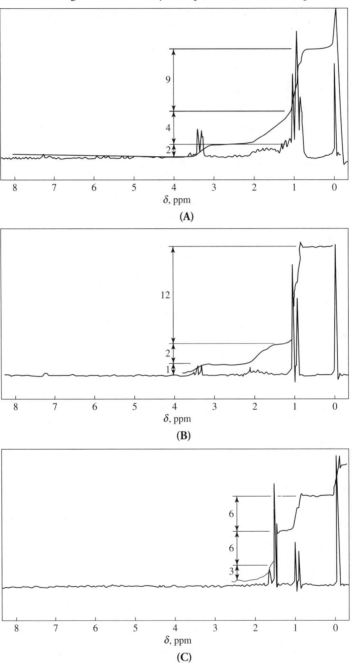

Figure 12-3

266. Discuss the validity of the following statements.

    (A) The presence of a peak whose mass is 1 more than the parent, P + 1, may be due to presence of a naturally abundant D (^{2}H) replacing an H.

    (B) The presence of the P + 1 peak may be attributable to the natural abundance of ^{13}C.

    (C) For oxycompounds, a P + 2 peak may be attributable to the natural abundance of ^{18}O.

    (D) For compounds with N atoms, some of the P + 1 peak may be due to the natural abundance of ^{15}N.

    (E) For organic compounds with N atoms, a P + 2 peak could arise from the presence of ^{15}N and ^{13}C.

267. (A) Give molecular formulas of hydrocarbon cations with *m/z* values of
        I. 29
        II. 51
        III. 91

    (B) Give a combination of C, H, and N to account for *m/z* values of
        I. 29
        II. 57

268. Give the structure of a compound, $C_{10}H_{12}O$, whose mass spectrum shows *m/z* values of 15, 43, 57, 91, 105, and 148.

269. (A) What information can be obtained from the mass spectrum in Figure 12-4 about the structure of an aromatic hydrocarbon?

    (B) What other spectroscopies could help pinpoint the compound?

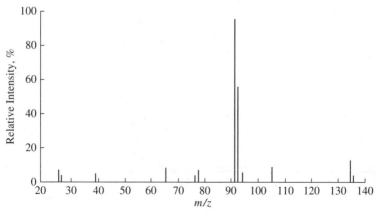

Figure 12-4

270. Summarize the kinds of information provided by the following kinds of spectral techniques:

(A) UV

(B) IR

(C) PMR

(D) ^{13}C NMR

(E) Mass

271. (A) Briefly discuss the salient similarities and differences between the following spectroscopies:

 I. IR and Raman

 II. NMR and ESR (*electron spin resonance*, also called *electron paramagnetic resonance or* EPR)

(B) Discuss the origin and applications of microwave spectroscopy.

CHAPTER 13

Alcohols and Thiols

272. Give the IUPAC name for each of the following alcohols and classify each as 1°, 2°, or 3°:

(A) $CH_3(CH_2)_3CHCH(CH_3)_2$
|
OH

(B) $(CH_3)_3CCH_2OH$

(C) $(CH_3)_2COH$
|
Ph

(D) $BrH_2CCH_2CHC(CH_3)_3$
|
OH

(E) $H_2C{=}CHCHCH_3$
|
OH

(F) $PhCH_2OH$

(G) $HOCH_2CH_2CH_2CH_2Ph$

273. Write the structure for each of the following alcohols:

(A) *sec*-Butyl alcohol

(B) Cinnamyl alcohol

(C) 3-Chloro-2-methyl-1-butanol

(D) *erythro*-3-Chloro-2-butanol

(E) 3,3-Dimethylcyclopentanol

(F) 4,4-Dimethyl-2-cyclohexen-1-ol

274. Give the synthesis of each of the following alcohols from an alkene with the same number of carbons:

(A) 2-Butanol

(B) 1-Methylcyclohexanol

(C) Isobutyl alcohol

(D) Cyclopentylcarbinol

(E) 2-Methyl-2-butanol

275. Outline a synthesis of each alcohol from the indicated starting materials:

(A) Isopropyl alcohol from a hydrocarbon

(B) *n*-Butyl alcohol from acetylene

(C) Allyl alcohol from propane

(D) *t*-Butyl alcohol from *t*-butyl chloride

276. Give the Grignard reagent and carbonyl compound or ethylene oxide that can be used to prepare the following alcohols. List all pairs of possible combinations.

(A) $CH_3CH_2CH_2OH$

(B) $(CH_3)_2C(OH)CH_2CH_2CH_3$

(C) $PhCH_2CH(OH)CH_3$

(D) $CH_3CH_2C(CH_3)OH$
        |
        Ph

(E)

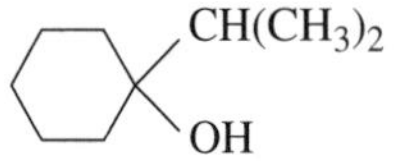

(F)

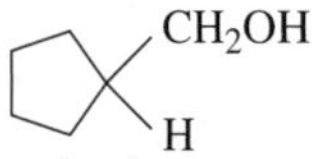

(G) $(CH_3)_2CHCH_2CH_2OH$

277. Compare the acidities of $ClCH_2CH_2OH$ and CH_3CH_2OH. Explain.

278. Use two methods for converting 3-pentanol into 3-bromopentane with little or no 2-bromopentane.

279. (A) Write an equation for the reaction of PBr_3 with an alcohol, ROH.

(B) Does the resulting alkyl bromide show inversion, retention, or racemization?

280. (A) Describe the Lucas test for distinguishing between 1°, 2°, and 3° alcohols.

(B) What is the theoretical basis for this test?

(C) Why is it useful only for alcohols with six or fewer Cs?

281. (A) What is the Jones reagent?

(B) Give the product of the oxidation of each of the following substances with Jones reagent:

    I. $CH_3CH=CHCH(OH)CH_3$

    II.

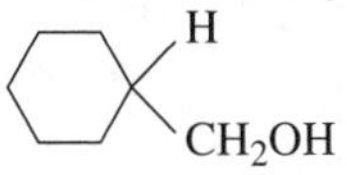

282. Give the product of oxidation by $KMnO_4$ of 1°, 2°, and 3° alcohols in acidic and basic media.

283. Give the structures for the unknown compounds **A** through **C**.

$$C_6H_{12}O(\textbf{A}) \xrightarrow[\Delta]{H_2SO_4} C_6H_{10}(\textbf{B}) \xrightarrow[\Delta]{HNO_3} C_6H_{10}O_4(\textbf{C}) \xleftarrow[\Delta]{HNO_3} \textbf{A}$$

284. A concentrated CCl_4 solution of *t*-butyl alcohol has a broad absorption band at 3440 cm^{-1}, accompanied by a small sharp band at 3620 cm^{-1}. As the solution is progressively diluted, the 3620 cm^{-1} band becomes more intense while the 3440 cm^{-1} band diminishes.

(A) Identify the two bands.

(B) Explain the change of relative intensities with dilution.

285. Give a simple chemical test that can distinguish between 2- and 3-pentanol.

286. Give a simple test tube reaction that distinguishes between the compounds in each of the following pairs. What would you *do*, *see*, and *conclude*?

(A) *t*-Butyl and *n*-butyl alcohol

(B) Ethyl and *n*-propyl alcohol

(C) Allyl and *n*-propyl alcohol

(D) Benzyl methyl ether and benzyl alcohol

(E) Cyclopentanol and cyclopentyl chloride

287. Name the following:

(A) $CH_3CH_2CH_2SH$

(B) $(CH_3)_2CHCH(SH)CH_2CH_3$

(C) $CH_2{=}CHCH_2CH_2SH$

(D) $PhCH_2SH$

(E)

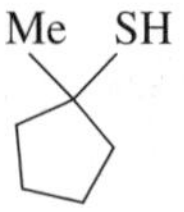

(F)

288. Write the structures for

(A) *t*-butyl mercaptan

(B) neopentyl mercaptan

(C) (*Z*)-2-penten-2-thiol

(D) *trans*-4-ethenylcyclohexanethiol

(E) allyl mercaptan

(F) 1-phenyl-2-propanethiol

(G) 3-mercapto-1-propanol (OH has priority over SH)

289. Which is a stronger nucleophile?

(A) RSH or RS⁻

(B) RS⁻ or RO⁻ (in a protic solvent)

Explain.

290. Distinguish between an alcohol and a thiol without using a chemical or physical test.

291. Distinguish between each pair of compounds by a simple chemical test.

(A) $(CH_3)_2CHOH$ and $(CH_3)_2CHSH$

(B) $CH_3CH_2CH_2OH$ and $(CH_3)_2CHOH$

(C) $CH_3CH_2SCH_3$ and $(CH_3)_2CHSH$

(D) $(CH_3)_2C(OH)CH_2CH_3$ and $CH_3CH_2CH(OH)CH_2CH_3$

CHAPTER 14

Ethers, Epoxides, Glycols, and Thioethers

292. Give the common names of the following ethers:

(A) $CH_3CH_2OCH_2CH_3$

(B) $(CH_3)_2CHOCH(CH_3)CH_2CH_3$

(C) $ClCH_2CH_2OCH_3$

(D) $C_6H_5OCH_3$

(E) $p\text{-}NO_2C_6H_4OC_2H_5$

(F) 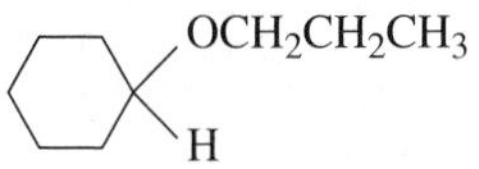 $OCH_2CH_2CH_3$ H

(G) $H_2C{=}CHOCH_2C_6H_5$

293. Write the structures for each of the following compounds:

(A) Cyclopentyl t-butyl ether

(B) m-Diethoxybenzene

(C) 5-Methoxy-2-pentanol

(D) 3-Cyclohexenyl isopropyl ether

(E) Dibenzyl ether

(F) 2,4-Dichlorophenyl 3-nitrophenyl ether

294. (A) Name

I. $CH_3OCH_2CH_2OCH_3$

II. $CH_3OCH_2CH_2OCH_2CH_2OCH_3$

(B) Name these polyethers by the oxa method.

295. Name each of the following compounds:

(A) 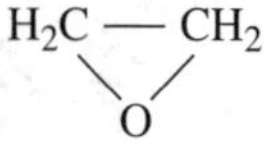 $H_2C \longrightarrow CH_2$
           \   /
            O

(B) 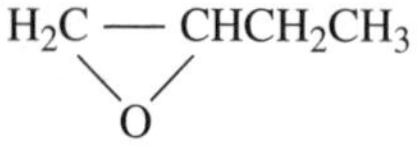 $H_2C \longrightarrow CHCH_2CH_3$
           \   /
            O

(C) 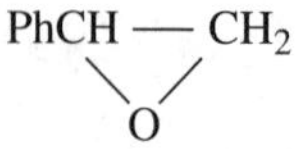   PhCH $\longrightarrow CH_2$
           \   /
            O

(D) 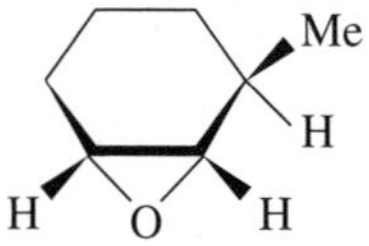   Me
                          H
        H   O   H

(E) 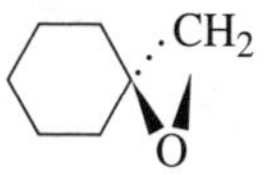 CH_2
                    O

(F) 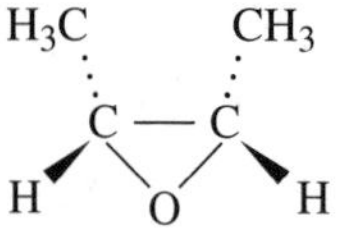 H_3C CH_3
           C — C
        H   O   H

296. Give the IUPAC ring names for the cyclic ethers, $(CH_2)_nO$, where $n =$ 2, 3, 4, 5, and 6.

297. Give the structural formulas for

(A)   phenyloxirane

(B)   3,3-dichloro-2-methyloxetane

(C)   *trans*-2-chloro-5-ethyloxepane

(D)   oxetene

298. Compare

(A)   boiling points

(B)   water solubilities

of ethers, such as diethyl ether and a hydrocarbon of comparable molecular weight and structure, e.g., *n*-pentane.

299. Prepare the following ethers via the Williamson synthesis:

(A)   di-*n*-propyl ether (**A**)

(B)   benzyl methyl ether (**B**)

(C)   phenyl ethyl ether (**C**)

(D)   *t*-butyl ethyl ether (**D**)

300. Rank the following alkyl halides in decreasing order of reactivity in the Williamson reaction:

$(CH_3)_3CCH_2Br$ **(A)** $ClCH_2CH{=}CH_2$ **(B)**

$ClCH_2CH_2CH_3$ **(C)** $BrCH_2CH_2CH_3$ **(D)**

301. (A) Synthesize tetrahydrofuran using the Williamson synthesis.

(B) Through which conformation does the substrate react?

(C) What by-product might one expect in this synthesis?

(D) Why is very little of this by-product formed?

302. Outline the steps in the following syntheses:

(A) $H_2O{=}CHCH_3$ (as the only organic reactant) $\longrightarrow$

$\qquad BrCH{=}CHCH_2OCH_2CH_2CH_3$ **(A)**

(B) $H_2C{=}CHCH_3$ and ethylene $\longrightarrow CH_3CH_2CH_2CH_2OCH(CH_3)_2$ **(B)**

(C) $PhCH(CH_3)OCH(CH_3)Ph$ **(C)** from PhH and any aliphatic compound

303. Give three methods for protecting the OH group of an alcohol by ether formation. In each case, indicate how the alcohol is liberated.

304. Give two syntheses of propylene oxide from propylene.

305. From organic compounds of three or fewer Cs prepare cis-$CH_3CH(OCH_3)CH_2CH{=}CHCH_3$ **(H)**.

306. Write the structure of

(A) propylene glycol

(B) glycerol (glycerin)

(C) sorbitol

(D) pentaerythritol

307. (A) Draw the conformational structures of the four isomeric 4-t-butyl-1,2-cyclohexane-diols.

(B) Which isomer cannot H-bond intramolecularly? Why not?

308. Prepare $HOCH_2CH_2OH$ from
(A) ethylene
(B) ethanol
(C) ethylene oxide
(D) 1,2-dibromoethane

309. (A) Give three ways of naming $(CH_3)_2CHSCH_2CH_2CH_2CH_3$.
(B) Name

      I. $CH_3SCH_2CH_2CH_2OH$

      II. $PhSCH_2CH_3$

      III. $ClCH_2CH_2SCH_2CH_2Cl$

      IV. $CH_3SCH(CH_3)SCH_3$

      V. 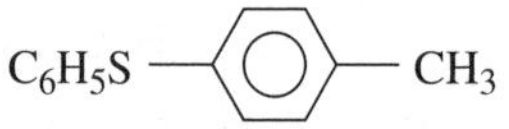 C_6H_5S —⟨○⟩— CH_3

      VI. 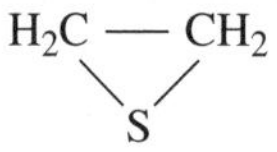 H_2C — CH_2
              \ /
              S

     VII. 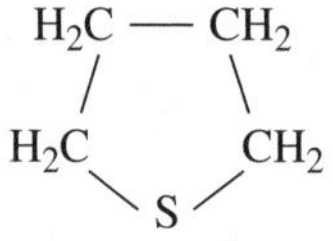 H_2C — CH_2
           /   \
      H_2C CH_2
         \ S /

310. Supply structures and names for compounds **A** through **K**. Different letters may indicate the same compound.

(A) $2CH_3CH_2CH_2Cl \xrightarrow{Na_2S_2} A \xrightarrow[H_2SO_4]{Zn} B \xrightarrow{I_2} C \xrightarrow[-20°C]{Cl_2} D$

           $\xrightarrow{CH_3CH_2S} E$; or $C \xrightarrow{CH_3CH_2S} E$

(B) 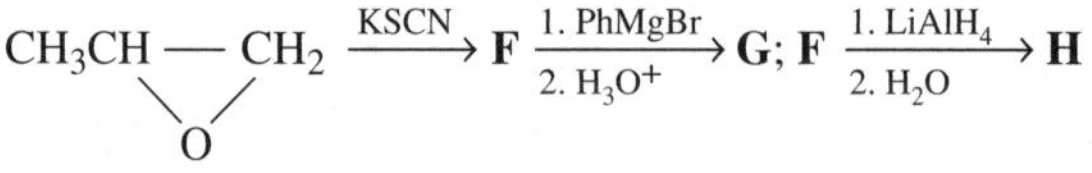 CH_3CH — CH_2 $\xrightarrow{KSCN} F \xrightarrow[2.\ H_3O^+]{1.\ PhMgBr} G$; $F \xrightarrow[2.\ H_2O]{1.\ LiAlH_4} H$
           \ /
            O

(C) $CH_3SCH_3 \xrightarrow[100°C]{H_2O_2} I \xrightarrow{C_2H_5O^-} J \xrightarrow{EtBr} K$

311. Describe simple chemical tests to distinguish between
(A) an ether and an alkyl bromide
(B) an ether and an alkene
(C) an ether and a 3° alcohol
(D) divinyl ether and chloromethyl vinyl ether

CHAPTER 15

Aldehydes and Ketones

312. Give the common names for

  (A) CH_3CHO

  (B) $CH_3CHClCHO$

  (C) $(CH_3)_2CHCHO$

  (D) $CH_2{=}CHCHO$

  (E) $CH_3CH_2CH(OH)CH_2CHO$

  (F) *trans*-$CH_3CH{=}CHCHO$

313. Give the IUPAC names for the compounds in Problem 312.

314. Write structures for each of the following:

  (A) 3-Formylcyclohexanol

  (B) γ-Bromobutyrophenone

  (C) 1, 3-Cyclopentanedione

  (D) 4, 4-Dimethylcydohexanecarbaldehyde

315. Discuss the ^{13}C NMR chemical shifts of carbonyl compounds.

316. Summarize the important features, including similarities and differences, in the IR spectra of aldehydes and ketones.

317. Give an industrial preparation of

  (A) formaldehyde

  (B) benzaldehyde

  (C) acetaldehyde

318. Synthesize each of the following compounds from alcohols of three or fewer carbons and acetylene:

(A) 3-hexanone

(B) pentanal

(C) 2-methyl-3-pentanone

You may reuse any intermediate or product once made.

319. Prepare an aldehyde by reduction of a carboxylic acid ester.

320. Give the product of each of the following reactions:

(A) $C_6H_5CH_3 + CrO_3$ in $(CH_3CO)_2O \longrightarrow A \xrightarrow{H_2O} B$

(B) $C_6H_5CH_3 + CO + HCl \xrightarrow[AlCl_3]{CuCl} C$

(C) $C_6H_5CH_2CH_2NO_2 \xrightarrow[2.\,H_3O^+]{1.\,OH^-} D$

321. Give the product of the reaction of RCOCl and an alkene, $R'CH{=\!=}CH_2$, in the presence of BF_3, and formulate a mechanism.

322. Give the product of the reaction of CO + HCl in the presence of $CuCl/AlCl_3$ with

(A) C_6H_6

(B) $CH_3OC_6H_5$

323. Write equations for the reaction with water of

(A) formaldehyde

(B) acetone

What is the general name for the product?

324. Show the Beckmann rearrangement of cyclohexanone oxime.

325. Select the best way for reducing the $\diagdown C{=\!=}O$ in each of the following:

(A) $BrCH_2CH_2CHO$

(B) $(CH_3)_2C(OH)CH_2CH_2COCH_3$

(C) $PhCH(OH)CH_2COCH_2CH_3$

(D) 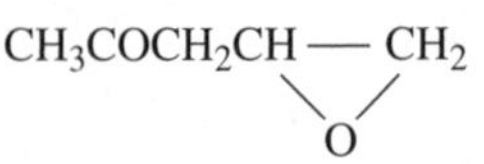 $CH_3COCH_2CH \overset{\diagup}{\underset{\diagdown O}{\diagup}} CH_2$

326. In the presence of concentrated OH^-, aldehydes lacking an α-hydrogen undergo the *Cannizzaro reaction*. Give the products of the reactions of

(A) benzaldehyde

(B) trimethylacetaldehyde

(C) furaldehyde

327. Find the products of the *crossed-Cannizzaro* reaction of

(A) H_2CO and PhCHO

(B) H_2CO and Me_3CCHO

328. Two isomers are formed from the reaction of butanone with Mg/Hg. Write their structures.

329. Suggest a mechanism for the following reaction that occurs in the presence of UV or peroxides (free-radical initiators):

$$CH_3CH_2CHO + H_2C{=}CHCH_3 \longrightarrow CH_3CH_2COCH_2CH_2CH_3$$

330. Give the product and a mechanism of the reaction

$$PhCH{=}O \xrightarrow{\text{KCN/EtOH}} C_{14}H_{12}O_2.$$

331. Give a simple chemical test to distinguish between the compounds in each of the following pairs:

(A) $PhCH{=}CHCH_2OH$ and $PhCH{=}CHCHO$

(B) $CH_3CH_2CH_2CH_2CHO$ and $CH_3CH_2COCH_2CH_3$

(C) $PhCH_2COCH_2CH_3$ and $PhCH(OH)CH_2CH_2CH_3$

(D) $PhCH_2CHO$ and $PHCOCH_3$

332. Compound **X**, $C_9H_{10}O$, is inert to Br_2 in CCl_4. Vigorous oxidation with hot alkaline permanganate yields benzoic acid. **X** gives a precipitate with semicarbazide hydrochloride and with 2, 4-dinitrophenylhydrazine (DNPH).

(A) Write all possible structures for **X**.

(B) How can these isomers be distinguished by using simple chemical tests?

CHAPTER 16

Carboxylic Acids

333. Give the common name of the following acids:

(A) $ClCH_2COOH$

(B) $O_2NCH_2CH_2COOH$

(C) $BrCH_2CH_2CH_2COOH$

(D) $CH_3C(CH_3)_2COOH$

(E) $O{=}CHCH_2CH_2CH_2CH_2COOH$

(F) $BrCH_2CHBrCHBrCOOH$

(G) $HOCH_2CH_2CHFCOOH$

(H) $CH_3CH_2COCH_2COOH$

334. Give the IUPAC name for these compounds:

I. $HCOOH$, formic acid (from ants)

II. CH_3COOH, acetic acid (from vinegar)

III. CH_3CH_2COOH, propionic acid (from fat)

IV. $n\text{-}CH_3CH_2CH_2COOH$, butyric acid (from butter)

V. $n\text{-}CH_3(CH_2)_3COOH$, valeric acid (from valerian)

VI. $n\text{-}CH_3(CH_2)_4COOH$, caproic acid (from goats)

335. (A) Give the IUPAC name for the following:

I. $PhCH_2CH_2COOH$

II. $CH_2{=}CHCOOH$

III. $CH_3CH{=}CHCOOH$

IV. $CH_3CH_2CH(CHO)CH_2COOH$

(B) Name —COOH as a substituent group.

336. Name the following:

(A)

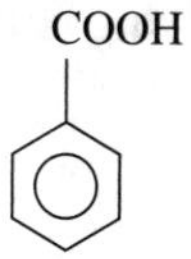

COOH

(B)

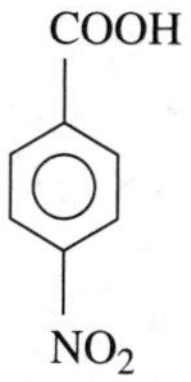

COOH

NO$_2$

(C)

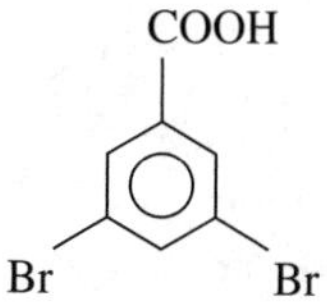

COOH

Br   Br

(D)

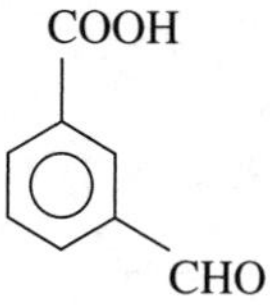

COOH

CHO

(E)

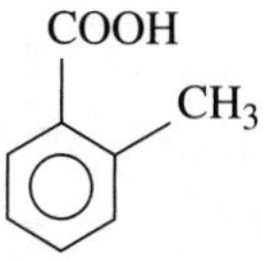

COOH

CH$_3$

(F)

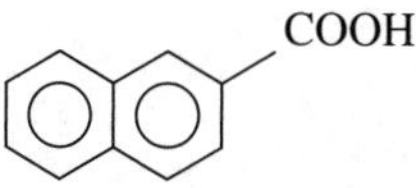

COOH

337. (A) Define the term *fatty acid*.

(B) Give the common and IUPAC names for the following fatty acids:

I. $CH_3(CH_2)_{14}COOH$

II. $CH_3(CH_2)_{16}COOH$

III. $CH_3-(CH_2)_7-\underset{\underset{H}{|}}{C}=\underset{\underset{H}{|}}{C}-(CH_2)_7COOH$

IV.

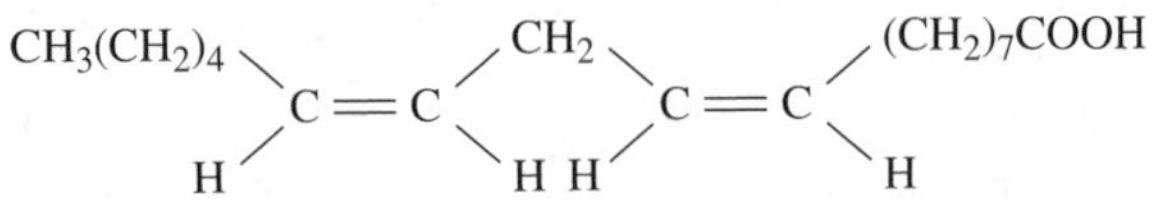

$$CH_3(CH_2)_4\underset{H}{\diagdown}C=C\diagup\overset{CH_2}{\underset{H\ H}{\diagdown}}C=C\diagup\overset{(CH_2)_7COOH}{\underset{H}{\diagup}}$$

V.

$$CH_3CH_2\underset{H}{\diagdown}C=C\diagup\overset{CH_2}{\underset{H\ H}{\diagdown}}C=C\diagup\overset{CH_2}{\underset{H\ H}{\diagdown}}C=C\diagup\overset{(CH_2)_7COOH}{\underset{H}{\diagup}}$$

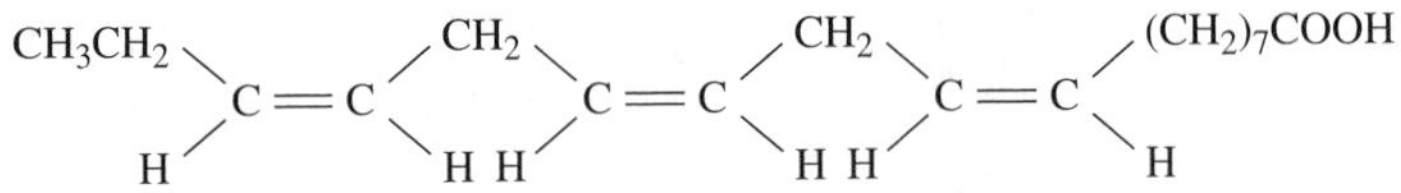

338. Write the structural formulas and give the IUPAC names for

(A) phthalic acid

(B) isophthalic acid

(C) terephthalic acid

(D) maleic acid

(E) fumaric acid

(F) tartaric acid

(G) citric acid

339. Acetic acid in the vapor state has a molecular weight of 120. Explain.

340. Synthesize

(A) $CH_3CH_2CH_2COOH$ from

I. $CH_3CH_2CH_2CH_2OH$

II. $CH_3CH_2CH_2CHO$

(B) $p\text{-}O_2NC_6H_4COOH$ from $PhCH_3$

(C) adipic acid from benzene

341. Starting with C_6H_6 and $C_6H_5CH_3$ prepare the following:

(A) C_6H_5COOH

(B) $p\text{-}CH_3C_6H_4COOH$

(C) 2-Methyl-5-chlorobenzoic acid

(D) $p\text{-}HOOCC_6H_4CH_2COOH$

(E) 2-Bromo-4-nitrobenzoic acid

(F) 1,2,4-Benzenetricarboxylic acid. Do not repeat the preparation of any needed intermediate compound.

342. Give industrial methods for the manufacture of

(A) acetic acid (use two ways, exclusive of fermentation)

(B) formic acid

343. Write balanced equations for the following reactions, and name the salt that is formed.

(A) $CH_3COOH + NaOH$

(B) $CH_3CH_2COOH + Ca(OH)_2$

(C) $CH_3(CH_2)_{16}COOH + Fe(OAc)_3$ (aq)

344. (A) Describe a micelle formed from a soap.

(B) Explain why these very small micelles do not coalesce.

(C) Describe the detergency (ability to remove oil and grease) role of these soap micelles.

345. (A) Write equations for the ionization of RCOOH and for K_a.

(B) Give the thermodynamic equation relating pK_a with $\Delta H°$ and $\Delta S°$ of the ionization reaction, and discuss the relationship.

(C) Name the factors that influence

   I. $\Delta H°$

   II. $\Delta S°$

(D) Must H_3O^+ be taken into account in rationalizing differences in acid strengths?

346. What is the correlation between the effect of a substituent on the acidity of ArCOOH and on the aromatic electrophilic substitution?

347. (A) Which reducing agent, LiAlH$_4$ or BH$_3$/THF, will reduce the following carboxylic acids to their corresponding 1° alcohols?

    I. CH$_3$CH(CH$_3$)CH$_2$COOH

    II. *p*-CH$_3$COC$_6$H$_4$COOH

    III. Cyclohexanecarboxylic acid

    IV. *m*-O$_2$NC$_6$H$_4$COOH

    V. (Z)-CH$_3$CH=CHCH$_2$COOH

    VI. BrCH$_2$CH$_2$CH$_2$COOH

  (B) Give the structure of the alcohol.

348. (A) Give the final product with the sequence of intermediates for the reaction of propanoic acyl with Br$_2$ and a trace of PBr$_3$ followed by addition of H$_2$O [*Hell–Volhard–Zelinsky* (HVZ) reaction].

  (B) What is the final product when 2 eq of reagent is used?

  (C) What is the reaction with Me$_3$CCOOH?

  (D) Find the product formed if

    I. PCl$_3$ replaces PBr$_3$

    II. Cl$_2$ replaces Br$_2$

349. (A) Compare the reaction of CH$_3$CH$_2$COOH with excess

    I. CH$_3$MgBr

    II. CH$_3$Li

350. Convert 2-chlorobutanoic acid into 3-chlorobutanoic acid.

351. Show the conversion of stearic acid to

  (A) 1-bromopentadecane

  (B) 1-nonadecanol

352. Prepare

  (A) I. 2-oxocyclopentanecarboxylic acid

    II. 1-cyclopentenylmethanol from cyclopentanol

  (B) *cis*-1, 2-cyclohexanedicarboxylic acid from any organic compound of four Cs or less.

Use as few steps as possible.

353. (A) Define the term *neutralization equivalent* of an acid.

(B) Find the number of ionizable Hs for a polycarboxylic acid (MW = 210 g/mol) with a neutralization equivalent of 70 g/eq. How many equivalents of NaOH would be neutralized by 1 mol of this acid?

(C) Find the neutralization equivalent of mellitic acid, $C_6 (COOH)_6$.

354. Identify the substances **A** through **D** in the sequence

Palamitic acid $\xrightarrow{\text{LiAlH}_4}$ **A** $\xrightarrow{\text{HCl}}$ **B** $\xrightarrow[\text{2. Ethylene oxide}]{\text{1. Mg/Et}_2\text{O}}$ **C** $\xrightarrow{\text{KMnO}_4}$ **D**

CHAPTER 17

Acid Derivatives

355. (A) Name each of the following acid halides using the IUPAC method:

       I. CH_3CH_2COCl

      II. $(CH_3)_3CCH_2COCl$

     III. $CH_3CH_2CH_2CHBrCOBr$

     IV. $CH_3CH_2CH=CHCH_2COCl$

      V.

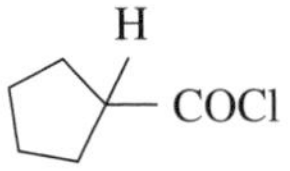

  (B) Give common names for compounds (I) through (III).

356. Give the common name for each anhydride:

  (A) $(PhCO)_2O$

  (B) $PhCOOCOCH_3$

  (C) $(CH_3CHClCO)_2O$

  (D) $CH_3(CH_2)_4COOCOCH_2CH_3$

  (E)

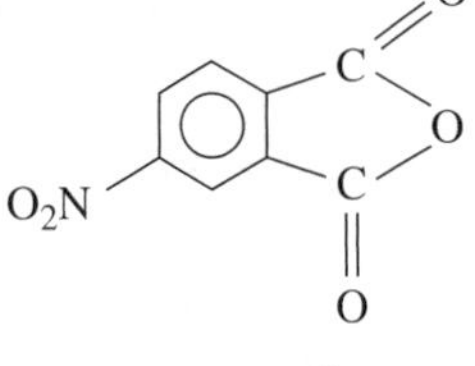

  (F)

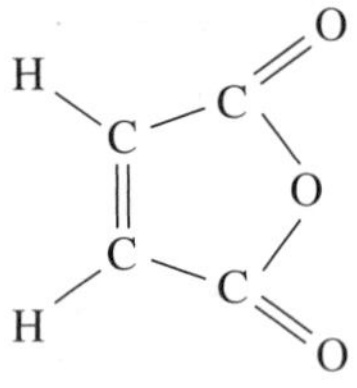

357. (A) Give common names of these esters:

     I. $CH_3COOCH_2CH_2CH_3$

     II. 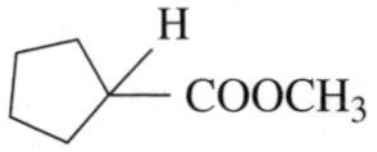 COOCH_3

     III. $CH_3CHBrCH_2COOCH(CH_3)_2$

     IV. $CH_2(COOCH_2CH_2CH_3)_2$

     V. $HOOCCOOC_2H_5$

     VI. $H_2C{=}CHCOOCH(CH_3)CH_2CH_3$

    (B) Give the IUPAC name for (I)–(IV) in (A).

358. Name the following amides:

    (A) $CH_3CH_2CONH_2$

    (B) $CH_3CONHPh$

    (C) $p\text{-}CH_3C_6H_4CONH_2$

    (D) $H_2NCOCH_2CH_2CH_2CONH_2$

    (E) $(CH_3)_2CHCONHC_2H_5$

    (F) 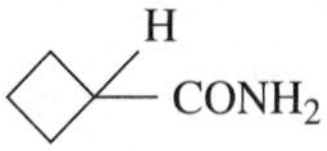 CONH_2

359. Write structures for the following compounds:

    (A) Benzanilide

    (B) Di-*n*-butyl adipate

    (C) 5-Oxohexanoyl bromide

    (D) N-bromosuccinimide

    (E) Phthalimide

    (F) γ-Valerolactone

    (G) Methyl *cis*-2-bromocyclohexane-carboxylate

    (H) *cis*-Cinnamoyl chloride

360. (A) Write a general structure for

     I. an acid hydrazide

     II. an acid azide

     III. a thioacid

     IV. a thioester

     V. a hydroxamic acid

    (B) Why are they classified as acid derivatives?

361. (A) Give the resonance structures for RCOG.

(B) What effect does resonance have on the stability and electrophilic character of the $C{=}O$ group?

362. Explain why esters have lower bps than

(A) ketones

(B) acids of comparable molecular weight

363. Show the general mechanism of nucleophilic acyl substitution on the acyl

$$\overset{\displaystyle O}{\overset{\|}{}}$$

derivative, $RC{-}G$, in

(A) a basic solution

(B) an acid solution

364. (A) List three reagents for converting a carboxylic acid to its acyl chloride.

(B) Select the most convenient of the three reagents, give a reason for your choice, and write a balanced equation for its reaction with RCOOH.

(C) Name the reagent that can convert

I. an acid to an acyl bromide

II. an acyl chloride to an acyl fluoride

365. (A) Define transesterification.

(B) Complete the following reaction:

$$CH_3COOH_2CH_3 \xrightarrow[n\text{-}C_5H_{11}O^-/n\text{-}C_5H_{11}OH]{H^+,\ n\text{-}C_5H_{11}OH\ or} ?$$

366. Give the product of each of the following reactions:

(A) Succinic anhydride $+$ MeOH $\longrightarrow$ A $\xrightarrow{PCl_3}$ B $\xrightarrow{MeONH_2}$ C

(B) Phthalic acid $+ NH_3 \longrightarrow$ D $\xrightarrow{300°C}$ E

(C) $MeCH(CH_2COOH)_2 \xrightarrow[\Delta]{(CH_3CO)_2O}$ F

367. (A) Why does an acyl chloride undergo nucleophilic attack more rapidly than does an alkyl chloride?

(B) What is the essential difference between nucleophilic attack on the $C{=}O$ of an aldehyde or ketone and on an acyl derivative?

368. List the reagent for converting benzoyl chloride to

(A) benzaldehyde

(B) benzylamine

(C) benzyl alcohol

(D) benzoyl benzoate

(E) benzoic anhydride

(F) N-benzylbenzamide

369. Give the structures of **A** through **F**.

(A) $CH_3CH_2COCl + PhH \xrightarrow{AlCl_3} \mathbf{A}$

(B) $i\text{-BuBr} \xrightarrow[2.CuI]{1.Li} \mathbf{B} \xrightarrow{PhCOCl} \mathbf{C}$

(C) $PhH + (CH_3CO)_2O \xrightarrow[2.H^+]{1.AlCl_3} \mathbf{D}$

(D) $PhCH_2COOCH_3 \xrightarrow[2.H^+]{1.2eq\ of\ n\text{-}BuLi} \mathbf{E}$

(E) $H_2C{=}CHCH_2CN \xrightarrow[2.H^+]{1.PhMgBr} \mathbf{F}$

370. Write equations for the reaction with nitrous acid of

(A) a 1° amide

(B) a 2° amide

(C) a 3° amide

371. What are the structures of **A** through **E**?

(A) $CH_3CH_2COOCl \xrightarrow{HN_3} \mathbf{A} \xrightarrow{\Delta} \mathbf{B}(C_3H_5NO) \xrightarrow{H_2O} \mathbf{C}(C_2H_7N)$

(B) $CH_3CH_2COOCH_3 \xrightarrow{H_2NOH} \mathbf{D}(C_3H_7NO_2) \xrightarrow{OH^-} \mathbf{E}$

372. (A) Define

I. lipid

II. triglyceride

III. fat

IV. oil

V. wax

(B) What is the important chemical difference between a fat and an oil?

(C) What nonester compounds are classified as lipids?

373. (A) Write structures for

      I. trimethyl phosphate

      II. dimethyl ethylphosphonate

      III. cyclopentyl pyrophosphate

  (B) Write an equation for the preparation of a trialkyl phosphate

374. The Beckmann rearrangement of an oxime occurs with PCl_5, H_2SO_4, or $ArSO_3H$.

  (A) Give the products of the reaction of

      I. $Me_2C{=}NOH$

      II. $\underset{\underset{\displaystyle NOH}{\|}}{Ph{-}C{-}Me}$

      III. $\underset{\underset{\displaystyle HON}{\|}}{Ph{-}C{-}Me}$

      IV. 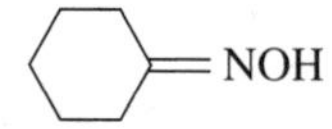 ⬡= NOH

  (B) Suggest a mechanism.

375. A pleasantly smelling, optically active compound **F** has an SE = 186. It does not react with Br_2 in CCl_4. Hydrolysis of **F** gives two optically active compounds, **G**, which is soluble in NaOH, and **H**. Compound **H** gives a positive iodoform test, and on warming with conc. H_2SO_4 gives **I** with no diastereomers. When the Ag^+ salt of **G** is reacted with Br_2, racemic **J** is formed. Optically active **J** is formed when **H** is treated with tosyl chloride (TsCl) and then NaBr. The IR spectrum of **F** shows a single C=O stretching peak. Give structures of **F** through **J** and explain your choices.

CHAPTER 18

Carbanion-Enolates and Enols

376. (A) Account for the fact that nitroform, $HC(NO_2)_3$ (trinitromethane), and cyanoform, $HC(CN)_3$ (tricyanomethane), are both strong acids ($K_a > 1$) but chloroform is a very weak acid.

(B) Why is $CH_3SO_2CH_3$ ($pK_a \cong 31$) much less acidic than CH_3NO_2 ($pK_a \cong 10$)?

377. (A) Write the structure of another product that can be formed when H^+ from H_2O adds to a carbanion-enolate anion.

(B) What are the names given to the isomeric products and to the equilibrium in (**A**)?

378. Show structures for the tautomer of each of the following compounds:

(A) CH_3CHO

(B) $C_6H_5COCH_3$

(C) CH_3NO_2

(D) $Me_2C{=}NOH$

(E) $CH_3CH{=}NCH_3$

379. (A) Write structures for the stable keto and enol tautomers of 2,4-pentanedione (**A**), a typical dicarbonyl compound.

(B) Why are such enols of β-dicarbonyl compounds more stable than those of monocarbonyl compounds?

(C) Account for the fact that the enol content of **A** is 15% in H_2O and 92% in hexane.

(D) How can the enol be chemically detected and separated?

380. Account for the PMR spectrum of $PhCH_2COCH_3$ that shows four main types of signals roughly in the ratio of 1:5:1:3 in decreasing order of chemical shift.

381. Describe the steps in the formation of HCI_3 from the haloform reaction of $PhCOCH_3$ with NaOH and I_2 (NaOI).

382. Give formulas for **A** through **D** in the following reactions.

$$RCH_2\text{—}\overset{\displaystyle |}{C}\text{=}O + (i\text{-pr})_2N^-Li^+ \longrightarrow A + B \quad A + R'X \longrightarrow C + D$$

$$\text{Lithium diisopropylamide,}$$

$$\text{LDA}$$

383. (A) Give the two possible enamines and C-alkylation products resulting from the Stork reaction, using 2-methylcyclohexanone and $PhCH_2Cl$.

(B) Predict the major product and explain your choice.

384. Give structural formulas of **A** through **C** in this modified enamine synthesis:

$$\text{Cyclohexanone} + \text{cyclohexylamine} \longrightarrow A(C_{12}H_{21}N) \xrightarrow{\text{EtMgBr}}$$

$$B(C_{12}H_{20}NMgBr) \xrightarrow[\text{2. } H^+]{\text{1. ethylene oxide}} C(C_8H_{14}O_2)$$

385. (A) Show the general steps for using diethyl malonate (DEM) in the synthesis of mono-(RCH_2COOH) and disubstituted acetic acids $(RR'CHCOOH)$.

(B) Discuss the chemistry.

(C) Why can R_3CCOOH not be made by this synthesis?

386. Use DEM to prepare

(A) 3-methylbutanoic acid

(B) 2-ethylbutanoic acid

(C) 2-methylbutanoic acid

387. (A) Give general equations for use of acetoacetic ester (AAE) to prepare CH_3COCH_2R and $CH_3COCHRR'$.

(B) Discuss the chemistry.

(C) Why can CH_3COCR_3 not be made this way?

388. (A) Which three isomers may be present in the equilibrium mixture created when $CH_2{=}CHCH_2CHO$ (**D**) is treated with aq. NaOH?

(B) Indicate the most stable isomer (99.9%).

389. (A) Define the terms

  I. *aldol addition*

  II. *mixed aldol addition*

(B) What reagents are used as catalysts?

(C) What kinds of products are formed from these additions?

(D) Name the bond that forms the products in (**C**).

(E) Write a general equation for the aldol addition.

(F) What further reaction of the product in (**C**) may occur?

(G) What effect does the step in (**F**) have on the equilibrium of the overall reaction?

(H) What are aldol-type additions?

390. (A) Show the net reactions for the formation of the aldol adduct from

  I. propanal in dilute NaOH

  II. acetone with $Ba(OH)_2$

Name the products.

(B) Give the major difference between these two additions.

(C) How can we increase the poor yields of aldol-addition products from ketones?

391. Give the final products of the reaction of an aryl aldehyde $PhCH{=}O$ with

(A) CH_3CHO

(B) CH_3COCH_3

392. Prepare the following compounds from CH_3CH_2CHO. Do not repeat precursor syntheses.

(A) $CH_3CH_2CH{=}C(CH_3)CHO$ (**A**)

(B) $CH_3CH_2CH_2CH(CH_3)CHO$ (**B**)

(C) $CH_3CH_2CH{=}C(CH_3)CH_2OH$ (**C**)

(D) $CH_3CH_2CH_2CH(CH_3)CH_2OH$ (**D**)

(E) $CH_3CH_2CH_2CH(CH_3)_2$ (**E**)

(F) $CH_3CH_2CH(OH)CH(CH_3)COOH$ (**F**)

393. Give structures of the products from the following condensations:

(A) $p\text{-}CH_3C_6H_4CHO + (CH_3CH_2C)_2O \xrightarrow{CH_3CH_2COO^-Na^+}$

where the reagent bears:

$$\overset{\displaystyle O}{\overset{\displaystyle \|}{}}$$

(B) Cyclohexanone $+ CH_3CH_2NO_2 \xrightarrow{OH^-}$

(C) $C_6H_5CHO + C_6H_5CH_2C{=}N \xrightarrow{OH^-}$

(D) Benzophenone $+$ cyclopentadiene $\xrightarrow{OH^-}$

(E) $CH_3COCH_3 + 2C_6H_5CHO \xrightarrow{OH^-}$

(F) 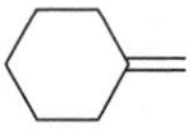 $\langle \rangle{=}O + N{\equiv}CCH_2COOCH_3 \xrightarrow{CH_3COO^-NH_4^+}$

394. Give the product and the mechanism for the OEt^--catalyzed Claisen condensation of CH_3COOEt.

395. Compare the Claisen condensation with the aldol addition in terms of the mechanism and nature of the product.

396. Synthesize 3-ethyl-2pentanone, using acetic acid as the only organic compound.

397. Give the structures for compounds **A** through **E** and justify your answers.

$$C_{10}H_{16}(A) \xrightarrow[\text{Zn or } H_2O_2]{O_3} C_{10}H_{16}O_2(B) \xrightarrow{aq.OH^-}$$

$$C_{10}H_{14}O(C)(\lambda_{max} = 300 \text{ nm}) \xrightarrow{Zn/Hg,HCl}$$

$$C_{10}H_{16}(D) \xrightarrow{H_2/Pd} C_{10}H_{18}(E)$$

E is also obtained from the complete catalytic hydrogenation of azulene.
$$A \xrightarrow[\Delta]{S} \text{naphthalene}, C_{10}H_8.$$

CHAPTER 19

Amines

398. Define amines and identify the following amines as primary (1°), secondary (2°), or tertiary (3°):

(A) $CH_3CH_2CHCH_3$
$\quad\quad\quad\quad |$
$\quad\quad\quad NH_2$

(B) $(CH_3)_3N$

(C) CH_3CHNH_2
$\quad\quad\quad |$
$\quad\quad C_6H_5$

(D) $CH_2{=}CHCH_2NHCH_3$

(E) 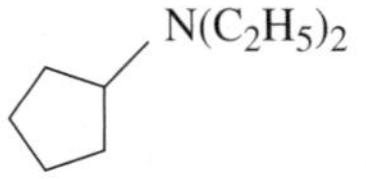

(F) 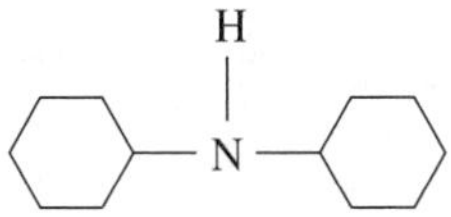

399. Give the IUPAC names for:

(A) $Me_2CHCH_2NHCHMe_2$

(B) $H_2N(CH_2)_4NH_2$

(C) $CH_3CH_2N(CHClCH_3)_2$

(D) $HOCH_2CH_2CH_2NH_2$

(E) $CH_3CH_2CHNMe_2$
$\quad\quad\quad |$
$\quad\quad CH_3$

400. Give the chemical abstract (CA) names for

(A)

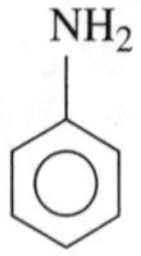

NH$_2$

(B)

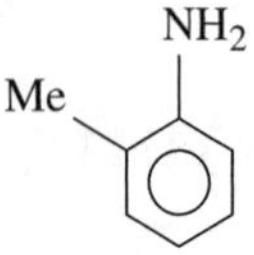

Me, NH$_2$

(C)

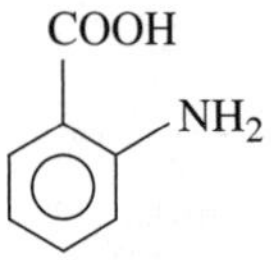

COOH, NH$_2$

(D)

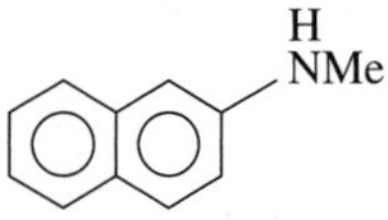

$\overset{H}{N}$Me

(E)

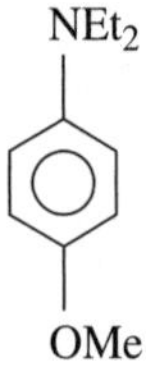

NEt$_2$, OMe

(F)

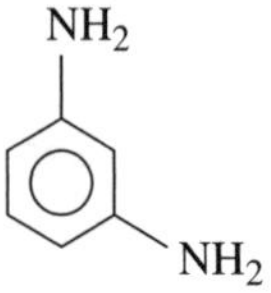

NH$_2$, NH$_2$

(G)

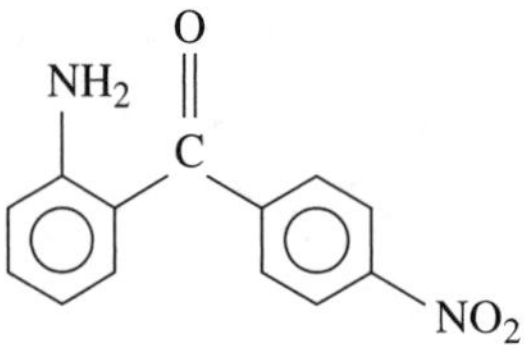

NH$_2$, $\overset{O}{\underset{||}{C}}$, NO$_2$

401. Give the chemical abstract (CA) names for

(A) $CH_3CH_2NH_2$

(B) $CH_3CH_2CH_2CH_2NHCH_3$

(C) $H_2NCH_2CH_2NH_2$

(D) $PhNH_2$

(E)

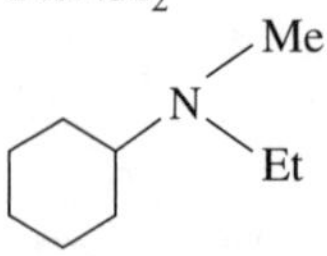

$N\overset{Me}{\underset{Et}{\diagdown}}$

(F) $CH_3CH_2N(CHClCH_3)_2$

402. Write structures for the following compounds:

(A) *o*-Phenetidine

(B) 2-Ethylpyrrolidine

(C) Piperidine-3-carboxylic acid

(D) *cis*-4-Methyl-1-cyclohexanamine

(E) Aziridine

(F) Morpholine

403. Discuss the solubility of amines in

(A) water

(B) alcohol

404. (A) Write chemical equations for the reactions of $MeNH_2$ with

I. H_2O

II. gaseous HCl

III. $B(Me)_3$

(B) Characterize the chemical behavior of $MeNH_2$ in each case in (**A**).

405. (A) Write the equilibrium expression (K_b) for the reaction of $MeNH_2$ in water.

(B) Given $K_b = 4.3 \times 10^{-4}$, find the pK_b.

(C) Find the pK_a for $MeNH_3^+$, the conjugate acid.

406. (A) Write the equilibrium expression for the dissociation constant, K_{diss}, for the complex $MeH_2\overset{+}{N}$—$\bar{B}Me_3$.

(B) How are the values of K_{diss} and the reactivity of the amine toward the trialkylborane related?

407. Explain the diminished basicities of 3° amines as their Rs become bulkier.

408. Summarize the factors that affect relative basicities.

409. Give the generic name for the conjugate base of an amine.

410. (A) Prepare *n*-butylamine by a *Gabriel synthesis*.

(B) Why is the synthesis in (**A**) not a viable method for preparing

    I. *t*-butylamine

    II. neopentylamine

    III. diethylamine

    IV. *p*-toluidine

from the corresponding halide or tosylate?

411. Identify **A** through **E** in the following:

$$PhSO_2Cl + EtNH_2 \xrightarrow{-HCl} A \xrightarrow{NaOH} B \xrightarrow{EtBr} C \xrightarrow{H_3O^+} D + E.$$

412. The reaction of (*S*)-2-methylbutanamide with Br_2 and OH^- produces an optically active amine. Give the structure of the product, including its stereochemical designation and the mechanism for its formation.

413. Discuss the environmental and biochemical importance of nitrosamines.

414. (A) Supply the structures for **A** through **C** in

$$RCH_2CH_2NH_2 \xrightarrow{MeI \ (excess)} A \xrightarrow{AgOH} B \xrightarrow{\Delta} C.$$

(B) Classify the reaction.

(C) What is the leaving group in the last step?

(D) Why does $RCH_2CH_2NH_2$ not undergo an E2 elimination?

415. Describe how aniline may be

(A) monobrominated

(B) mononitrated

416. Prepare $PhCH_2NH_2$ (**A**) by

(A) Gabriel synthesis

(B) alkyl halide amination

(C) nitrile reduction

(D) reductive amination

(E) Hofmann degradation

417. Prepare

(A) the local anesthetic benzocaine, $p\text{-}H_2NC_6H_4COOC_2H_5$, from *p*-nitrotoluene

(B) the antibiotic sulfanilamide, $p\text{-}H_2NC_6H_4SO_2NH_2$, from $PhNH_2$

418. Deduce the structure of the following amines from the following exhaustive methylation and Hofmann elimination data.

(A) A resolvable amine is subjected to exhaustive methylation with 3 eq of MeI, followed by a Hofmann elimination. On reductive ozonolysis, the isolated alkene yields an equimolar mixture of $H_2C{=}O$ and $O{=}CHCH_2CH_2CH_3$.

(B) $C_5H_{13}N$ **(B)** reacts with 1 eq of MeI and eventually gives propene.

(C) $C_5H_{13}N$ **(C)** reacts with 2 eq of MeI and Ag_2O/Δ to give $H_2C{=}CH_2$ and a 3° amine. The amine reacts further with 1 eq of MeI to eventually give $H_2C{=}CHCH_3$.

419. Deduce the structure of a compound ($C_9H_{11}NO$) that is soluble in dilute HCl and gives a positive test with $Ag(NH_3)_2^+$. Its IR spectrum has a strong band at 1695 cm^{-1} and a smaller one at 2720 cm^{-1}, but no bands in the 3300 to 3500 cm^{-1} region. The proton-decoupled ^{13}C spectrum shows six signals which display the following splitting patterns in the proton-coupled spectrum: one quartet, two singlets, and three doublets, one of which is very downfield.

CHAPTER 20

Phenols and Their Derivatives

420. Distinguish among alcohols, enols, phenols, and naphthols.

421. (A) Account for the fact that phenols are much more stable than enols.
  (B) Give the two keto forms with type and name.

422. Give the structural formulas and
  (A) the IUPAC names
  (B) the common names
  (C) the CA names
  of the phenyl isomers of C_7H_8O.

423. Name each of the following compounds. Include the common names when applicable.

(A)

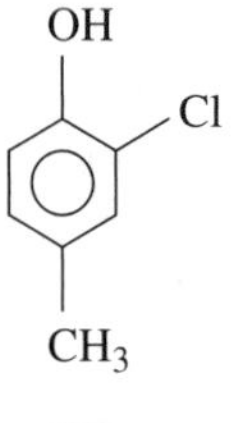

OH, Cl, CH$_3$ substituents on benzene ring

(B)

OH, NH$_2$ substituents on benzene ring

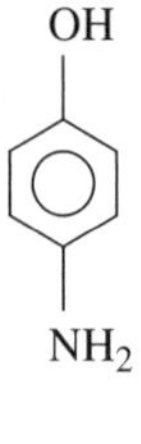

(C)

NHCOCH$_3$

OH

(D)

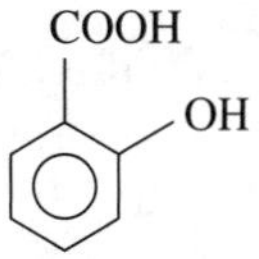

COOH

OH

(E)

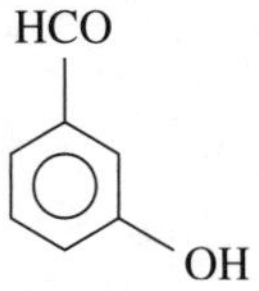

HCO

OH

(F)

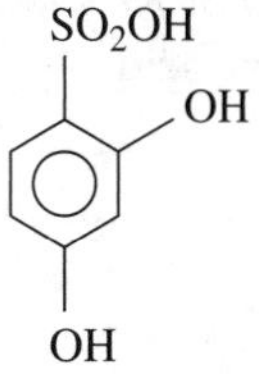

SO$_2$OH

OH

OH

(G)

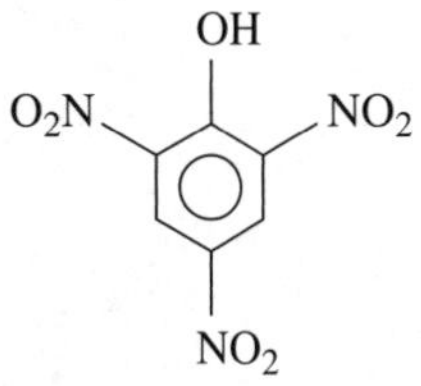

OH

O$_2$N

NO$_2$

NO$_2$

(H)

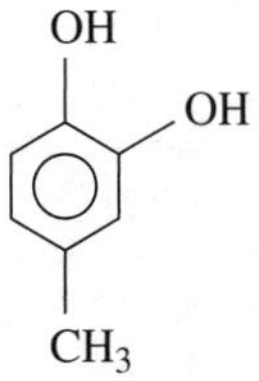

OH

OH

CH$_3$

424. Give the structural formulas for

(A) 2-nitro-4-acetylphenol

(B) *p*-vinylphenol

(C) 4-*n*-hexylresorcinol (an antiseptic)

(D) ethyl salicylate

(E) β-naphthol

(F) 2-hydroxy-3-phenylbenzoic acid

(G) *m*-allylphenol

(H) 6-bromo-1-naphthol

425. Give a laboratory method for converting PhH to PhOH via $PhNO_2$.

426. Synthesize
   (A) α-naphthol from naphthalene
   (B) β-naphthol from naphthalene

427. Explain why $PhOH(pK_a = 10)$ is much more acidic than EtOH ($pK_a = 18$).

428. Compare the acidities of
   (A) *p*-chlorophenol and *p*-nitrophenol
   (B) 2,4-dinitrophenol and 2,4,6-trinitrophenol
   (C) *o*-aminophenol and *m*-aminophenol

429. Explain why a substituent such as NO_2 bonded *ortho* or *para* has a much greater effect on the acidity of a phenol than a benzoic acid.

430. Give the structural formula and name of the principal organic product (if any) from the reaction of *p*-cresol with
   (A) hot conc. HCl
   (B) Me_2SO_4, aq. NaOH
   (C) benzyl chloride, aq. NaOH
   (D) PhCl, aq. NaOH
   (E) CH_3COOH, H_2SO_4
   (F) benzoyl chloride, NaOH
   (G) acetic anhydride
   (H) phthalic anhydride
   (I) $PhSO_2Cl$ (benzenesulfonyl chloride)
   (J) SO_2Cl
   (K) 2,4-dinitrochlorbenzene, aq. NaOH

431. (A) Give the structures of the products resulting from the reaction of PhO^-Na^+ and CO_2 at 6 atm and 125°C followed by addition of aq. acid.
   (B) Medically, why is this *Kolbe reaction* one of the most important organic syntheses?
   (C) Suggest a mechanism for this reaction.

432. Predict the product of the Claisen rearrangement of
    (A) allyl phenyl ether
    (B) 2,6-dimethylphenyl allyl ether

433. (A) Write the ionic equation for the reduction of p-benzoquinone (often called p-quinone) to hydroquinone.
    (B) The rapid reversibility of this reaction makes it possible to determine experimentally a standard electrode reduction potential $E°$, for every quinone. Define $E°$.
    (C) What is the relationship between $E°$ and the stability of the quinone?
    (D) How is the reverse of the reaction in (A) utilized in photography?

434. Prepare from benzene
    (A) resorcinol
    (B) hydroquinone

435. Devise laboratory syntheses in good yields of the following phenols from PhH or PhMe and any aliphatic or inorganic reagents:
    (A) m-Iodophenol
    (B) 3-Bromo-4-methylphenol
    (C) 2-Bromo-4-methylphenol
    Do not repeat a synthesis.

436. (A) From vanillin, **A** prepare
       I. caffeic acid **B** found in coffee beans
      II. noradrenaline **C** an adrenal hormone
    (B) From anethole, **D**, prepare tyramine, **E**, found in ergot, a toxic growth on plants.

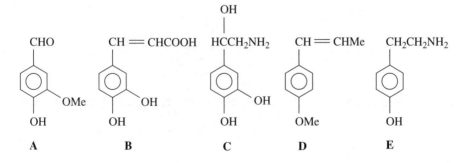

437. Identify compounds (**A**) through (**E**) in the following.

$$p\text{-}NO_2C_6H_4OH \xrightarrow[\text{2. EtBr}]{\text{1. OH}^-} A \xrightarrow{\text{Zn/HCl}} B \xrightarrow[5°C]{\text{NaNO}_2/\text{HCl}} C \xrightarrow{\text{PhOH}}$$

$$D \xrightarrow{\text{LiAlH}_4} E + F \text{ (dissolves in NaOH)}$$

438. Find the structure of safrole (**C**), $C_{10}H_{10}O_2$, a sweet-smelling liquid isolated from oil of sassafrass, given the following properties: It does not dissolve in NaOH or give a color with $FeCl_3$. It adds 1 eq of H_2 on catalytic hydrogenation. Reductive ozonolysis affords $H_2C{=}O$ and $C_9H_8O_3$ (**D**) that gives a positive Tollens' test. Oxidation of **C** with $KMnO_4$ gives an acid (**E**) (N.E. = 166) which gives no color with $FeCl_3$. When **E** is refluxed with conc. HI, $H_2C{=}O$ and 3,4-dihydroxybenzoic acid are isolated and identified.

439. A compound, $C_{10}H_{14}O$ (**F**), dissolves in NaOH but not in $NaHCO_3$. It reacts with aq. Br_2 to give $C_{10}H_{12}Br_2O$. The IR spectrum of **F** shows a broad peak at 3250 cm^{-1} and a strong peak at 750 cm^{-1}. The PMR spectrum shows signals at the following δ values: $δ = 1.3$ ppm, *s*, nine H; $δ = 4.9$ ppm, *s* (broad), one H; and $δ = 7.0$, *m*, four H. Deduce the structure of **F**.

440. Why is the ring of PhOH more easily oxidized than that of PhH?

CHAPTER 21

Aromatic Heterocyclic Compounds

441. What structural features are necessary for a heterocyclic compound to be aromatic?

442. (A) Give the common name for each of the following compounds using numbers and Greek letters.

(B) Give the ring index name for compound III.

I.

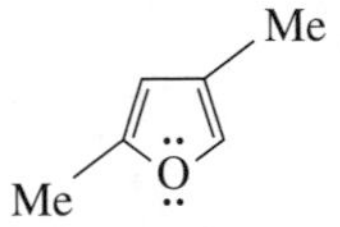

II. 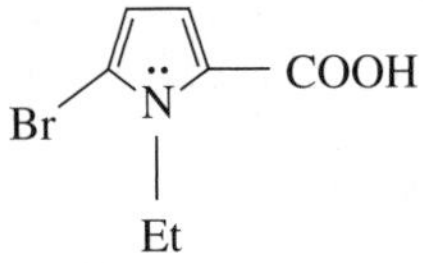 Br COOH

III.

IV.

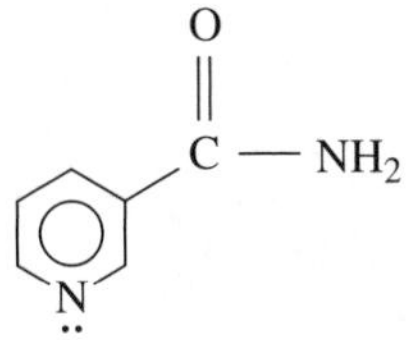

443. Name the following benzene-fused heterocyclic compounds:

(A)

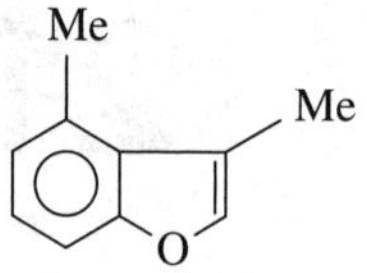

(B)

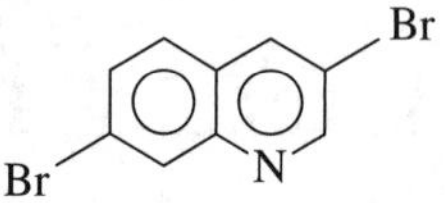

(C)

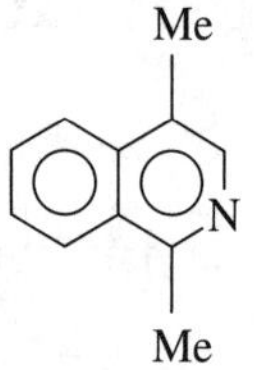

(D)

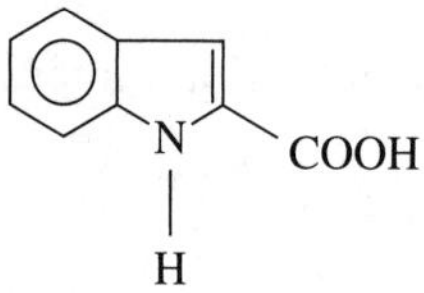

444. Name each of the following aromatic five-member ring compounds with more than one heteroatom:

(A)

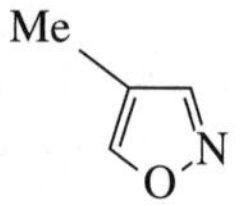

(B)

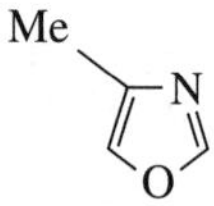

(C)

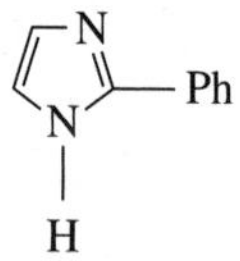

(D)

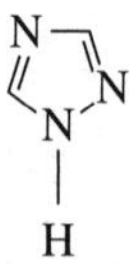

(E)

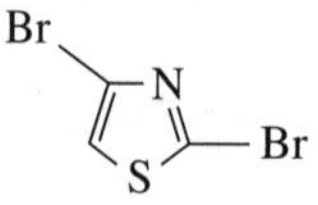

445. Name the following monocyclic aromatic ring compounds with more than one heteroatom:

(A)

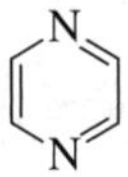

(B)

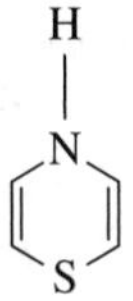

(C)

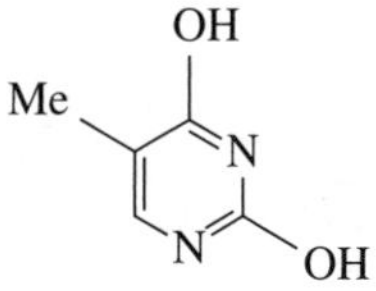

(D)

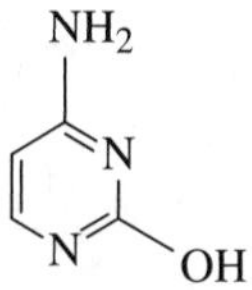

(E)

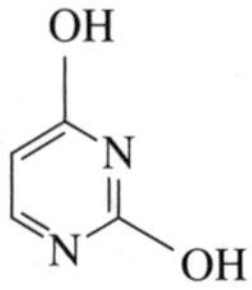

(F)

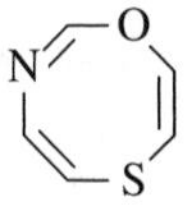

446. Give the following industrial syntheses:
(A) Thiophene from butane
(B) Pyrrole from $HC\equiv CH$ and $H_2C=O$
(C) Furan from corncobs

447. Prepare the following compounds by heating a 1,4-dicarbonyl compound with the appropriate inorganic reagent. (This is an often used method for making five-member ring heterocyclics.)
(A) 3, 4-dimethylfuran
(B) 2,5-dimethylthiophene
(C) 2,3-dimethylpyrrole

448. Show how pyridines can be synthesized from $2RCOCH_2COOEt + R'CHO + NH_3$.

449. Why is $PhNH_2$ ($K_b = 4.2 \times 10^{-10}$) less basic than pyridine ($K_b = 2.3 \times 10^{-9}$)?

450. Give the product of the reaction of pyridine (PyH, C_5H_5N) with
(A) HCl
(B) BMe_3
(C) MeI
(D) t-BuCl

451. Name the products obtained from the reaction of
(A) furan with
I. CH_3CONO_2 (acetyl nitrate)
II. $(CH_3CO)_2O/BF_3$
(B) pyrrole with
I. SO_3/pyridine
II. $CHCl_3$/KOH
III. PhN_2^+ Cl^- (give the structure)
(C) thiophene with
I. H_2SO_4
II. Br_2/PhH
III. $H_2C{=}O/HCl$

452. Give the expected product of the monobromination of quinoline, and explain the orientation.

453. Give the oxidation product of quinoline.

454. Provide structures for **A** and **B**:
Thiophene + phthalic anhydride $\xrightarrow{\text{AlCl}_3}$ **A** $\xrightarrow{\text{H}_2\text{SO}_4}$ **B**.

455. Give the structures and names of the products from the reactions of furfural, 2-furancarboxaldehyde, with

(A) conc. aq. NaOH

(B) $CH_3CHO/NaOEt$

(C) $(CH_3CH_2CO)_2O + CH_3CH_2COO^-Na^+$

(D) $PhCH_2CN/OH^-$

(E) cyclopentadiene/OH^-

Identify each reaction. (Disregard stereochemistry.)

456. Prepare 4-bromopyridine from pyridine.

457. Supply the structural formulas for **E** through **L** given

(A) $o\text{-}H_2NC_6H_4COOH + ClCH_2COOH \xrightarrow{-HCl}$

$\quad E \xrightarrow[\Delta(-H_2O)]{base} [F] \xrightarrow{-CO_2} [G] \longrightarrow C_8H_7ON(H)$

(B) $o\text{-}H_2NC_6H_4COOEt + H_2C(COOEt)_2 \longrightarrow$

$\quad I(\text{acid-insoluble}) \xrightarrow{NaOEt} J \xrightarrow[\Delta]{H^+} K \text{ or } L(C_9H_7O_2N)$

458. How can pyridine, pyrrole, and piperidine be distinguished by IR spectroscopy? Give the key characteristic absorptions. (There is no need to give a complete analysis.)

459. An acid-insoluble compound (**A**), C_6H_9N, reacts with H_2/Pd to give an acid-soluble compound (**B**), $C_6H_{13}N$. **B** reacts with 1 eq of MeI to give **C** which, after treatment with Ag_2O, is heated to give **D**, $C_7H_{15}N$. **D** undergoes another sequence of exhaustive methylation and Hofmann degradation to form 2-methyl-1,3-butadiene (**E**). Determine the structures of **A** through **D**.

460. Write structures for **A** through **D**, and name **A** and **D** in the following reactions:

(A) $Urea + O{=}CHCH_2COOEt \xrightarrow{OEt^-} A$

(B) $H_2NCSNH_2 + MeI \xrightarrow{-HI} B$ and

$\quad B + O{=}CHCHMeCOOEt \longrightarrow C \xrightarrow{aq.\ HBr} D(C_5H_6O_2N_2)$

CHAPTER 22

Amino Acids, Peptides, and Proteins

Table 22-1 may be useful in solving some of the questions in this chapter.

Table 22-1 Natural α-Amino Acids

Name	Symbol	Formula
Monoaminomonocarboxylic		
Glycine	Gly	$H_3\overset{+}{N}CH_2COO^-$
Alanine	Ala	$H_3\overset{+}{N}CH(CH_3)COO^-$
Valine*	Val	$H_3\overset{+}{N}CH(i\text{-}Pr)COO^-$
Leucine*	Leu	$H_3\overset{+}{N}CH(i\text{-}Bu)COO^-$
Isoleucine*	Ileu	$H_3\overset{+}{N}CH(s\text{-}Bu)COO^-$
Serine	Ser	$H_3\overset{+}{N}CH(CH_2OH)COO^-$
Threonine*	Thr	$H_3\overset{+}{N}CH(CHOHCH_3)COO^-$
Monoaminodicarboxylic and Amide Derivatives		
Aspartic acid	Asp	$HOOCCH_2CH(\overset{+}{N}H_3)COO^-$
Asparagine	Asp(NH$_2$)	$H_2NCOCH_2CH(\overset{+}{N}H_3)COO^-$
Glutamic acid	Glu	$HOOC(CH_2)_2CH(\overset{+}{N}H_3)COO^-$
Glutamine	Glu(NH$_2$)	$H_2NCOCH_2CH_2CH(\overset{+}{N}H_3)COO^-$
Diaminomonocarboxylic		
Lysine*	Lys	$H_3\overset{+}{N}(CH_2)_4CH(NH_2)COO^-$
Hydroxylysine	Hylys	$H_3\overset{+}{N}CH_2CHCH_2CH_2CH(NH_2)COO^-$ $\quad\qquad\ |$ $\quad\qquad OH$
Arginine*	Arg	$\begin{array}{c} H_2N^+ \\ \diagdown \\ \qquad C - NH(CH_2)_3CH(NH_2)COO^- \\ \diagup \\ H_2N \end{array}$

Name	Symbol	Formula
Sulfur-Containing		
Cysteine	CySH	$H_3\overset{+}{N}CH_2(CH_2SH)COO^-$
Cystine	CySSCy	$^-OOCCH(\overset{+}{N}H_3)CH_2S{-}SCH_2CH(\overset{+}{N}H_3)COO^-$
Methionine*	Met	$CH_3SCH_2CH_2CH(\overset{+}{N}H_3)COO^-$
Aromatic		
Phenylalanine*	Phe	$PhCH_2CH(\overset{+}{N}H_3)COO^-$
Tyrosine	Tyr	$p\text{-}HOC_6H_4CH_2CH(\overset{+}{N}H_3)COO^-$
Heterocyclic		
Histidine*	His	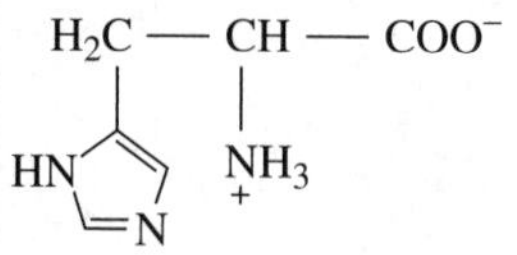
Proline	Pro	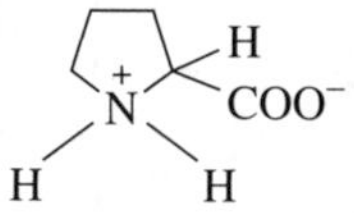
Hydroxyproline	Hypro	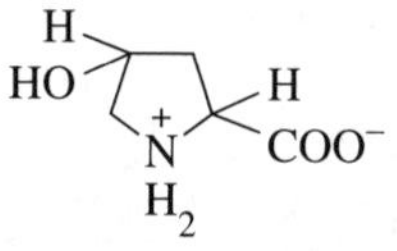
Tryptophane*	Try	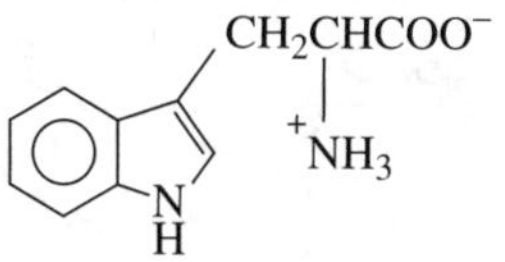

461. (A) Give a general structural formula for the naturally occurring α-amino acids (AA) and indicate their importance.

   (B) Explain their classification as essential and nonessential.

462. (A) Which AA is achiral?

   (B) Give the AAs with more than one chiral center.

463. Write equilibrium equations to show the amphoteric behavior of an AA in H_2O. Include the net charge of each species.

464. Write equilibrium equations for the dissociation of lysine, a basic AA, and calculate its isoelectric point. See Table 22-2 for the pK_a values.

465. How are AAs separated and identified by *electrophoresis?*

Table 22-2 Acid-Base Properties or Amino Acids

Amino acid	With Neutral Side Chains		
	pK_{a1}^*	pK_{a2}^*	PI
Glycine	2.34	9.60	5.97
Alanine	2.34	9.69	6.00
Valine	2.32	9.62	5.96
Leucine	2.36	9.60	5.98
Isoleucine	2.36	9.60	6.02
Methionine	2.28	9.21	5.74
Proline	1.99	10.60	6.30
Phenylalanine	1.83	9.13	5.48
Tryptophan	2.83	9.39	5.89
Asparagine	2.02	8.80	5.41
Glutamine	2.17	9.13	5.65
Serine	2.21	9.15	5.68
Threonine	2.09	9.10	5.60

Amino acid	With Ionizable Side Chains			
	pK_{a1}^{**}	pK_{a2}	pK_{a3}	PI
Aspartic acid	1.88	3.65	9.60	2.77
Glutamic acid	2.19	4.25	9.67	3.22
Tyrosine	2.20	9.11	10.07	5.66
Cysteine	1.96	8.18	10.28	5.07
Lysine	2.18	8.95	10.53	9.74
Arginine	2.17	9.04	12.48	10.76
Histidine	1.82	6.00	9.17	7.59

*In all cases pK_{a1} corresponds to ionization of the carboxyl group; pK_{a2} corresponds to ionization of the ammonium ion.

**In all cases pK_{a1} corresponds to ionization of the carboxyl group of $RCHCO_2H$.

$$\overset{|}{\underset{+}{N}H_3}$$

466. Prepare valine, $Me_2CHCH(\overset{+}{N}H_3)COO^-$ (Val) by

(A) a Hell–Volhard–Zelinsky reaction

(B) a reductive amination

(C) a Gabriel synthesis

467. Use the *Strecker synthesis* to prepare phenylalanine (Phe).

468. (A) What is a peptide bond or linkage?

(B) Distinguish between a peptide, oligopeptide, polypeptide, and protein.

(C) Give the standard way of describing the sequential order of AAs.

(D) Name the tripeptide Tyr.Thr.Try.

469. (A) List and name all the different dipeptides that can be made from alanine and glycine.

(B) How many tripeptides are possible using alanine, glycine, and tyrosine?

(C) How many tripeptides in (B) are possible if each is used only once?

(D) How many tetrapeptides can be formed from the three AAs in (B)?

470. Write structures for

(A) alanylvaline

(B) valylalanine

471. Discuss the precautions in synthesizing peptides.

472. How are different peptides separated from one another?

473. A tripeptide (**B**) is hydrolyzed completely to 2 eq of Glu and 1 eq each of Ala and NH_3. **B** has only one free carboxyl group and does not react with 2,4-dinitrofluorobenzene. Ala is released first when **B** is incubated with carboxypeptidase. Provide a structure for **B**.

474. A hexapeptide (**C**) is completely hydrolyzed to give Ala, Arg, Gly, Lys, Try, Val, and NH_3. Incubation of **C** with chymotrypsin gives a dipeptide identified as Arg. Try and a tetrapeptide (**D**) containing Gly, Lys, Ala, and Val. When **C** or **D** is incubated with carboxypeptidase, there is no reaction. On partial hydrolysis, **D** yields Ala.Val, Gly.Lys, Lys.Ala, and NH_3. **E**, given below, is produced when **D** is subjected to a single Edman degradation. Deduce the structure of **C**.

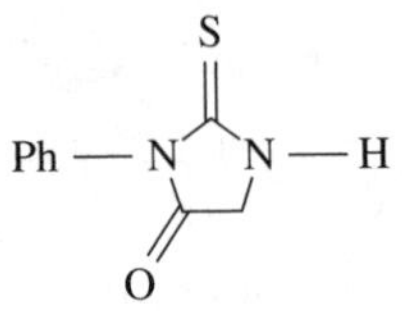

E

475. The disulfide bond in a peptide is reduced to —SH by adding a large excess of $HSCH_2CH_2OH$.

(A) Write an equation for the reaction of RS — SR with 2-mercaptoethanol and explain its action.

(B) How is this reaction used in determining the sequence of AAs of proteins?

476. Categorize proteins according to

(A) shape

(B) biological function

477. Define the primary, secondary, tertiary, and quaternary structure of a protein.

478. (A) What kind of bonding is greatly responsible for the secondary structure?

(B) Describe the three types of secondary structures.

479. Describe the kind of bonding responsible for the tertiary structure.

480. Describe the kind of bonding responsible for quaternary structure.

CHAPTER 23

Carbohydrates

481. Account for the name *carbohydrate* in terms of the general formula.

482. (A) What is the common name for carbohydrates?

(B) Name the suffix that indicates a simple carbohydrate.

483. Define

(A) *saccharide*

(B) *monosaccharide*

(C) *disaccharide*

(D) *oligosaccharide*

(E) *polysaccharide*

484. Classify the following monosaccharides using the suffix *-ose*.

(A) $HOCH_2CHOHCOCH_2OH$

(B) $HOCH_2(CHOH)_4CHO$

(C) $HOCH_2(CHOH)_2CH_2CHO$

485. Deduce the molecular formula of glucose from the following data: The % composition is C = 40.0, H = 6.7, O = 53.3. A solution of 9.0 g in 100 g of H_2O freezes at 0.93°C.

486. (A) Write Fischer formulas for the D and L isomers of the simplest known aldosugar.

(B) Give the sign of rotation of these enantiomers.

(C) Give the *R/S* designations.

487. (A) How many chiral Cs are there in an aldotetrose?

   (B) Give the Fischer formulas and common names for the stereoisomers of an aldotetrose, and classify them as D and L sugars.

488. Define the term *epimer,* and illustrate with threose and erythrose.

489. (A) Compare the reactions of an aldohexose and a 2-ketohexose with
   I. Tollens' reagent
   II. Fehling's solution
   III. Benedict's reagent
   IV. Br_2/H_2O
   Describe the changes that signal a positive test and give formulas for the reagents.

   (B) Classify the product from the aldohexose.

490. (A) Give the two isomeric products from the reaction of D-threose with NaCN/HCN.

   (B) What is the net result of this reaction?

491. (A) Give structures for **E** through **G**, given an aldohexose

$$\xrightarrow{\text{aq.Br}_2} \textbf{E} \xrightarrow{\text{CaCO}_3} \textbf{F} \xrightarrow[\text{Fe(III)}]{\text{H}_2\text{O}_2} \textbf{G}.$$

   (B) What is the net structural change?

   (C) Name this overall method.

   (D) Discuss the possibility of epimer formation.

492. Emil Fischer, the father of carbohydrate chemistry, used synthetic L-gulose (whose structure he knew) to distinguish between the known epimers D-glucose and D-mannose, whose structures were not yet established. How would he have deduced this?

493. Do the anomers of D-glucose have specific rotations of the same magnitude but opposite signs?

494. Name the enantiomer of α-D-(+)-glucose.

495. What size of rings is most frequently observed in hemiacetals? Name each type.

496. Draw the *Haworth* projection for α-D-glucopyranose. How does the β-anomer differ?

497. Draw the Haworth projections for the anomers of D-fructofuranose.

498. (A) Discuss the general structure of disaccharides.

   (B) What sequence is used for drawing the unit monosaccharides of the disaccharides?

499. (A) What is glycogen and how does it differ from starch?

   (B) What is cellulose and how is it structurally different from starch?

500. (A) Find the average molecular weight of starch given that an aqueous solution of 10.0 g/L of starch has an osmotic pressure $\Pi = 5.6 \times 10^{-3}$atm at 25°C.

   (B) What is the approximate average number of glucose units in this sample of starch?

ANSWERS

Chapter 1: Structure and Properties

1. In general, organic compounds
    (A) react more slowly and require higher temperatures for reaction
    (B) undergo more complex reactions and produce more side products
    (C) have lower melting and boiling points and are generally insoluble in water
    (D) are less stable and therefore often decompose on heating to compounds of lower energy content
    (E) are classified into families of compounds such as alcohols, which have similar reactive groups and chemical properties
    (F) are far more numerous than inorganic compounds

2. (A) *Aliphatic* compounds with Cs bonded in chains are called *acyclic* to distinguish them from *cyclic* compounds, which have Cs bonded in rings (not circular).

    (B) *Aromatic* compounds, originally so named because of their pleasant odors, include derivatives of the parent hydrocarbon benzene (C_6H_6) and other ring systems with unusual stability.

    (C) *Heterocyclics* are compounds with rings having at least one element other than C in the ring.

3. (A) Ionic
    (B) covalent
    (C) covalent
    (D) ionic

4. Individual atoms lose, gain, or share e^-s to attain electronic configurations (stable outer shells with eight e^-s) of the nearest noble gas. In ionic bonding an e^- is transferred to form a cation and an anion: $A \cdot + \cdot \ddot{B}: \rightarrow A^+ + :\ddot{B}:^-$. For example, $Na \cdot$ transfers the lone e^- in its outer (valence) shell to $:\ddot{F} \cdot$ with seven e^-s in its outer shell, leaving both cation and anion with outer shells of eight (an octet) e^-s.

$$Na(2,8,1) + F(2,7) \rightarrow Na^+(2,8) + F^-(2,8) \qquad \text{or} \qquad Na^+ : \ddot{F}:^-$$

Octets are also formed by transferring more than one e^-.

$$Mg(2,8,2) + 2\,Cl(2,8,7) \rightarrow Mg^{2+}(2,8) + 2\,Cl^-(2,8,8) \qquad \text{or} \qquad Mg^{2+}\,2:\ddot{Cl}:^- (\text{or Mg Cl}_2)$$

Noble gas configurations are attained during covalent bonding by sharing of e^- pairs, with each e^- having an opposite spin as required by the Pauli exclusion principle: $:\ddot{Cl} \cdot + \cdot \ddot{Cl}: \rightarrow :\ddot{Cl}:\ddot{Cl}:$.

5.

	Acceptor	*Donor*	
(A)	H^+	$+ H:\ddot{O}:H$	$\rightarrow [H:\ddot{O}:H]^+$

(B) Cu^{2+} $+ 4 : NH_3$ $\rightarrow [H_3N:\ddot{C}u:NH_3]^{2+}$ (with NH_3 above and below)

(C) $AgCl$ $+ :\ddot{C}l:^-$ $\rightarrow AgCl_2^-$

(D) BF_3 $+ : NH_3$ $\rightarrow F_3B:NH_3$

6. Electron-dot structures show all bonding and unshared valence e⁻s. First write the *skeleton* of the molecule, showing the bonding arrangement of the atoms. In molecules with three or more atoms there is at least one central atom, which has the highest covalency. If there is more than one multicovalent atom in the molecule [as in **(B)** and **(E)**], bond them to each other to get the skeleton; then bond the univalent atoms (H, F, Cl) to them in order to satisfy their normal multicovalencies. In their bonded state, second-period elements should have eight e⁻s, but not more. (Exceptions are Be and B which may have less than eight.) The number of e⁻s in the Lewis structure should equal the sum of the valence e⁻s of all the individual atoms.

(A) $:\ddot{F}:\ddot{O}:\ddot{F}:$

(B) $H:\ddot{O}:\ddot{O}:H$

(C) $:\ddot{C}l:\overset{:\ddot{C}l:}{\underset{}{P}}:\ddot{C}l:$

(D) $H:\underset{H}{\overset{H}{C}}:\ddot{C}l:$

(E) $H:\overset{H}{N}:\overset{H}{N}:H$

7. The charge on a species is numerically equal to the total number of valence electrons of the unbonded atoms, minus the total number of electrons shown (as bonds or dots) in the Lewis structure.

    (A) The sum of the valence electrons (six for O, four for C, and three for three Hs) is 13. The electron-dot formula shows 14 e⁻s. The net charge is $13 - 14 = -1$, and the species is the methoxide anion, $CH_3\ddot{O}:^-$.

    (B) There is no charge on the formaldehyde molecule, because the 12 e⁻s in the structure equal the number of valence electrons, i.e., six for O, four for C, and two for Hs.

    (C) This species is neutral, because there are 13 e⁻s shown in the formula and 13 valence electrons: eight from two Cs and five from five Hs.

    (D) There are 15 valence electrons: six from O, five from N, and four from four Hs. The Lewis dot structure shows 14 e⁻s. It has a charge of $15 - 14 = +1$ and is the hydroxyl-ammonium cation, $[H_3NOH]^+$.

    (E) There are 25 valence electrons, 21 from three Cls and four from C. The Lewis dot formula shows 26 e⁻s. It has a charge of $25 - 26 = -1$ and is the trichloromethide anion, CCl_3^-.

8. Structural formulas omit the outer unshared e⁻s of Lewis structures.

(A) H — O — Cl

(B) 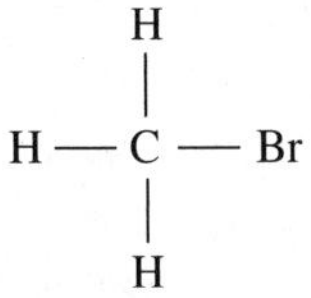
$$\text{H} - \overset{\displaystyle \text{H}}{\underset{\displaystyle \text{H}}{\text{C}}} - \text{Br}$$

(C) H — O — N＝O

(D) Cl — C≡N

9. The three atoms with the largest covalencies (C, C, O) can be bonded to one another in two ways, resulting in two structures:

(A) 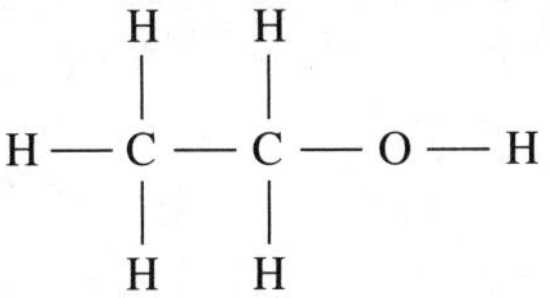
$$\text{H} - \overset{\displaystyle \text{H}}{\underset{\displaystyle \text{H}}{\text{C}}} - \overset{\displaystyle \text{H}}{\underset{\displaystyle \text{H}}{\text{C}}} - \text{O} - \text{H}$$

Ethyl alcohol

(B) 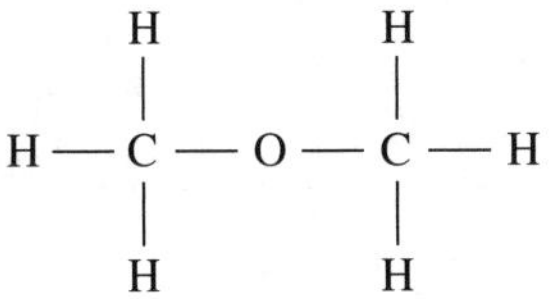
$$\text{H} - \overset{\displaystyle \text{H}}{\underset{\displaystyle \text{H}}{\text{C}}} - \text{O} - \overset{\displaystyle \text{H}}{\underset{\displaystyle \text{H}}{\text{C}}} - \text{H}$$

Dimethyl ether

10. (A) There is only one possible structure:
$$\text{H} - \overset{\displaystyle \text{H}}{\underset{\displaystyle \text{H}}{\text{C}}} - \overset{\displaystyle \text{H}}{\underset{\displaystyle \text{H}}{\text{C}}} - \overset{\displaystyle \text{H}}{\underset{\displaystyle \text{H}}{\text{C}}} - \text{H}.$$

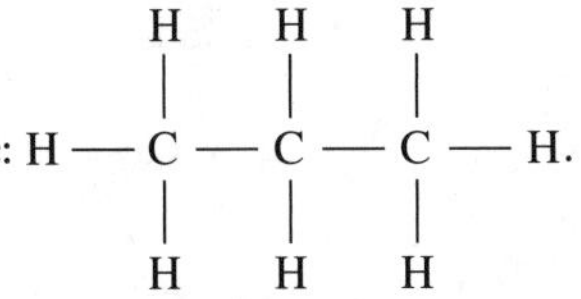

(B) The four Cs can lie in a straight (unbranched) or branched chain.

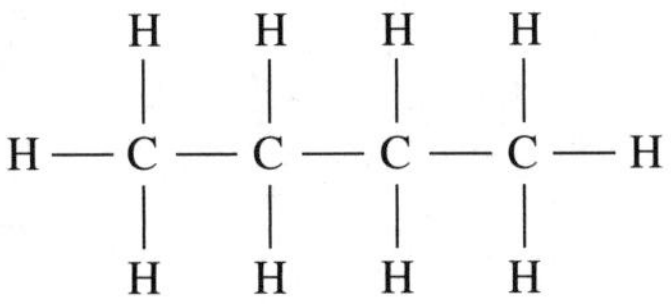

$$\text{H} - \overset{\displaystyle \text{H}}{\underset{\displaystyle \text{H}}{\text{C}}} - \overset{\displaystyle \text{H}}{\underset{\displaystyle \text{H}}{\text{C}}} - \overset{\displaystyle \text{H}}{\underset{\displaystyle \text{H}}{\text{C}}} - \overset{\displaystyle \text{H}}{\underset{\displaystyle \text{H}}{\text{C}}} - \text{H}$$

n-Butane

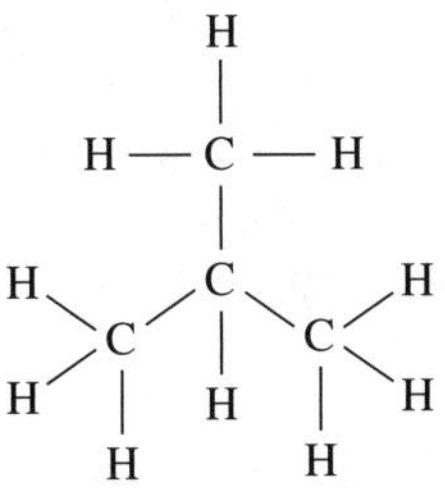

Isobutane

(C) The three isomers of pentane are as follows:

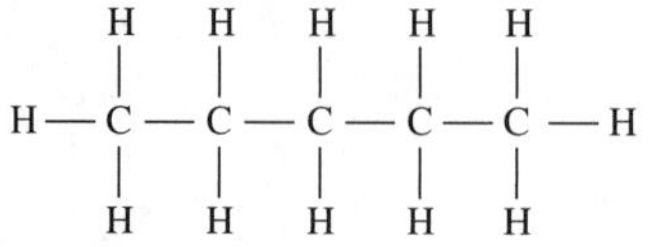

n-Pentane 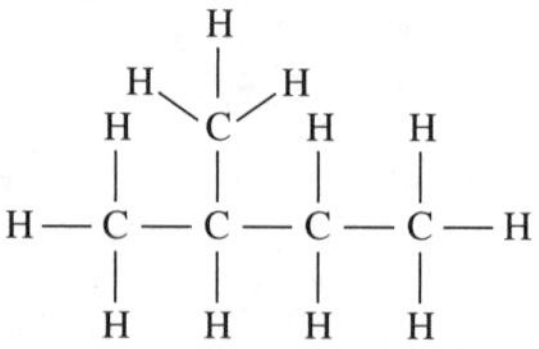   Isopentane 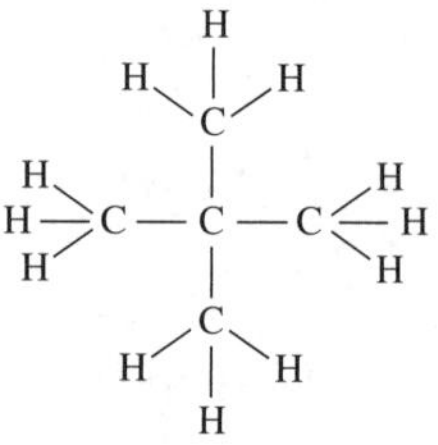   Neopentane

11. There are two fewer Hs in C_4H_8 than in C_4H_{10}, from which it is deduced that the isomers have either a double bond or a cyclic structure. The double bond structures (alkenes) are as follows:

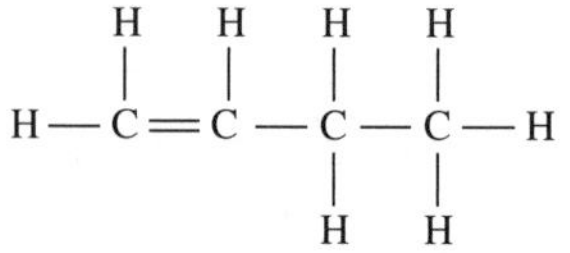

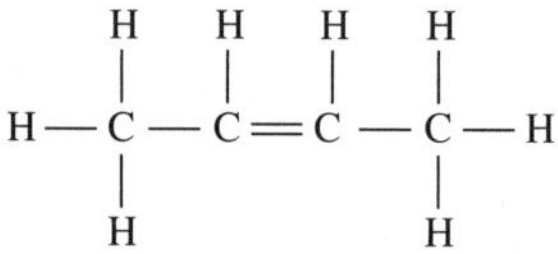

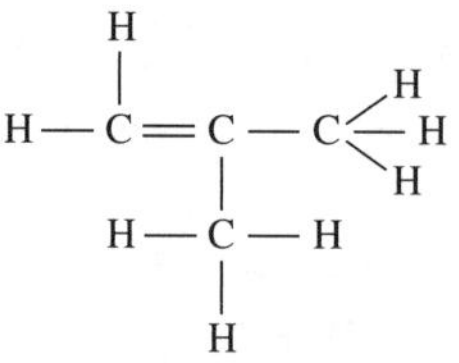

Two cyclic structures are possible: one is a four-C ring, and the other is a three-C ring with an attached fourth C.

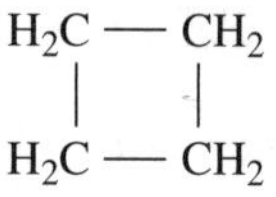

Cyclobutane 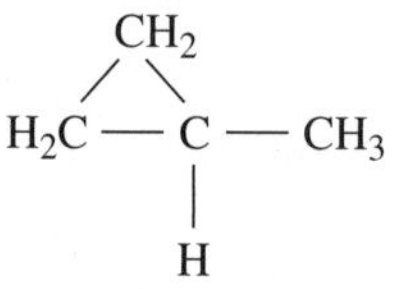   Methylcyclopropane

12.

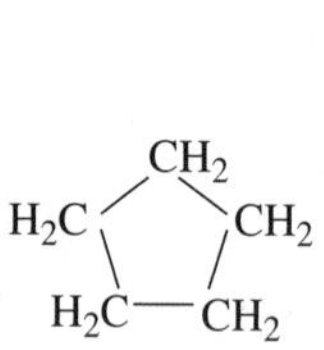

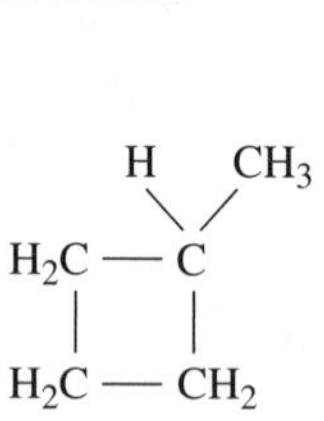

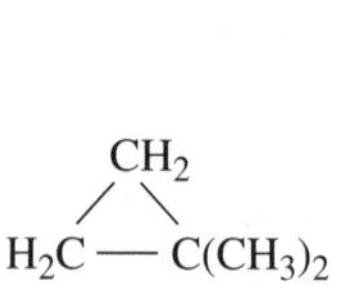

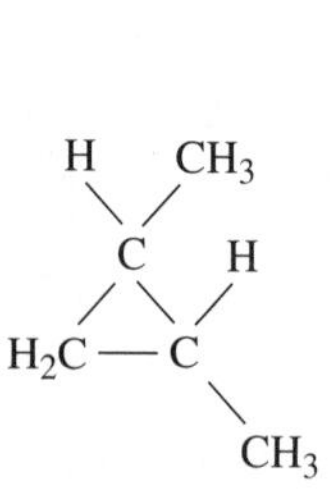

13. (A) $H = 1 - [0 + \frac{1}{2}(2)] = 1 - 1 = 0$; $O = 6 - [4 + \frac{1}{2}(4)] = 6 - 6 = 0$; $Cl = 7 - [6 + \frac{1}{2}(2)] = 0$.
  (B) Each $H = 1 - [0 + \frac{1}{2}(2)] = 0$; $N = 5 - [0 + \frac{1}{2}(8)] = +1$ (equal to charge on ion).
  (C) Each $H = 0$; $O = 6 - [2 + \frac{1}{2}(6)] = +1$; $B = 3 - [0 + \frac{1}{2}(8)] = -1$ (total FC = 0).

14. (A)

$$\text{H} - \text{O} - \overset{\overset{\displaystyle :\ddot{\text{O}}:^{-}}{\displaystyle |}}{\underset{+}{\text{N}}} = \ddot{\text{O}}:$$

(B)

$$\text{H} - \text{O} - \overset{\overset{\displaystyle :\ddot{\text{O}}:^{-}}{\displaystyle |}}{\underset{\underset{:\ddot{\text{O}}:^{-}}{\displaystyle |}}{\text{S}^{2+}}} - \text{O} - \text{H}$$

15. (A) The first structure has FCs of −1 on O and +1 on the central Cl; the second structure, with no FCs, is preferred.

(B) The second structure with *both* Ns having a FC of −1 and O having a FC of + 2 is unlikely. The first structure has less FC, the central N has a FC of +1 and O a FC of −1).

16. (A) A functional group is an atom or group of atoms in a compound that determines its chemical properties and in most cases is one of the sites of its chemical reactions.

(B) Organic compounds, while large in number, are classified into a relatively small number of categories whose properties are defined by their functional groups. Common functional groups are the double bond ($\overset{\diagdown}{}\text{C} = \text{C}\overset{\diagup}{}$), hydroxyl (—OH), and amine (—NH_2).

17. (A)

$$\text{CH}_3\text{CH}_2\overset{\overset{\displaystyle\|}{\displaystyle }}{\text{C}}\text{OH}$$
$$\text{O}$$

(B) I. $\text{CH}_3\text{CH}_2\text{COR}$ where R is an alkyl group
$$\overset{\displaystyle\|}{\text{O}}$$

II. $\text{CH}_3\text{CH}_2\text{CCl}$
$$\overset{\displaystyle\|}{\text{O}}$$

III. $\text{CH}_3\text{CH}_2\text{CNH}_2$
$$\overset{\displaystyle\|}{\text{O}}$$

18. (A) Divide the percentage of each element by its atomic weight to give the mass ratio. Convert to the simplest whole-number ratio to get the empirical formula.

C:92.25 ÷ 12.01 g /mol = 7.68 mol/g   H:7.743 ÷ 1.008 g/mol = 7.68 mol/g

The mass ratio is 1:1 and the empirical formula is (C_1H_1).

(B) The sum of the atomic weights in the empirical formula is 13.02. One molecular formula contains 78.11 ÷ 13.02 = 6 CH units, or $(CH)_6$. The molecular formula is C_6H_6.

19. The ideal gas law, $PV = nRT$, is used, where $n = g/MW$ and $MW = g\,RT/PV$.

$$MW = \frac{(11.75\text{ g})(0.0821\text{ L}\cdot\text{atm/mol}\cdot\text{K})(373\text{ K})}{(1\text{ atm})(5.0\text{ L})} = 72\text{ g/mol}$$

Since the hydrocarbon contains only C and H, the maximum number of Cs possible in a MW of 72 is five $(5 \times 12 = 60)$; the remainder of the molecule is 12 Hs, or C_5H_{12}.

20. **(A)** The mass of C in 2.63 g of CO_2 from the sample is

$$\frac{\text{AW of C}}{\text{MW of CO}_2} \times \text{mass of CO}_2 = \frac{12.01\text{ g C/mol}}{44.01\text{ g CO}_2/\text{mol}}(2.63\text{ g CO}_2) = 0.718\text{ g C}$$

which is $\dfrac{0.718\text{ g C}}{0.858\text{ g X}}(100\%) = 83.7\%$ of **X**.

The mass of H in 1.28 g of H_2O from the sample is

$$\frac{\text{AW of H}}{\text{MW of H}_2\text{O}} \times \text{mass of H}_2\text{O} = \frac{2.016\text{ g H/mol}}{18.02\text{ g H}_2\text{O/mol}}(1.28\text{ g H}) = 0.143\text{ g H}$$

which is 16.7% of **X**.

Since the sum of C and H percentages is 100.4%, O is absent.

(B) C:$83.7 \div 12.01 = 6.97$; $697 \div 6.97 = 1$ H:$16.7 \div 1.01 = 16.5$;$16.5 \div 6.97 = 2.37$

Multiplying 1:2.37 by 3 gives a ratio of 3.00:7.11, and if we round off, the empirical formula seems to be C_3H_7. But this formula doesn't fit any Lewis structure for a hydrocarbon, C_nH_{2n+2} (try it); a hydrocarbon cannot have an odd number of Hs. The formula is thus C_6H_{14}, and the MW is 86 g/mol.

21. Raoult's law gives the molality as

$$m = \frac{\Delta T_f}{K_{f\cdot p.}} = \frac{179°\text{C} - 166°\text{C}}{40°\text{C}\cdot\text{kg/mol}} = 0.325\text{ mol/kg}$$

Now 0.325 mol of **A** is dissolved in 1 kg of camphor. And 0.108 g of **A** in 0.90 g camphor is the same concentration as 120 g of **A** in 1,000 g camphor. Therefore, 120 g of **A** is 0.325 mol, and so the mass of 1 mol of **A** is

$$\frac{120\text{ g}}{0.325\text{ mol}} = 369\text{ g/mol}$$

22. A balanced equation must be written first:

$$C_6H_6 + HNO_3 \xrightarrow{\text{H}_2\text{SO}_4} C_6H_5NO_2 + H_2O$$

(A) The equation shows that 1 mol of benzene (MW = 78 g/mol) would give 1 mol of nitrobenzene (MW = 123 g/mol) if the yield were 100% (the theoretical yield in percent). Starting with 10.0 g of benzene, a 100% yield would be 10.0 g ÷ 78.0 g/mol of nitrobenzene (0.128 mol), which is (10/78 mol) (123 g/mol) = 15.8 g of nitrobenzene, the theoretical yield in grams.

(B) The actual yield is 13.2 g, and the percentage yield = 13.2 g/15.8 g (100%) = 83.5%.

Chapter 2: Bonding and Molecular Structure

23. The values of n are whole numbers starting with 1.
  (A) The maximum number of e⁻s in a shell, n, is $2n^2$.
  (B) The number of sublevels equals the value of n.
  (C) I. 18
    II. 3

24. **(A)** I. A sphere [Figure A2-1(A)].
    II. Touching spheres or "dumbbell" [Figure A2-1(B)]

To avoid using + and – signs that erroneously may be confused with electric charges, one p AO lobe (associated with the + sign) is shaded and one (associated with the – sign) is unshaded, as shown in Figure A2-1(B).

  (B) From solutions of the Schrödinger equation, the lowest energy AO, the s, has no trigonometric function, indicating that it has no angle dependency. The shape that fits this criterion is the sphere. The solution for the next-higher energy AO has a trigonometric function, and a plot of the solutions gives the "dumbbell" shape for the p AO. Since there are three solutions, there are three p AOs.

  (C) (I) The s AO has no node, and the e⁻ can be any place in the sphere *including* the nucleus. (II) The p AO has one node at the nucleus; an e⁻ cannot be at the nucleus. This nodal point (the nucleus) lies on a nodal plane that separates the two lobes.

  (D) The question is specious because it restricts the behavior of an e⁻ to being a particle. As a particle it could not make the questioned move, but as a wave it can. The two lobes together form the electron cloud, and each has the same amount of electron density. It is meaningless to talk about the e⁻ being in one lobe or the other; it is in both lobes.

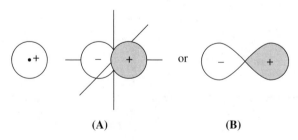

(A)   **(B)**

Figure A2-1

25. (A) The AOs are filled in order of increasing energies.

   (B) Each degenerate orbital is half-filled before electrons are paired in an AO. There is less electrostatic repulsion between electrons in different orbitals than between paired electrons in a single orbital.

   (C) I. $\underset{1s^2}{\uparrow\downarrow}\ \underset{2s^2}{\uparrow\downarrow}\ \underset{2p_x^1}{\uparrow}\ \underset{2p_y^1}{\uparrow}\ \underset{2p_z}{\ \ }$ (correct)

Energies of orbitals increase from left to right. Large space between orbitals shows an increase in energy, and less space is left between degenerate orbitals. The choice of p_x and p_y is arbitrary; any two p AOs can be used.

   II. $\underset{1s^2}{\uparrow\downarrow}\ \underset{2s^2}{\uparrow\downarrow}\ \underset{2p_x^2}{\uparrow\downarrow}\ \underset{2p_y}{\ \ }\ \underset{2p_z}{\ \ }$ (incorrect)

   (D) C atoms with the correct distribution, having some number of unpaired electrons, are *paramagnetic*; they are drawn into a magnetic field. Cs with the incorrect distribution, having only paired electrons, would be *diamagnetic*; they would be somewhat repelled by a magnetic field.

   (E) The valence electrons for representative elements are those in the outermost shell, the one with the highest principal energy number, n. For C this is the second shell ($n = 2$), and there are four valence electrons in the $2s$ and the two $2p$ AOs.

26. Two AOs combine (overlap) to form two MOs, one by reinforcement having a lower energy and the other by cancellation having a higher energy.

$$\text{Relative energy} \left| \begin{array}{ccc} & \text{MO*}\_ & \\ \text{AO}\_ & & \text{AO}\_ \\ \text{MO}\_ & & \end{array} \right.$$

27. (A) The subscript s indicates that this MO comes from overlap of two s AOs. See Figure A2-2(A).

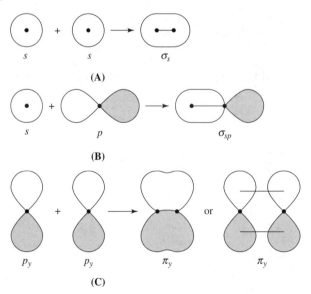

Figure A2-2

(B) This σ MO comes from head-to-head overlap of an s and p AO. See Figure A2-2(B).

(C) Side-to-side (lateral) overlap of two p_y AOs forms a π MO, as shown in Figure A2-2(C). Only one π bond is formed by the overlap of the top lobes with each other and the overlap of the bottom lobes with each other, as indicated by the tie-lines.

28. The asterisks indicate that these are antibonding molecular orbitals. See Figure A2-3.

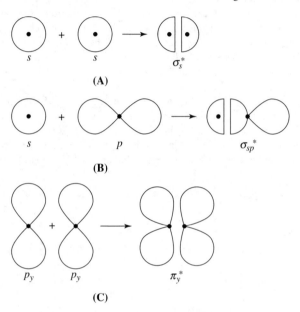

(A)

(B)

(C)

Figure A2-3

29. (A) The total number of electrons in the molecule or ion is placed in the molecular orbitals following the Aufbau principle and Hund's rule, discussed in Problem 25.

(B) The e^-s are indicated with arrows representing the spins.

$\sigma_{1s_-}^*$	—	↑	↑	↑↓
σ_{1s}↑	↑↓	↑↓	↑↓	↑↓
H_2^+	H_2	H_2^-	HHe	He_2
$(\sigma_{1s})^1$	$(\sigma_{1s})^2$	$(\sigma_{1s})^2(\sigma_{1s}^*)^1$	$(\sigma_{1s})^2(\sigma_{1s}^*)^2$

(C) Any species can exist if there are more e^-s in MOs than in MO*s. The greater the excess of e^-s in MOs, the more stable is the molecule or ion.

(D) He_2 has an equal number of e^-s in the MO and MO* and therefore does not exist.

(E) H_2 (two bonding e^-s) > H_2^+, H_2^-, HHe (one excess bonding e^-) ≫ He_2 (no excess bonding e^-). Since electrons exert some repulsive force, H_2^+ may be slightly more stable than H_2^- and HHe because it has fewer electrons.

30. (A) Bond order = $\dfrac{\text{(number of e's in MO's)} - \text{(number of e's in MO*'s)}}{2}$

   (B) For C_2, $4/2 = 2$; for N_2, $6/2 = 3$; for O_2, $4/2 = 2$; for NO, $5/2 = 2.5$; for CN^-, $6/2 = 3$.

31. (A) (I) Since the bond angle is close to the tetrahedral angle, 109.5°, N must use three sp^3 HOs for bonding with H, and the unshared pair resides in the fourth sp^3 HO. The unshared pair exerts a greater repulsive force than do the shared pairs, which causes a contraction of the bond angles to somewhat less than 109.5°. (II) H_2O also uses sp^3 HOs. Two of them are half-filled and are used for bonding with Hs; the other two contain the unshared pairs. Since there are two unshared pairs, the repulsion is greater than in NH_3, and the bond angle shrinks even more to 105°.

   (B) Yes. Ground state N has three half-filled p AOs ($1s^2 2s^2 2p_x^1 2p_y^1 2p_z^1$), and O has two half-filled p AOs ($1s^2 s^2 2p_x^2 2p_y^1 2p_z^1$) available for overlap.

   (C) HOs give stronger bonds than do p AOs. Furthermore, when p AOs form bonds, the bond angle should be close to 90°, the angle between the axes of any two p AOs. There is greater repulsion between the bonding pairs of e⁻s with bond angles of 90° than there is in the tetrahedral angle.

Note that knowledge of the bond angle permits the prediction of the kind of orbital an atom uses for bonding.

32. (A) I.

$$\begin{array}{c} H \\ \diagdown \\ H \diagup N{-}H^+ \\ H \end{array}$$

4 σ bonds, sp^3

II.

$$\begin{array}{c} H \quad\quad H \\ \diagdown \quad\quad \diagup \\ C{-}N{:} \\ H \diagup \quad \diagdown H \end{array}$$

C, 4 σ bonds, sp^3
N, 3 σ bonds + 1 lone pair, sp^3

III.

$$\begin{array}{c} H \\ \diagdown \\ C{=}\ddot{O}{:} \\ \diagup \\ H \end{array}$$

3 σ bonds, sp^2

IV.

$$\begin{array}{c} H \quad\quad H \\ \diagdown \quad\quad \diagup \\ C{=}N{:} \\ \diagup \\ H \end{array}$$

C, 3 σ bonds, sp^2
N, 2 σ bonds, 1 lone pair, sp^2

V.

$$H{-}C{\equiv}N{:}$$

C, 2 σ bonds, sp
N, 1 σ bond, 1 lone pair, sp

   (B) (I) Tetrahedral, 109.5° bond angles. (II) The tetrahedral C is joined to a *pyramidal* N to give a nonplanar molecule. The bonds on N have a pyramidal shape because the lone pair replaces one of the tetrahedral bonds. A pyramid and terahedron have similar shapes except that in a pyramid the central atom is at a corner rather than in the center of the tetrahedron. All bond angles are approximately 109°. (III) $H_2C{=}O$ is a planar trigonal molecule. The π bond is formed from lateral overlap of the p_z AOs of C and O, and the bond angles are 120°. (IV) Both the C and N have a trigonal array and bond through sp^2 σ bonds to give a planar molecule with 120° bond angles. The remaining p_z AOs on C and N overlap to give the π bond which has no effect on the shape. (V) Molecular shape is always dictated by the hybrid state of central atoms, in this case C, and never by terminal atoms, in this case N. The sp HOs of C are diagonal and HCN is a linear molecule.

33. (**A**) sp^3
(**B**) p
(**C**) sp^3
(**D**) C, N, both sp
(**E**) sp
(**F**) C^1, sp^2, and C^2 (center C), sp

34. (**A**) HF > HCl > HBr > HI. The electronegativities of the halogens decrease from F to I, which decreases the value of μ.
(**B**) The order generally follows the decrease in electronegativity of the halogens with an exception. The apparent anomaly of CH_3F having a smaller μ than CH_3Cl is explained by the shorter C—F bond distance, which tends to decrease the value of μ even though F is more electronegative than Cl.

35. (**A**) The smaller the electronegativity of the metal, the more likely its bond to C will be ionic.
(**B**) (I) Ionic, $CH_3\ddot{C}H_2^-K^+$, (II) highly polar covalent, $\overset{\delta-}{CH_3}-\overset{\delta+}{Mg}-\overset{\delta-}{CH_3}$.
(**C**) Covalent, $(CH_3)_2Hg$, $(CH_3CH_2)_4Pb$.

36. (**A**) $(ON)_C + 2(ON)_O = 0$ (charge on molecule); $(ON)_C + 2(-2) = 0$; $(ON)_C = +4$
(**B**) +3
(**C**) +5
(**D**) $(ON)_S + 3(-2) = -2$ (charge on the ion); $(ON)_S = +4$
(**E**) -3

37. (**A**) An increase in ON (more positive or less negative) is an *oxidation,* and a decrease is a *reduction.*
(**B**) (I) The ON of C goes from -4 to -2—oxidation, (II) ON is zero for both— neither (III) -2 to -3—reduction (IV) The ON of both Cs has changed, one from -1 to -3, and the other from -1 to +2. Thus the average value must be compared for both reactant and product; this is -1, unchanged—neither.

38. The strongest force is the *hydrogen bond,* which consists of a bond between an H attached to a highly electronegative atom, X, and an electronegative atom bearing an unshared pair of electrons, either in another molecule or in a different part of the same molecule. It is considerably stronger than *dipole-dipole* interactions, which result from the attraction of the $\delta+$ end of one polar molecule for the $\delta-$ end of another polar molecule. The *van der Waals (London) forces* are the weakest. They are present to some extent between all molecules, but are important only in nonpolar molecules when the other two forces are absent. They are a result of a momentary imbalance in charge distribution in neighboring molecules, resulting in a temporary dipole moment. Although constantly changing, these induced dipoles result in a weak net attractive force. Molecules with higher molecular weights engender greater van der Waals attractive forces because they have a greater number of electrons.

39. One molecule of HF H-bonds at most with two other molecules, but each H_2O molecule contributes both Hs for H-bonding with the Os of two other molecules and uses its O for H-bonding with an H of a third molecule.

40. The three pentanes and their corresponding boiling points are: *n*-pentane, $CH_3CH_2CH_2CH_2CH_3$, 36°C; isopentane, $CH_3CH_2CH(CH_3)_2$, 28°C; and neopentane, $(CH_3)_4C$, 9.5°C. Alkanes are either very slightly polar or nonpolar. The forces holding nonpolar molecules to one another are thus weak van der Waals forces which exert themselves on the surface of the molecules only. The straight-chain isomer may be thought of as a zig-zag chain with the greatest surface area, and two such molecules can touch each other along the length of the chain. The greater the contact between molecules, the greater the van der Waals forces and the higher the boiling point. A branched-chain isomer such as isopentane may be regarded more as spherelike. Spheres touch only at a point, and thus the van der Waals forces are smaller. This isomer has a lower boiling point than the straight-chain isomer. Neopentane with the most branching has the lowest boiling point since it has the least surface area.

41. (A) Structural isomers are real molecules whose atoms are linked together in different ways to form different "skeletons." *Contributing structures are not real.* They are written whenever one electronic structure cannot adequately represent the actual structure. Their atoms are σ-bonded to one another in the same way (same skeleton), but π bonds and unshared pairs are distributed differently, with the consequence that the presence and position of formal charges may be different. A double-headed arrow (↔) is written between them to indicate resonance, *not* equilibrium.
   (B) The *resonance hybrid* is the real structure that is considered to be a "blend" of the hypothetical contributing structures.

42. (A)

(B)

(C)

(D)

43. (A) (I) N has three sp^2 HOs. Two form σ bonds with the two Os, and the third holds the unshared pair. Its *p* AO overlaps laterally with a *p* AO of *each* O, resulting in extended π bond overlap encompassing both Os and the N. The charge is thus spread out over both Os. See Figure A2-4(A). NO_3^- is much like NO_2^- except that a third O is involved in the extended π bond. The – charge is delocalized over three Os; each O has a −2/3 charge. See Figure A2-4(B).

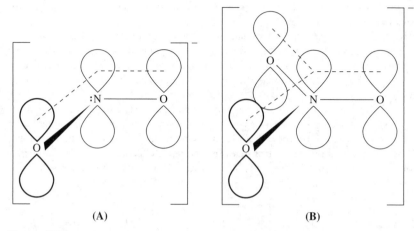

(A)   (B)

Figure A2-4

(B) The energy of the hybrid is always *lower* than that of any of the individual resonance structures. The greater the number of contributing structures with similar energies, the lower is the energy of the hybrid (more stable). The presence of more similar energy-contributing structures results in more extended π bonding, permitting e^-s to move in a larger space, thereby lessening electron repulsion. This difference between the energy of a "nonresonance" hypothetical structure, which can only be calculated, and the experimentally determined energy of the actual hybrid is the resonance or delocalization energy.

(C) The negative charge in NO_3^-, with three contributing structures, is delocalized over all three Os rather than over two Os as in NO_2^-, with two contributing structures. NO_3^- has greater delocalization energy and, thus, is more stable than NO_2^-.

44. (A) Contributing structures must have the same number of paired electrons. Singlet and triplet states cannot be contributing structures.

(B) The second structure cannot exist; N has 10 electrons.

(C) These isomers differ in the placement of the H atom; in this special case they are called *tautomers*.

Chapter 3: Chemical Reactivity and Organic Reactions

45. (A) A singlet carbene
(B) A radical
(C) A carbanion
(D) A carbocation

46. (A) $(CH_3)_2CH^+$, a carbocation
(B) $CH_3 - \overset{+}{C}H - CH_2CH_3$, a carbocation
(C) $CH_3\overset{..}{C}H_2$, a radical
(D) $CH_3\overset{..}{C}H$, a singlet carbene
(E) $CH_3CH_2^+$, a carbocation
(F) $CH_3 - C \equiv C:^-$, a carbanion
(G) H_3C^+, a carbocation

47. (A) Any diminution of + or – charge or of electron deficiency on the C stabilizes the intermediate.

　(B) The *inductive effect* of a substituent affects the charge or electron density on the C. Electronegative groups such as O, N, and halogens tend to withdraw electron density from the C whereas electropositive groups such as alkyl groups tend to increase its electron density. This effect is transmitted through the chain of σ bonds and diminishes with increasing chain length.

　(C) The carbanion C, with an unshared electron pair, has a high electron density. Electron-releasing alkyl groups make this electron density even higher, thus destabilizing the carbanion. Since the Cs of the carbocation and radical are electron-deficient, these intermediates are stabilized by the electron-releasing inductive effect of an alkyl group, which diminishes their electron deficiency. The more Rs attached to the C, the greater is the effect on the stability, as shown:

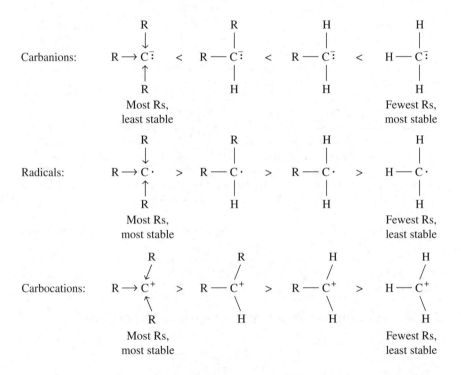

48. (A) Addition and redox. The oxidation number (ON) of each C has changed from −2 to −1 (oxidation). The ON of each Br changed from 0 to −1 (reduction). (See Question 37.)

　(B) Displacement

　(C) Displacement

　(D) α-Elimination

　(E) Addition

　(F) β-Elimination and redox. Zn is oxidized (Zn → Zn^{2+}), the dihalide is reduced

　(G) Rearrangement

　(H) Substitution (an H is displaced) and redox Cl_2 is reduced and C_6H_6 is oxidized

(I) γ-Elimination (a ring is formed) and redox [see **(F)**]
(J) Decomposition
(K) Rearrangement

49. (A) $CH_4 + Cl_2 \longrightarrow CH_3Cl + HCl$, a substitution reaction.
(B) $H_3C \cdot$ and $:\ddot{C}l \cdot$, each of which is consumed in ensuing steps.
(C) All—each step involves formation of radicals.
(D) Decomposition.
(E) In step 2, $:\ddot{C}l \cdot$ displaces $H_3C \cdot$ from an H. In step 3, a $:\ddot{C}l \cdot$ is displaced from $:\ddot{C}l:\ddot{C}l:$ by $H_3C \cdot$.
(F) No.
(G) Step 2.
(H) *Chain* reactions.
(I) $H_3C \cdot + \cdot CH_3 \longrightarrow H_3C:CH_3$, ethane, formed by a combination reaction.

50.

Reaction	(A)	(B)	(C)	(D)	(E)
Species I	Nu	Nu	E	Nu	E
Species II	E	E	Nu	E	Nu

51. (A) I. $CH_3COOH + H_2O \rightleftharpoons H_3O^+ + CH_3COO^-$
 Acid$_1$ Base$_2$ Acid$_2$ Base$_1$
 (weaker) (weaker) (stronger) (stronger)

 II. $CH_3NH_2 + H_2O \rightleftharpoons OH^- + CH_3NH_3^+$
 Base$_1$ Acid$_2$ Base$_2$ Acid$_1$
 (weaker) (weaker) (stronger) (stronger)

The conjugate pairs have the same subscript and are linked together.

(B) The net direction favors the formation of the weaker acid and base at the expense of the stronger acid and base as shown in the equations.
(C) H_2O can act either
 I. as a base or
 II. as an acid substances with such dual character are said to be *amphoteric*.

52.

Reaction	(A)	(B)	(C)	(D)	(E)	(F)
Reactant I	B	A	A	A	A	B
Reactant II	A	B	B	B	B	A

53. Acid and base strengths are measured by the position of equilibrium in reactions with water. The further the reactions go to the right, the greater the acid or basic strength.
(A) The equation for the acid equilibrium is: $H:A + H:OH \rightleftharpoons H_3O^+ + :A^-$. The expression for the equilibrium constant, K_a, is

$$K_a = \frac{[H_3O^+][:A]}{[H:A][H_2O]} \quad \text{or simply} \quad \frac{[H_3O^+][:A^-]}{[H:A]}$$

The brackets indicate molar concentrations, mol/L. H_2O is always the solvent, and its molar concentration, $[H_2O]$, equals 1000 g/L $\times 1$ mol/18 g $= 55.5$ mol/L, a constant. This term is included in the K values and doesn't appear in the equilibrium expressions. The stronger the acid, the more it ionizes, the larger is the numerator, and the larger is K_a. Then the *stronger* the acid, the *smaller* is the value for p K_a.

(B) The equilibrium for a base is: $B: + H:OH \rightleftharpoons B:H^+ + :OH^-$, and the equilibrium expression is

$$K_b = \frac{[B:H^+][:OH^-]}{[B:]}$$

Then the *stronger* the base, the *smaller* is the value for p K_b.

54. The equilibrium

$$HOAc + H_2O \rightleftharpoons OAc^- + H_3O^+$$

lies more to the right than does

$$HOAc + MeOH \rightleftharpoons OAc^- + MeOH_2^+$$

This difference could result if MeOH were a weaker base than H_2O. However, this may not be so. The difference arises mainly from the solvents' abilities to solvate the product ions. The more polar water is a better solvator of ions than is MeOH, thereby shifting the equilibrium in water more to the right.

55. (A) The greater inductive effect of an increasing number of electron-attracting Cls that is responsible for decreasing base strengths increases acid strengths. The relative order is: $Cl_3CCOOH > Cl_2CHCOOH > ClCH_2COOH$.

(B) The order is reversed: $CH_3COO^- > ClCH_2COO^- > Cl_2CHCOO^- > Cl_3CCOO^-$.

56. The cation formed by addition of H^+ has three equivalent contributing structures. This greatly stabilizes the conjugate acid, making it very weak and the base strong.

$$H_2\ddot{N} - \underset{\underset{:NH}{\|}}{C} - \ddot{N}H_2 \xrightarrow{H^+} \left[H_2\ddot{N} - \underset{\underset{NH_2^+}{\|}}{C} - \ddot{N}H_2 \leftrightarrow H_2\overset{+}{\ddot{N}} = \underset{\underset{:NH_2}{|}}{C} - \ddot{N}H_2 \leftrightarrow H_2\ddot{N} - \underset{\underset{:NH_2}{|}}{C} = \overset{+}{\ddot{N}}H_2 \right]$$

57. (A) The symbol for heat is q. For reactions at constant pressure the change in heat, q_p, is expressed as ΔH, called the *change* (the meaning of Δ) *in enthalpy*. At constant volume the change in heat, q_u, is expressed as ΔE. Since most organic reactions are performed at atmospheric pressure (constant), ΔH is used more frequently than is ΔE. The unit for ΔH is kcal/mol (kilocalorie/mole) or kJ/mol (kilojoule/mole).

(B) As is true for all thermodynamic functions, $\Delta H = H_{products} - H_{reactants}$. (We are never concerned about the individual H values, only about the ΔH values.)

   I. For an *exothermic* reaction (heat is evolved), $H_{products} < H_{reactants}$, making ΔH negative ($-\Delta H$).

   II. For an *endothermic* reaction (heat is absorbed), the reverse is true and ΔH is positive ($+\Delta H$).

(C) I. Bond breaking is always endothermic; ΔH is positive.

II. Bond formation is always exothermic; ΔH is negative.

(D) The *standard state* of any pure substance is its stable state (gas, liquid, or solid) at a *pressure of one atmosphere* and a *standard temperature*, usually 25°C. Under these conditions, $\Delta H°$ is the symbol used. The ° superscript is always used for standard-state functions and reactions.

58. (A) *Bond-dissociation energy* is the energy needed for *homolytic* breaking of one mole of a covalent bond into one mole of particles in the gas phase: $A{:}B \rightarrow A \cdot + \cdot B$. Actually, the term *enthalpy* rather than *energy* should be used since we use ΔH's.

(B) I. Bond-breaking is always endothermic, and the sign of ΔH is positive.

II. Bond formation is always exothermic, and the sign of ΔH is negative.

(C) In a molecule like CH_4 with four C—H bonds, ΔH for the process $CH_4 \rightarrow CH_3 \cdot + H \cdot$ is the bond-dissociation energy for breaking the first C—H bond *only*. The ΔH_d values for the stepwise breaking of each of the other three bonds are not the same. If it is necessary to break all four bonds in a reaction, the average value, calculated from the sum of all four individual ΔH's, called the *bond energy*, is used.

(D) Since most reactions involve the breaking of a single bond, the values found in tables are bond-dissociation energies. However, these are often loosely (incorrectly) called bond energies.

(E) The larger the ΔH_d value, the more energy is needed to break the bond, and the stronger is the bond.

59. The *heat of reaction*, ΔH_r, is the sum of the ΔH_d values for the broken bonds plus the sum of the ΔH_d values for the bonds formed. When a bond is formed, a minus sign is placed in front of the bond-dissociation energies found in the tables (where the entries are always positive).

$$\Delta H_r = \Sigma \left[+\Delta H \text{ (bonds broken)} \right] + \Sigma \left[-\Delta H \text{(bonds formed)} \right]$$

(A) The C—H and Br—Br bonds are broken, and C—Br and H—Br bonds are formed. Therefore,

$$\Delta H_r = (+102 + 46) + [(-70) + (-88)] = -10 \text{ kcal/mol}$$

(B) Since ΔH_r is negative, the reaction is exothermic.

60. The value 590 is for breaking both bonds of the C=C.

$$\Delta H_r = (590 + 435) + [(-368) + 2(-410)] = -163 \text{ kJ/mol}; \quad \text{exothermic reaction}$$

The C—H value in CH_3CH_3 was doubled because two C—H bonds were formed.

61. (A) The *standard heat of formation* $\Delta H_f°$ is the change in enthalpy when one mole of substance in its standard state (Problem 57) is formed from its elements in their standard states. By definition, $\Delta H_f°$ for any *element* in its standard state is zero.

(B) $2C \text{ (graphite)} + H_2(g) \longrightarrow C_2H_2(g)$

(C) To find ΔH_f° for the reaction in (B) that cannot be experimently determined, equations (I), (II), and (III) in (C) are manipulated by using Hess' law. Units of ΔH° are in kJ/mol.

Transpose (I): $\quad 2CO_2(g) + H_2O(l) \longrightarrow C_2H_2(g) + 2.5O_2(g) \qquad \Delta H^\circ = +1300$
Double (II): $\quad 2C(\text{graphite}) + 2O_2(g) \longrightarrow 2CO_2(g) \qquad \Delta H^\circ = 2(-394)$
Rewrite(III): $\quad H_2(g) + 0.5O_2(g) \longrightarrow H_2O(l) \qquad \Delta H^\circ = -286$

Adding these three equations gives the equation in (B). Adding the individual ΔH° values gives

$$\Delta H_f^\circ \text{ for } C_2H_2 = 1300 + (-788) + (-286) = +226 \text{ kJ/mol}$$

(D) Acetylene is unstable because it has a positive ΔH_f°. When heated, it explodes.

62. $\Delta G^\circ = -2.30 RT \log K_e = (-2.30)(2.00 \text{ cal/mol} \cdot K)(1 \text{ kcal}/10^3 \text{cal})(298 K)\left[\log(4.8 \times 10^{18})\right]$
$\qquad = (-26 \text{ kcal/mol})(4.18 \text{ kJ/kcal}) = -1.1 \times 10^2 \text{ kJ/mol}$

Since ΔG° is both negative and large, the forward reaction is favored.

63. (A) $-\Delta G$; forward; $K_e > 1$
   (B) $+\Delta G$; reverse; $K_e < 1$
   (C) If ΔH has a large negative value, it usually overwhelms a negative ΔS: $-\Delta G$; forward; $K_e > 1$. However, if T is very high, $T\Delta S$ can be high enough to overcompensate for a negative ΔH, and ΔG can become positive, the reaction is reversed, and $K_e < 1$.
   (D) If ΔH is very positive, it overrides the effect of a positive $T\Delta S$ term: $+\Delta G$; reverse; $K_e < 1$. At elevated T's, the positive $T\Delta S$ term becomes more important, and it can cause a reaction to occur. A small positive ΔH with a large positive ΔS also results in $-\Delta G$, forward, and $K_e > 1$. Predictions cannot be made exclusively from the signs in (C) and (D) without knowing the actual values of ΔH, ΔS, and T's.

64. (A) The data given for Reaction 1 show that the reaction rate depends on concentrations of both reactants raised to the first power. Had one of the concentrations been raised to the second power, doubling it would have resulted in quadrupling the rate when the other concentration was kept constant. The rate equation of Reaction 1 is rate = $k[CH_3Br][OH^-]$. This equation is of first order for each reactant but is of second order overall (1 + 1).
   The rate equation of Reaction 2 depends on $[(CH_3)_3CBr]$ raised to the power of 1: rate = $k[(CH_3)_3CBr]$. It is of the first order with respect to $[(CH_3)_3CBr]$, of zeroth order with respect to $[OH^-]$, and of first order (1 + 0) overall.
   (B) The rate equations are different because the reactions have different mechanisms.

65.

| | H partially broken | |
| Methane | Transition state | Methyl radical |

The brackets show the transient character of the TS that is further indicated by the symbol $\ddagger$.

66. **(A)** Enthalpy diagrams show the relationship between the enthalpies of reactants, transition state, and products along the y axis. The x axis shows the progress of the reaction. The y axis may indicate free energy or potential energy as well as enthalpy. See Figure A3-1.

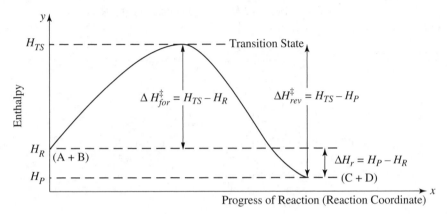

Figure A3-1

Because the reaction is exothermic, $H_P < H_R (\Delta H_r = H_P - H_R)$.

    (B) Both reactions must proceed through the same TS. Since the reaction is exothermic and the enthalpy of the product is lower, $\Delta H^{\ddagger}_{reverse} > \Delta H^{\ddagger}_{forward}$.

    (C) They are rarely related. An exception occurs when the TS shows only the breaking of bonds.

67. In some combination, two As and one B are needed to participate in the slow rate-determining step. The three do not collide simultaneously since termolecular steps are very rare and therefore disregarded. This dictates multisteps in which there are initial fast reactions to produce the intermediate necessary for the slow step. The second mole of B, which is in the chemical equation but not in the rate equation, is used in a fast step following the slow step. Two possible mechanisms are:

Mechanism 1	Mechanism 2
$A + B \xrightarrow{\text{fast}} AB$	$A + A \xrightarrow{\text{fast}} A_2$
$AB + A \xrightarrow{\text{slow}} A_2B$	$A_2 + B \xrightarrow{\text{slow}} A_2B$
$A_2B + B \xrightarrow{\text{fast}} C + D$	$A_2B + B \xrightarrow{\text{fast}} C + D$

The rate equation alone does not determine which is the correct mechanism.

Chapter 4: Alkanes

68. (A) The general formula is C_nH_{2n+2} where n is an integer.
   (B)   I. C_4H_{10}
      II. C_7H_{16}
      III. $C_{10}H_{22}$
      IV. $C_{22}H_{46}$
   (C) The alkanes having from 1 to 7 Cs are, in order, methane, ethane, propane, butane, pentane, hexane, and heptane.

69. (A) In the condensed formula, all atoms or groups written after a C are bonded to it.

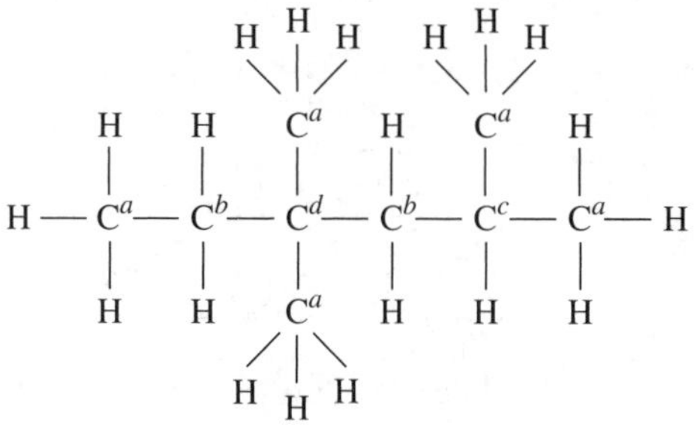

$a = 1°$ $b = 2°$
$c = 3°$ $d = 4°$

A $1°$ C is bonded to only one other C, a $2°$ C to two other Cs, a $3°$ C to three other Cs, and a $4°$ C to four other Cs. (The C of CH_4 is super $1°$.)
   (B) $1°$ Hs are those attached to $1°$ Cs, to $2°$ Hs and $2°$ Cs to $3°$ Cs Other atoms or groups bonded to C, like halogen, are similarly identified. (A $1°$ H cannot exit because all four bonds of a $4°$ C are to other Cs.)
   (C) 3, 2, 1, and 0
   (D) 1, 2, 3, and 4

70. (A) $CH_3 - CH - CH - CH_2CH_2CH_3$
                   | |
                  CH_3 Cl

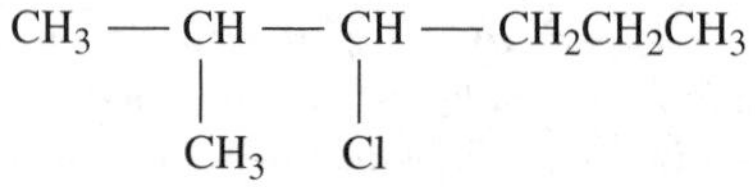

   (B) $CH_3 - CH - CH - CH - CH_3$
                   | | |
                  CH_3 CH_3 CH_3

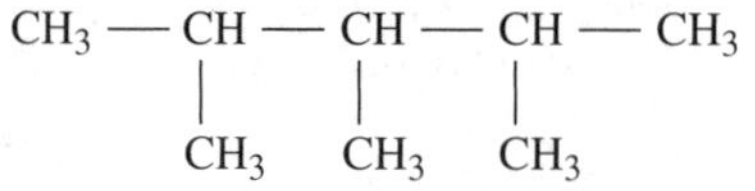

   (C) $BrCH_2 - CH - CH_2 - CH_2Br$
                      |
                     CH_3

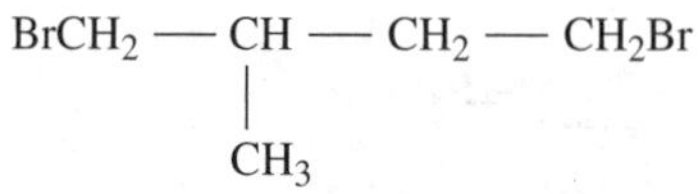

   (D) $CH_3 - CH_2 - CH_2 - C - CH_3$
                                 |
                                CH_3 (with CH_3 above the C)

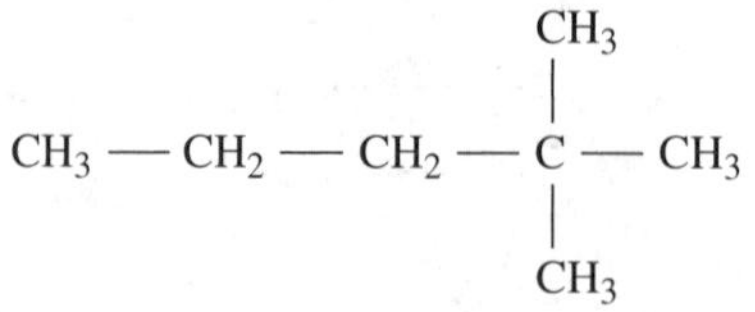

   (E) $CH_3 - CH_2 - CH_2 - CH - CH_2 - CH_2 - CH_3$
                               |
                           CH_3CHCH_3

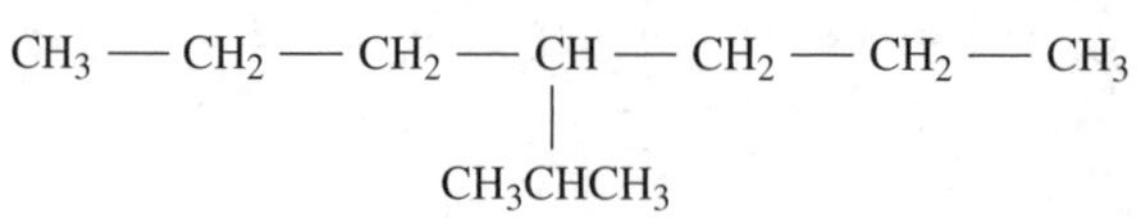

71. (**A**) 2, 2, 4, 4-Tetramethylpentane
  (**B**) 2, 2,-dimethylpropane
  (**C**) 2,2,-dichloro-3-methylbutane
  (**D**) 3-ethyl-4-methylhexane

72. Start with the longest chain, hexane, $CH_3CH_2CH_2CH_2CH_2CH_3$. Going to a five-carbon chain, a CH_3 may be placed either on C^2 to produce 2-methylpentane or on C^3 to give 3-methylpentane. Starting with a four-carbon chain, either a CH_3CH_2 or two CH_3s must be added as side chains for a total of six Cs. The CH_3CH_2 cannot be placed anywhere on the chain because that would lengthen it. A CH_3 would also extend the chain if it were placed on either terminal C. Placing one CH_3 on each of the central Cs gives 2,3-dimethylbutane; and if both are placed on the same central C, the isomer is 2,2-dimethylbutane. Note that each isomer has a distinctive name. If two structural formulas have the same correct names, they are identical even if they are drawn differently.

$$CH_3CHCH_2CH_2CH_3 \quad CH_3CH_2CHCH_2CH_3 \quad CH_3-CH-CH-CH_3 \quad CH_3-\overset{CH_3}{\underset{CH_3}{C}}-CH_2CH_3$$

CH_3	CH_3	CH_3 CH_3	CH_3
2-Methylpentane	3-Methylpentane	2,3-Dimethylbutane	2,2-Dimethylbutane

73. The two Brs are placed first on the same C and then on different Cs.

$Br_2CHCH_2CH_3$	$CH_3CBr_2CH_3$	$BrCH_2CHBrCH_3$	$BrCH_2CH_2CH_2Br$
1, 1-Dibromopropane	2, 2-Dibromopropane	1, 2-Dibromopropane	1, 3-Dibromopropane

74. With a lower molecular weight, C_5H_{12} has a lower bp than both C_6H_{14} isomers. The branched 2, 3-dimethylbutane has a lower bp than the straight-chain isomer because it is a more compact molecule with less surface area, and thus has weaker intermolecular van der Waals attractive forces. The actual bp's are: pentane, 36°C; 2,3-dimethylbutane, 58°C; hexane, 69°C.

75. (**A**) (I) 1-Chloropentane. It is a more polar compound (the C—Cl bond has an appreciable dipole moment) and has a higher molecular weight. (II) 2-Methylhexane. It has a longer, less-branched chain. Less branching leads to greater touchable surface area and, thus, greater van der Waals attractive forces.
  (**B**) CF_4 is spherical and has less approachable surface area for intermolecular attractive forces than the unbranched hexane. Think of two balls that can touch only at a point and two strands of uncooked spaghetti in contact along their entire length.

76. (**A**) See Figure A4-1.
  (**B**) $\Delta G \cong \Delta H$, and so $\Delta G = -RT \ln K_{eq}$ for the equilibrium: eclipsed $\rightleftharpoons$ staggered.

$$K_{eq} = \frac{\text{[staggered]}}{\text{[eclipsed]}} \quad \text{and} \quad \ln K_{eq} = -\Delta G/RT = \frac{-3000 \text{ cal/mol}}{(1.99 \text{ cal/mal} \cdot \text{K})(298 \text{ K})} = 5.059; \quad K_{eq} = 157$$

A K_{eq} of 157 signifies that at 25°C over 99% (157/158) of the molecules are in a staggered conformation, even though there is rapid rotation about the C—C bond.

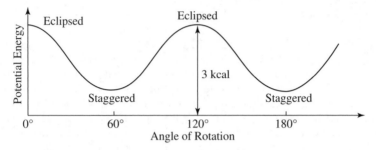

Figure A4-1

77. See Figure A4-2. (The O is not visible; it is behind the C.)

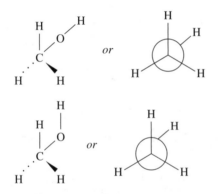

Figure A4-2

78. **(A)** The *dihedral angle* is the angle formed from the H on one C and the H of the other C as sighted along the C—C bond.

  (B) The values of the angles in the staggered and the eclipsed conformations are 60° and 0°, respectively.

  (C) See Figure A4-3. Hs are understood to be attached to each bond.

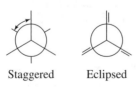

Staggered   Eclipsed

Figure A4-3

79. See Figure A4-4.

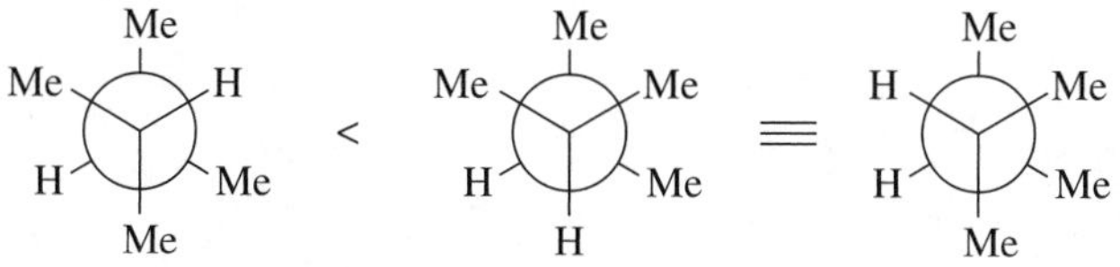

Figure A4-4

80. See Figure A4-5.

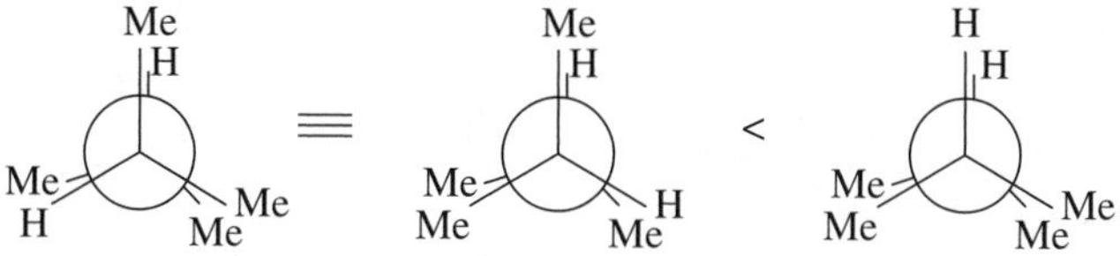

Figure A4-5

81. The equation for the reaction must be balanced first:

$$H_3C-CH_2-CH_3 + 5O_2 \rightarrow 3CO_2 + 4H_2O$$

Bond breaking requires energy, and bond formation liberates energy. Thus

Bonds broken: $2\ C-C\ (166) + 8H-C\ (792) + 5O=O\ (595) = +1553$ kcal/mol

Bonds formed: $6\ C=O\ (-1152) + 8O-H\ (-888) = -2040$ kcal/mol

$$\Delta H_c^\circ = \text{bonds broken} + \text{bonds formed} = +1553 + (-2040) = -487 \text{ kcal/mol}$$

82. Reduction using
   (A) Zn, H^+
   (B) $LiAlH_4$
   (C) Mg/anh. ether followed by H_2O

83. $(CH_3\ddot{C}H_2)-(MgBr)^+ + CH_3\ddot{O}H \longrightarrow CH_3CH_3 + (MgBr)^+ CH_3\ddot{O}:^-$

   Base$_1$ Acid$_2$ Acid$_1$ Base$_2$

84. **(A)** $R'\ddot{N}H_2 + R:^-Li^+ \longrightarrow Li^+(R'\ddot{N}H)^- + RH$
   (B) The H in an alkane is not sufficiently acidic. In fact, it is one of the least acidic Hs. Hs attached to hetero atoms such as O, N, and S in H_2O, alcohols, acids, amines, and thiols do react.

85. $2\,CH_3CH_2Cl + 2\,Na \longrightarrow CH_3CH_2CH_2CH_3 + 2\,NaCl$

86. The structure is

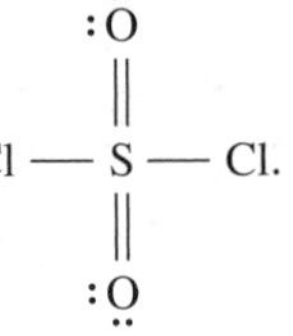

$$Cl - \overset{\displaystyle :\ddot{O}}{\underset{\displaystyle :O}{\overset{\displaystyle \|}{\underset{\displaystyle \|}{S}}}} - Cl.$$

87. Step 1. $ROOR \longrightarrow 2\,RO\cdot$
Step 2. $RO\cdot + R'H \longrightarrow ROH + \cdot R'$
Step 3. $\cdot R' + SO_2Cl_2 \longrightarrow R'Cl + \cdot SO_2Cl$
Step 4. $\cdot SO_2Cl \longrightarrow SO_2 + Cl\cdot$
Step 5. $Cl\cdot + R'H \longrightarrow HCl + \cdot R'$

Steps 1 and 2 are initation step; steps 3, 4, and 5 are propagation steps.

88. **(A)** The only alkene having the same carbon skeleton as A is $(CH_3)_3\overset{\displaystyle \overset{\textstyle CH_3}{|}}{C}C\!=\!CH_2$.

$$(CH_3)_3\overset{\displaystyle \overset{\textstyle CH_3}{|}}{C}C = CH_2 \xrightarrow{\text{H}_2,\text{Pt or Ni catalyst}} (CH_3)_3CCH(CH_3)_2$$

(B) 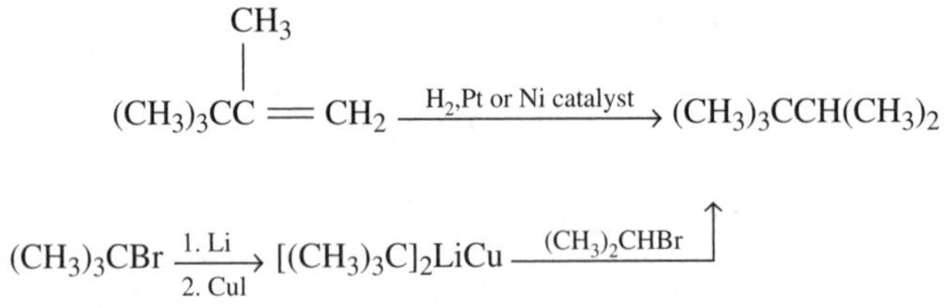 $(CH_3)_3CBr \xrightarrow[\text{2. CuI}]{\text{1. Li}} [(CH_3)_3C]_2LiCu \xrightarrow{(CH_3)_2CHBr} \uparrow$

89. **(A)** Both starting material and product have the same carbon skeleton.

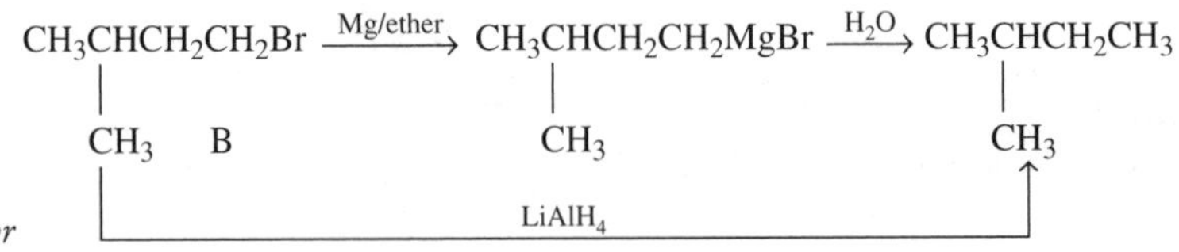

$$CH_3\underset{\underset{\textstyle B}{\overset{\textstyle |}{CH_3}}}{CH}CH_2CH_2Br \xrightarrow{\text{Mg/ether}} CH_3\underset{\overset{\textstyle |}{CH_3}}{CH}CH_2CH_2MgBr \xrightarrow{\text{H}_2\text{O}} CH_3\underset{\overset{\textstyle |}{CH_3}}{CH}CH_2CH_3$$

or $\underbrace{\hspace{5cm}}_{\text{LiAlH}_4}$

(B) $B \xrightarrow[\text{2. CuI}]{\text{1. Li}} [(CH_3)_2CHCH_2CH_2]_2CuLi \xrightarrow{B} (CH_3)_2CHCH_2CH_2CH_2$
$CH_2CH(CH_3)_2$ *or* 2 mol $B \xrightarrow{\text{Na}}$ product (Wurtz reaction)

(C) $B \xrightarrow[\substack{\text{2. CuI}\\\text{3. CH}_3\text{CH}_2\text{Br}}]{\text{1. Li}} CH_3CH(CH_3)CH_2CH_2CH_2CH_3$

Chapter 5: Cycloalkanes

90. **(A)** The *cycloalkane* homologous series consists of hydrocarbons with the general formula C_nH_{2n}, where C—C bonds form a ring.

(B) I. C_3H_6 C_4H_8 C_5H_{10} C_6H_{12}

II. $CH_2 — CH_2$ $CH_2 — CH_2$ $CH_2 — CH_2$ $CH_2 — CH_2$
          $\diagdown \diagup$ $|$ $|$ $\diagup$ $\diagdown$ $\diagup$ $\diagdown$
           CH_2 $CH_2 — CH_2$ CH_2 CH_2 CH_2 CH_2
                                                            $\diagdown \diagup$ $\diagdown$ $\diagup$
                                                               CH_2 $CH_2 — CH_2$

III. △   □   ⬠   ⬡

91. **(A)** 1,1-Dimethyl-3-isopropylcyclopentane
   (B) 3-Iodo-2-methyl-1-ethylcyclohexane
   (C) 1,1,2,3-tetramethylcyclobutane
   (D) 3-cyclopropyl-2-methylheptane
   (E) 1-cyclobutyl-3-methylcyclopentane

92. **(A)**
Bicyclo[1.1.0]butane

(B)
Bicyclo[4.1.0]heptane   Bicyclo[3.2.0]heptane

(C)
Bicyclo[5.1.0]octane   Bicyclo[4.2.0]octane   Bicyclo[3.3.0]octane

Check your answer by adding 2 for the bridgehead Cs to the total of the numbers in the brackets. Your answer should be the same as the number of Cs in the alkane name.

93. To number bicyclics, start at one bridgehead C and move along the longest chain to the next bridgehead C. Continue along the next-longest chain to the first bridgehead C so that the shortest bridge is numbered last. For decalins, C^1 is next to a bridgehead C and is chosen so substituents have the lowest possible numbers—the bridgehead Cs get the last number, 9 and 10.

(A)

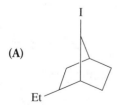

(B) 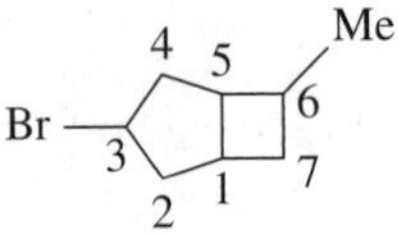 Br —

$$\begin{array}{c} \text{Me} \\ \underset{3}{\overset{4 \quad 5}{\diagup}} \overset{6}{\underset{2 \quad 1}{\square}} 7 \end{array}$$

(C)

$$\begin{array}{c} \text{Me} \\ \text{Me} \end{array}$$

Me

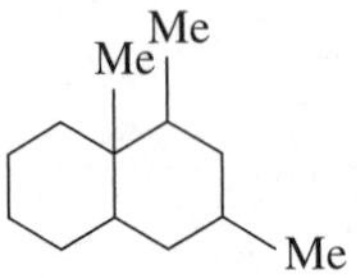

94. (A)

$$\begin{array}{c} \text{Me} \\ \text{Me} \\ \end{array} \begin{array}{c} R \\ C \quad D \\ A \quad B \end{array}$$

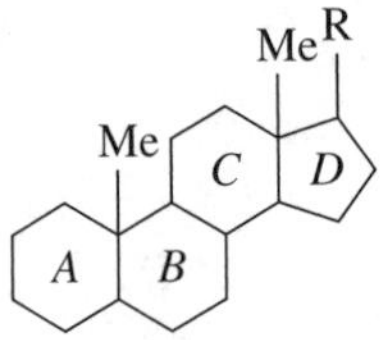

There is an angular Me at the upper bridgehead C of rings *A* and *B*, and one at *C* and *D*. The R indicates the position of an attached side chain.

(B) Tetracyclic.

95. (A)

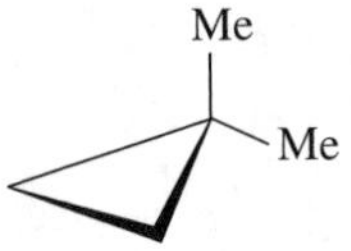

Me

Me

1,1-Dimethylcyclopropane

(B)

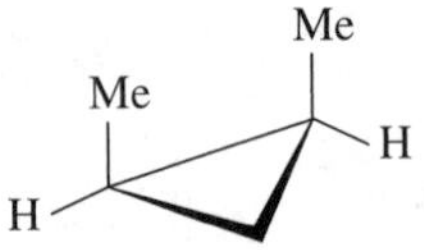

Me

Me

H

H

cis-1,2-Dimethylcyclopropane

(C)

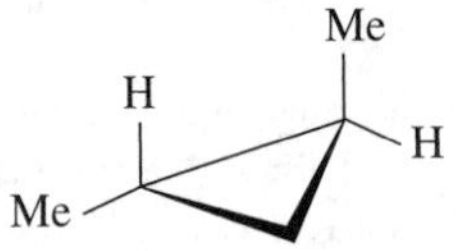

Me

H

H

Me

trans-1,2-Dimethylcyclopropane

96. (A) No! We could write structures that resemble *cis-trans* isomers:

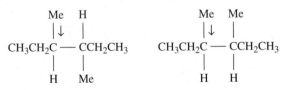

$$\begin{array}{ccc} \text{Me} & \text{H} & \\ |{\downarrow} & | & \\ \text{CH}_3\text{CH}_2\text{C} & \!\!-\!\! & \text{CCH}_2\text{CH}_3 \\ | & | & \\ \text{H} & \text{Me} & \end{array} \qquad \begin{array}{ccc} \text{Me} & \text{Me} & \\ |{\downarrow} & | & \\ \text{CH}_3\text{CH}_2\text{C} & \!\!-\!\! & \text{CCH}_2\text{CH}_3 \\ | & | & \\ \text{H} & \text{H} & \end{array}$$

However, these are not isomers because they rapidly interconvert by rotation about the indicated bond and consequently they are not isolable. They are conformations.

(B) There must be a rigid site to preclude easy rotation which rapidly interconverts the structures. In cyclic compounds such a site is the ring.

97. (A) None

(B)

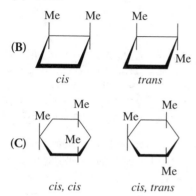

cis   trans

cis, cis   cis, trans

(C)

The stereochemical designations given in **(C)** indicate the positions of the substituents relative to the one at C^1.

98. (A) *Small rings* (C_3–C_4) have large ring strain.
(B) *Common rings* (C_5–C_6) have little or no strain.
(C) *Medium rings* (C_7–C_{12}) have little strain.
(D) *Large rings* (>C_{12}) are strain-free.

99. *Bond-angle strain* is caused by distortion of the tetrahedral C angle in closing the ring. *Eclipsing (torsional) strain* results from eclipsing of adjacent pairs of C—H bonds. Other factors are *gauche interactions,* which are similar to those in *n*-butane, and *transannular* (across the ring) *strain* arising from the proximity of H atoms not on adjacent Cs.

100. (A) To minimize angle strain, the Cs develop more *p* character in the orbitals forming the ring (and consequently more *s* character in the external C—H bonds). Since bond angles generated from overlapping *p* orbitals are 90°, additional *p* character in the internal bonds decreases the ring strain. To get more *s* character, the HOs for the external bonds are somewhere between sp^3 and sp^2, leading to enlargement of the angle. This is another example of deviations from pure *p*, *sp*, sp^2, sp^3 hybridization.

(B) The more *s* character in the HO used by C to form a bond, the shorter is the bond. The C—H bond in cyclopropane is shorter than in propane.

101. Cyclobutane is not a flat ring but rather exists as two equilibrating *puckered* ("folded") conformations (Figure A5-1) in which eclipsing is eliminated and replaced by staggered Hs. Puckering more than offsets the slight increase in angle strain because the new angles are 88°. The four boxed Hs in Figure A5-1 alternate between up-and-down, and the other four project outward from the perimeter of the ring.

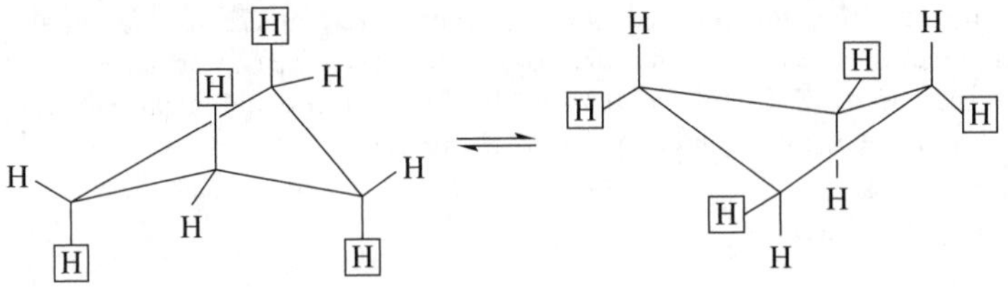

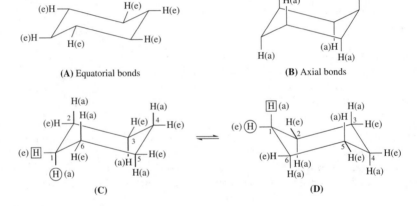

Figure A5-1

102. (A) See Figure A5-2 (A) and (B). Although the cyclohexane ring is not flat, we can consider that the Cs lie roughly in a plane for the purpose of identifying and naming the types of Hs. Six Hs are *equatorial* (e); they project out from the perimeter or equator of the ring. The other six Hs are *axial* (a), alternating, perpendicularly, up from the ring plane (toward the north axis) and down (toward the south axis), hence the designation of the names *axial* and *equatorial*.

    (B) Each C has one equatorial and one axial C—H bond, and in the conversion the equatorial bonds become axial while the axial bonds become equatorial [Figure A5-2 (C) and (D)].

(A) Equatorial bonds

(B) Axial bonds

(C)

(D)

Figure A5-2

103. (A) See Figure A5-3.

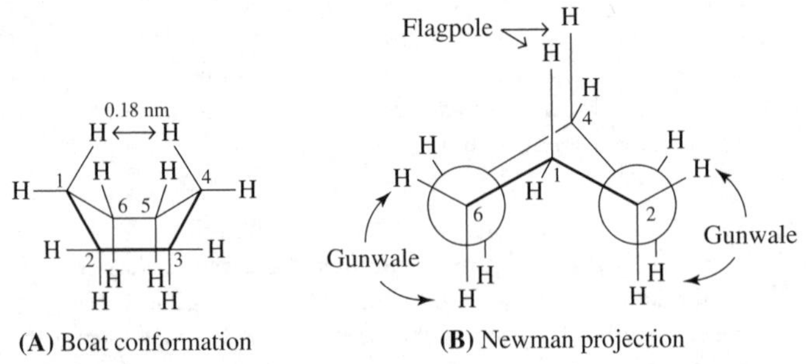

(A) Boat conformation

(B) Newman projection

Figure A5-3

(B) Flipping the chair conformer moves up C^1 to place it and C^4 on the same side of the plane composing the remaining four Cs, called the *gunwale* Cs.

(C) Like the chair, the boat conformation has no angle strain, but it has eclipsing strain from the two pairs of Hs on each set of gunwale Cs. There is also transannular strain from the crowding of the "flagpole" Hs on C^1 and C^4, which point toward each other and tend to occupy the same space.

104. (A) See Figure A5-4.

 (B) I. **E** and **F** are identical (e, a) conformers with the same energy.

   II. **G** is (e, e) and is more stable than **H** (a, a).

 (C) *cis*-**G** (e, e) is more stable than **E** or **F**.

 (D) All *cis*-dialkylcycloalkanes were expected to be less stable because of steric interaction of the Rs that were thought to be on the same side of the ring. Conformational analysis in terms of axial and equatorial orientations nicely explains the "anomaly."

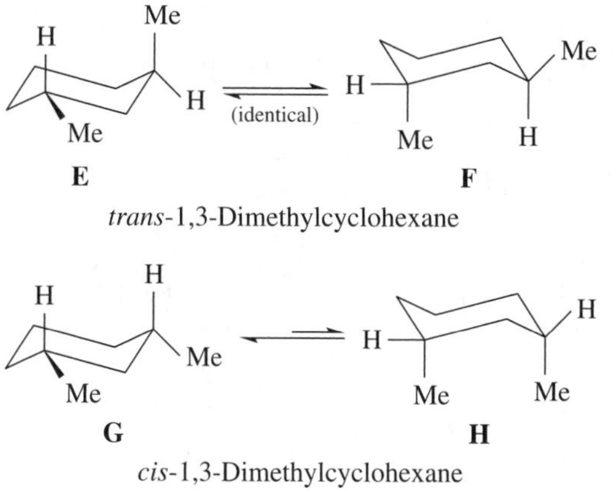

trans-1,3-Dimethylcyclohexane

cis-1,3-Dimethylcyclohexane

Figure A5-4

105. (A)

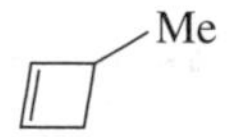

3-Methylcyclobutene

 (B)

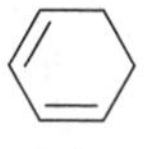

1,3-Cyclohexadiene

106. (A) **A** = cyclohexene, **B** = cyclohexane

 (B) Diels–Alder

 (C) six

107. (A)

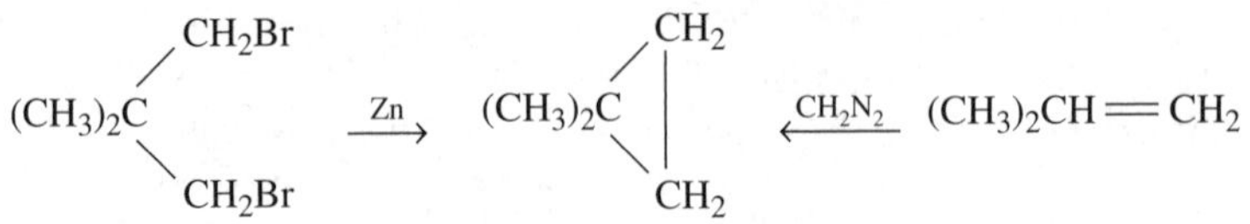

$$(CH_3)_2C \overset{CH_2Br}{\underset{CH_2Br}{\Big\langle}} \xrightarrow{Zn} (CH_3)_2C \overset{CH_2}{\underset{CH_2}{\Big|}} \xleftarrow{CH_2N_2} (CH_3)_2CH = CH_2$$

1,3-Dibromo-2,2-   1,1-Dimethylcyclopropane
dimethylpropane

(B)

$$CH_2 \overset{CHBrCH_3}{\underset{CHBrCH_3}{\Big\langle}} \xrightarrow{Zn} CH_2 \overset{CHCH_3}{\underset{CHCH_3}{\Big|}} \xleftarrow{CH_2N_2} CH_3CH = CHCH_3$$

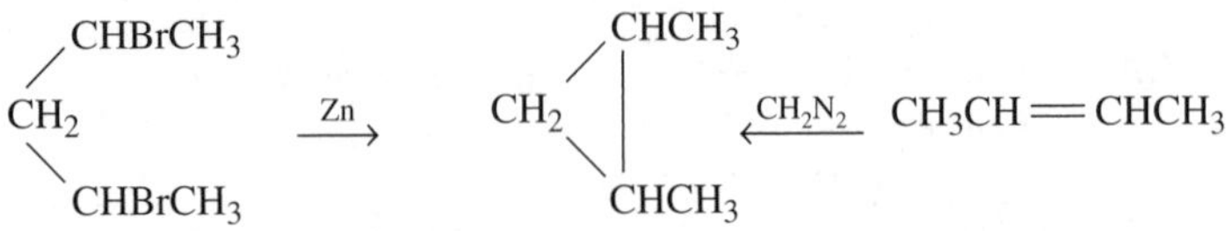

2,4-Dibromopentane   1,2-Dimethylcyclopropane

108. (A) I. $2H_2C = CH_2 \xrightarrow{h\nu} A$ or $H_2C = CHCH = CH_2 \xrightarrow{heat} \square \xrightarrow{H_2/Pd} A$

II. 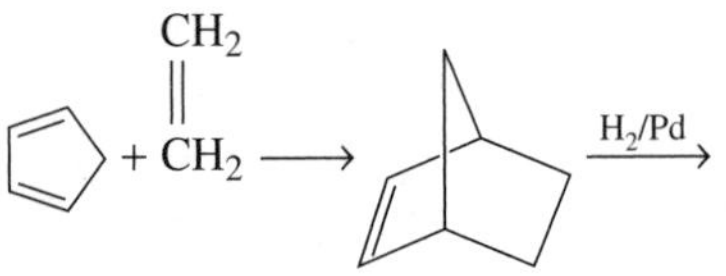 + $\overset{CH_2}{\underset{CH_2}{\|}} \longrightarrow$ $\xrightarrow{H_2/Pd}$ norbornane **B**

(B)   I. Electrocyclic
II. cycloaddition

109. (A) The ring and the CH_3 are monobrominated, giving a complex mixture of structural as well as geometric isomers of the 2-, 3-, and 4-bromomethylcyclohexanes.

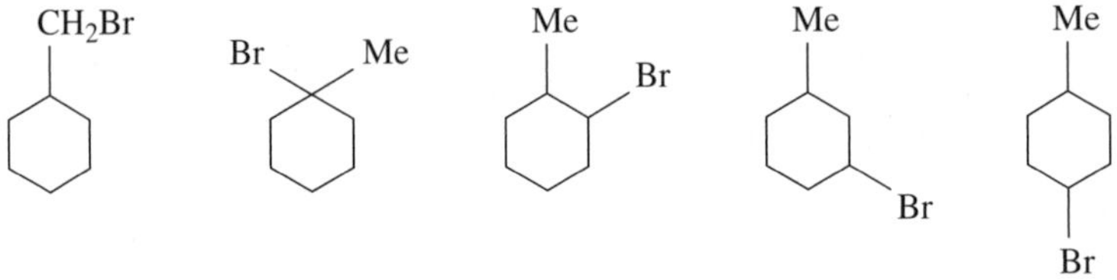

  A   B   C   D   E

cis and trans isomers

A is bromomethylcyclohexane; **B, C, D,** and **E** are 1-, 2-, 3-, and 4-bromomethylcyclohexanes, respectively.

(B) The intermediate Br · is a selective radical and preferentially attacks the 3^0 H, giving **B** as the major product.

(C) Cl · is much less selective, and the statistical factor plays a significant role in determining the product distribution. There would be more of each isomer with none dominating.

110. (A) :CCl$_2$ adds *cis* to the C$=$C, but the resulting three-member ring can be either *cis* or *trans* to Me (**A** and **B** in Figure A5-5).

(B) The anion formed, $ClBr_2C:^-$, loses Br^-, a better leaving group than Cl^-, to give the carbine, ClBrC:, which adds to the C = C so that either Cl or Br is *cis* to Me (**C** and **D** in Figure A5-5).

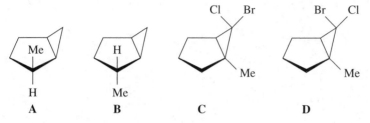

Figure A5-5

Chapter 6: Stereochemistry

111. (A) Structural isomers have the same molecular formula, but the atoms are joined in a different order. *Stereoisomers* have the same molecular formula, their atoms are attached in the same order, but they are arranged differently in space.

    (B) *Configuration* is the spatial arrangement of stereoisomers.

112. Stereoisomers consist of *enantiomers* (optical isomers) and *diastereomers*.

    (A) *Enantiomers* are stereoisomers whose mirror images are not identical, i.e., they are not *superposable* on each other, in the same way that a left and right hand are not superposable.

    (B) *Diastereomers* are stereoisomers which are not mirror images of each other, as, for example, *cis-trans* isomers in cycloalkanes.

113. (A) A *chiral* molecule is a stereoisomer whose mirror image is not superposable. It lacks a plane or center of symmetry.

    (B) An *achiral* molecule has a superposable mirror image.

114. The objects with at least one plane of symmetry are **(D)**, **(E)**, and **(G)**, as shown in Figure A6-1. For **(F)**, a spool of thread has the thread wound onto it in either a clockwise or counterclockwise fashion.

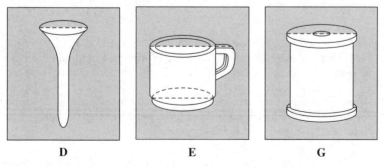

Figure A6-1

115. **(A)**

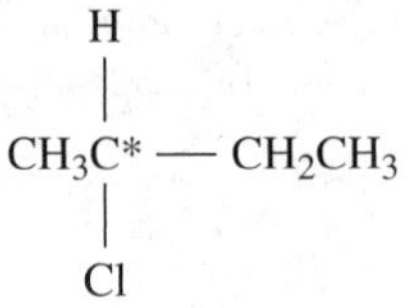

$$\overset{\displaystyle H}{\underset{\displaystyle Cl}{\overset{|}{\underset{|}{CH_3C^*}}}} - CH_2CH_3$$

(B)

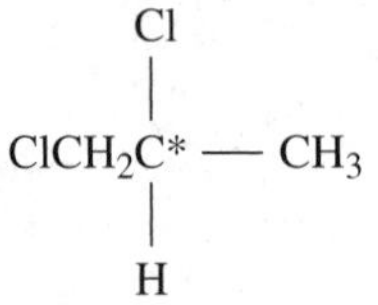

$$\overset{\displaystyle Cl}{\underset{\displaystyle H}{\overset{|}{\underset{|}{ClCH_2C^*}}}} - CH_3$$

(C)

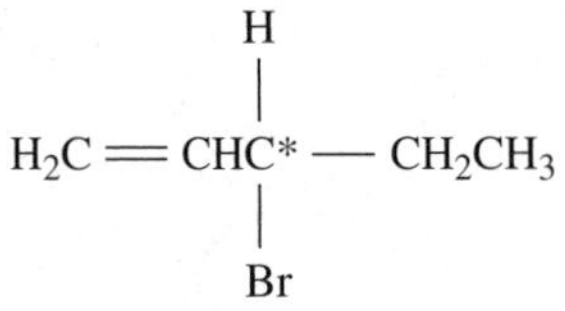

$$H_2C = \overset{\displaystyle H}{\underset{\displaystyle Br}{\overset{|}{\underset{|}{CHC^*}}}} - CH_2CH_3$$

(D)

$$\overset{\displaystyle CH_3}{\underset{\displaystyle Cl}{\overset{|}{\underset{|}{CH_3CH_2Si^*}}}} - CH_2CH_2CH_3$$

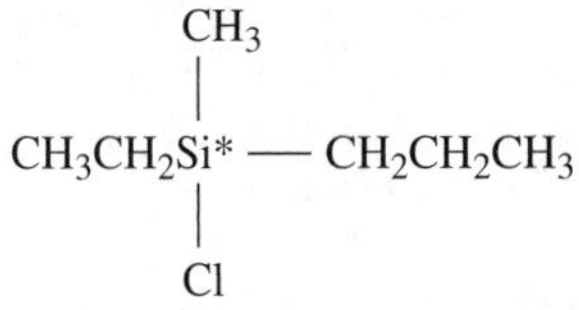

Note that in **(D)** the chiral center is an sp^3 hybridized (tetrahedral) Si atom.

116. Theoretically it can, but not in practice. A rapid "umbrella" type of inversion converts either enantiomer to a racemic mixture. The energy required for this inversion is very low at room temperature; thus racemization is unavoidable, and typically the enantiomers cannot be separated or isolated.

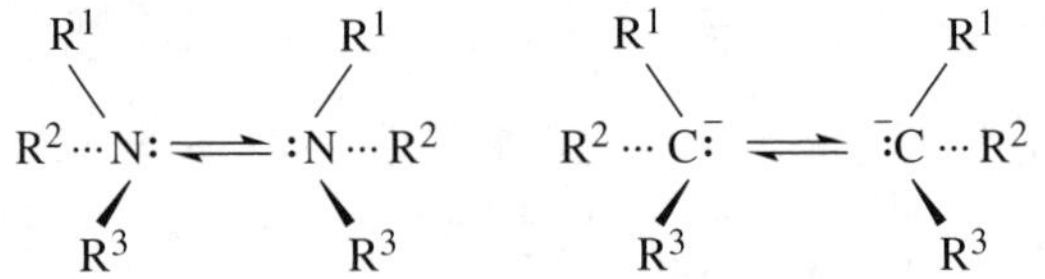

$$R^1 \searrow \atop R^2 \cdots N: \qquad :N \cdots R^2 \atop \swarrow R^1 \qquad \qquad R^1 \searrow \atop R^2 \cdots C: \qquad :C \cdots R^2 \atop \swarrow R^1$$

Inversion

117. Plane-polarized light is produced in an instrument called a *polarimeter*, and it passes through a polarimeter tube containing either the liquid enantiomer or its solution. The angle through which the polarized light has been rotated is measured in an analyzer. The observed rotation, α_{obs}, is expressed in degrees. If the polarized light plane is rotated to the left (counterclockwise), the enantiomer is said to be *levorotatory*. A rotation to the right (clockwise) is called *dextrorotatory*. The symbols (−) and (+) designate rotation to the left and right, respectively.

118. **(A)** Absolute configuration is the special arrangement of substituents attached to a chiral center.

(B) A priority sequence (proposed by Cahn, Ingold, and Prelog) is assigned to the four ligands attached to the chiral center. The directly attached atom having the highest atomic number has the highest priority, and the other ligand atoms follow in order of decreasing atomic number. When two ligands are isotopes, i.e., H and D, the one with the higher atomic weight has the higher priority. The molecule is then visualized with the ligand of lowest priority directed away from the viewer, behind the plane of the paper. The arrangement of the other ligands determines the classification: if the sequence from the highest to the lowest priority is clockwise, the molecule is specified *R*; and if the sequence is counterclockwise, the molecule is called *S*.

(C) The priority sequence is Br > Cl > CH_3 > H. The configurations and designations are as follows:

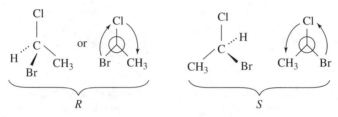

119. **(A)** *R*
     (B) *S*
     (C) *S*
     (D) *R*

120. In **E**, the priority order is CH_2Cl > $CH(CH_3)_2$ > CH_3 > **H**. The compound is *S*. In **F**, the priority order is CH_2OH > CN > C≡CH > CH_3. The compound is *S*. — CH_2OH has priority over C≡N because one O counts before three Ns. In **G**, the priority order is NH_2 > COOH > CHO > H. The compound is *R*.

121. In proline the chiral C is part of a five-member ring. It is attached to an N (the amino group), and this part of the ring has first priority. The carboxyl group is second and the C in the ring attached to the chiral C is third. The compound is *S*.

$$HN \overset{COOH}{\underset{CH_2}{\rule{0pt}{0pt}\vert}} H$$

122. There are two chiral Cs (C^2 and C^3), and the four stereoisomers are shown below with their *R/S* designation.

	CH_2Br		CH_2Br		CH_2Br		CH_2Br	
H—²—CH_3		CH_3——H		H——CH_3		CH_3——H	
H—³—Br		Br——H		Br——H		H——Br	
	CH_3		CH_3		CH_3		CH_3	
	2S, 3R		2R, 3S		2S, 3S		2R, 3R	

123. Diastereomers have different physical properties, e.g., melting and boiling points, refractive indices, solubilities in different solvents, crystalline structures, and specific rotations. Because of their differences in solubility they often can be separated from each other by fractional crystallization; because of slight differences in molecular shape and polarity, they often can be separated from each other by chromatography. Diastereomers have different chemical properties toward both chiral and achiral reagents. Neither any two diastereomers nor their transition states are mirror images of each other and so will not necessarily have the same energies. The $\Delta H^{\ddagger}$'s will be somewhat different, and thus the rates of reaction will differ. However, since the diastereomers have the same functional groups, their chemical properties are not too dissimilar.

124. Since the $2R,3S$ structure is identical with the $2S,3R$ structure, it can be called either R,S or S,R. (Numbers are not necessary because the two designations are equivalent.)

125. In (A) and (B), a plane of symmetry cuts through the center carbon and the two horizontal ligands revealing that the top half of the molecule is the mirror image of the bottom half. It does not matter which ligands are attached to this carbon because they are within the symmetry plane. This is also true in (C) if $n = 1$ or an odd number. However, if n is an even number, the symmetry plane cuts through the central C — C bond.

126. See Figure A6-2. Cyclopentane is best considered as a flat ring. All *trans*-isomers exist as a pair of enantiomers. All *cis*-isomers are *meso*.

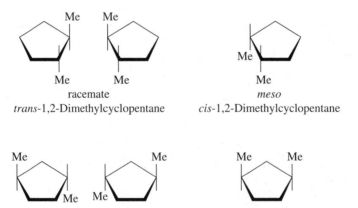

racemate
trans-1,2-Dimethylcyclopentane

meso
cis-1,2-Dimethylcyclopentane

racemate
trans-1,3-Dimethylcyclopentane

meso
cis-1,3-Dimethylcyclopentane

Figure A6-2

127. See Figure A6-3.

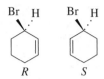

R   S

Figure A6-3

128. (A) (S)-$CH_3CHClCH_2CH_3$ → $ClCH_2CHClCH_2CH_3$ **(D)** + $CH_3C(Cl)_2CH_2CH_3$ **(E)** + $CH_3CHClCHClCH_3$ **(F)** + $CH_3CHClCH_2CH_2Cl$ **(G)**

　(B) **D** is still chiral, and the C^2 configuration is unchanged because no bonds have been broken. However, because of the change in priorities ($CH_2Cl > CH_2CH_3$), it is R. Since C^2 with two Cls has a plane of symmetry, **E** is achiral. Two diastereomers corresponding to **F** are formed. C^2 is still S, but C^3 can be R or S. These diastereomers are 2S, 3S which is optically active, and *meso* 2S, 3R. Attack at C^4 does not affect the configuration at C^2, nor does the priority order change; **G** is S.

129. (A), **(C)**, and **(D)** Retention; no bond breaking occurs at the chiral C.
　(B) Racemization; although the product has a chiral center (D being sufficiently different from H), both enantiomers are formed in equal amounts because D_2 adds to the enantiotopic faces of the alkene equally, **(E)** Inversion.

130. (A) False; the sign of rotation is not related to the configuration.
　(B) True; an example is a *meso* compound.
　(C) False; a racemate shows no optical activity.
　(D) False; the priority sequence of ligands may change.
　(E) False; if an optically active chiral co-reactant, solvent, or catalyst such as an enzyme is used, the product will likely be optically active.

131. In both **B** and **C**, one of the ligands on the chiral C must be — CH=CH$_2$ that adds H$_2$ to form a—C$_2$H$_5$ group. **B** already has a — C$_2$H$_5$ group on its chiral C, making the product achiral. However, since **C** does not have an ethyl ligand, the product remains active.

$$CH_3CH_2CHCH=CH_2 \xrightarrow{H_2, Pd} CH_3CH_2CHCH_2CH_3 \qquad ClCH_2CHCH=CH_2 \xrightarrow{H_2, Pd} ClCH_2CHCH_2CH_3$$
$$\underset{Cl}{|} \qquad\qquad\qquad \underset{Cl}{|} \qquad\qquad\qquad \underset{CH_3}{|} \qquad\qquad\qquad \underset{CH_3}{|}$$

　　　B 　　　　　　　　**D** 　　　　　　　　**C** 　　　　　　　　**E**

132. (A) False. The product could be *meso* or achiral.
　(B) True. Only by breaking a bond can the configuration be changed.

(C) True. Unlike a racemate, *meso* and achiral compounds cannot be resolved because they do not consist of enantiomers.

(D) True. Changing the configuration at one of the chiral Cs converts one diastereomer to the other.

(E) False. The terms D and L do not refer to the sign of rotation. They refer to the configuration of a stereoisomer relative to that of D-glyceraldehyde.

Chapter 7: Alkenes

133. (A) The number of pairs of Hs that a molecular formula lacks to be an alkane (C_nH_{2n+2}) is called the *degree* (or element) *of unsaturation*, or sometimes the *index of hydrogen deficiency*.

(B) (I) Zero. This molecular formula fits the alkane series. (II) A molecule with four Cs needs 10 Hs to be an alkane. The formula with six Hs lacks four Hs or two pairs of Hs, and so it has 2° of unsaturation. (III) A formula with six Cs and only six Hs lacks eight Hs or four pairs of Hs; it has 4° of unsaturation.

(C) Rings and multiple bonds.

134. Select the longest carbon chain or ring containing the largest number of double bonds, and change the suffix of the parent alkane from *-ane* to *-ene*. The alkenes use the same prefixes as the alkanes. The chain is numbered from the end closer to the C=C, whose position is indicated by assigning the lower possible number to the first doubly bonded C. Substituents are designated as for alkanes.

(A) 2-Pentene;

(B) 4-methyl-2-pentene;

(C) named as a hexene, the longest chain with C=C, not as a heptane which is the longest C chain but does not include the C=C; thus 3-*n*-propyl-1-hexene.

135. (A) 3-Nitro-2-pentene

(B) 2,3,4-trimethyl-2-pentene

(C) 3,6-dimethyl-1,4-heptadiene (note the use of *di* to indicate two C=Cs)

(D) 4-chloro-3-(1-methylpropyl or *s*-butyl)-7-methyl-1,5-octadiene

(E) 1-methyl-5-ethyl-1,3-cyclohexadiene

(F) the three C=Cs cannot be incorporated into a single chain; pick the longest chain with two C=Cs; 3-ethenyl-1,5-heptadiene

136. (A) *Z*, **(B)** *E*, **(C)** *Z*, **(D)** *E*.

137. (A)

(B) $CH_3 - \overset{\overset{\displaystyle Cl}{|}}{\underset{\underset{\displaystyle H}{|}}{C}}* - CH = CH_2$

(C) $\overset{\displaystyle CH_3CH_2}{\diagdown}\underset{\displaystyle CH_3 \diagup}{C} = \overset{\displaystyle \diagup H}{\underset{\displaystyle \diagdown CH_2 - \overset{\overset{\displaystyle H}{|}}{\underset{\underset{\displaystyle F}{|}}{C}}* - CH(CH_3)_2}{C}}$

138. In *elimination* reactions an atom or group is removed, with a net loss of 2 e⁻s, from each of two vicinal sp^3 Cs so that a C—C becomes a C=C:

$$-\overset{\overset{\displaystyle A}{|}}{\underset{|}{C}} - \overset{\overset{\displaystyle A}{|}}{\underset{|}{C}} - \xrightarrow{\text{reagent}} \overset{\diagdown}{\underset{\diagup}{C}} = \overset{\diagup}{\underset{\diagdown}{C}} + A{:}B$$

Since the groups are eliminated from adjacent Cs, these are called β- or 1, 2-eliminations.

139. Use Gibb's equation, $\Delta G = \Delta H - T\Delta S$. The best T has the most negative ΔG, as in **(III)**.

    (A) (I) At 25°C, $\Delta G = +27.6$ kcal/mol $- (298$ K$)(2.8 \times 10^{-2}$ kcal/mol · K$)$

$$= +19.3 \text{ kcal/mol.}$$

    (II) At 500°C, $\Delta G = +27.6$ kcal/mol $- (773$ K$)(2.8 \times 10^{-2}$ kcal/mol · K$)$

$$= +6.0 \text{ kcal/mol.}$$

    (III) At 1000°C, $\Delta G = +27.6$ kcal/mol $- (1273$ K$)(2.8 \times 10^{-2}$ kcal/mol · K$)$

$$= -8.0 \text{ kcal/mol.}$$

    (B) The $+\Delta H$ overwhelms the $+T\Delta S$ term at 25°C, giving $\Delta G = +19.3$. As the temperature rises, the positive $T\Delta S$ term becomes larger and ΔG becomes less positive. At 1000°C it predominates over the $+\Delta H$, ΔG becomes negative, and the reaction can occur.

    (C) When $\Delta G = 0$, $\Delta H = T\Delta S$, and

$$T = \frac{\Delta H}{\Delta S} = \frac{27.6 \text{ kcal/mol}}{2.8 \times 10^{-2} \text{ kcal/mol} \cdot \text{K}} = 986 \text{ K} = 713°C$$

Below this *crossover* temperature, ΔH dominates, ΔG is positive and there is no reaction. Above this temperature, $T\Delta S$ dominates, ΔG is negative, and the reaction occurs.

140. (A) $H-\overset{\displaystyle |}{\underset{\displaystyle |}{C}}-\overset{\displaystyle |}{\underset{\displaystyle |}{C}}-X + :B^- \rightarrow \overset{\displaystyle \diagdown}{\diagup}C=C\overset{\displaystyle \diagup}{\diagdown} + B:H + :\overset{\displaystyle ..}{\underset{\displaystyle ..}{X}}:^-$

(B) An H^+ and an anion, X^-, are lost from adjacent Cs; it is a β-elimination.

(C) KOH in ethanol (abbreviated as alc. KOH), where ethoxide ion, EtO⁻ may be the active base.

141. $(CH_3)_2 C=C(CH_3)CH_2CH_3 > CH_3CH=C(CH_3)CH(CH_3)_2$

Tetrasubstituted, $RC_2=CR_2$ Trisubstituted, $RHC=CR_2$

$> H_2C=C(CH_2CH_3)CH(CH_3)_2$

Disubstituted, $H_2C=CR_2$

142. (A) Cyclohexane $\xrightarrow[hv]{Cl_2}$ chlorocyclohexane $\xrightarrow{alc.\ KOH}$ cyclohexene

(B) $CH_3CH_2CH_3 \xrightarrow[hv]{Cl_2}$ mixture of $[CH_3CH_2CH_2Cl + CH_3CHClCH_3]$ $\xrightarrow{alc.\ KOH}$ propene

The mixture of chloropropanes need not be separated because they both give propene.

143. (A) Step 1.

$$CH_3\overset{\displaystyle \overset{H}{|}}{C}HCH_2 + H_2SO_4 \rightleftharpoons CH_3\overset{\displaystyle \overset{H}{|}}{C}HCH_2 + HSO_4^-$$

$$\underset{:\overset{..}{O}H}{} \qquad\qquad \underset{H:\overset{..}{O}H}{}$$

Base₁   Acid₂   Acid₁   Base₂
an onium ion

Step 2.

$$CH_3\overset{\displaystyle |}{C}-\overset{\displaystyle |}{C}H_2 \longrightarrow CH_3\overset{+}{C}HCH_2 + H_2O$$

$$\underset{H_2O^+}{} \quad \underset{H}{} \qquad\qquad \underset{H}{}$$

Isopropyl cation

Step 3.

$$CH_3\overset{+}{C}H-CH_2 + HSO_4^- \longrightarrow CH_3CH=CH_2 + H_2SO_4$$

$$\underset{H}{}$$

very strong
Acid₁   Base₂   Base₁   Acid₂

Instead of HSO_4^-, a molecule of alcohol could act as the base in Step 3 to give ROH_2^+.

(B) Step 2 is rate determining and is the slow step. Bond-breaking requires energy because it leads to a high-energy intermediate possessing a C with only six e⁻s and a + charge.

(C) Since an intermediate cannot appear in a rate expression, ROH_2^+ is replaced by starting materials. Brönsted acid-base reactions are among the fastest known, so the first step leading to formation of ROH_2^+ is fast and reversible. Hence,

$$K_e = [ROH_2^+]/[ROH][H^+] \quad \text{and} \quad [ROH_2^+] = K_e[ROH][H^+]$$

Substituting for $[ROH_2^+]$ in the rate expression for the slow second step,

$$\text{rate}_2 = k\,[ROH_2^+], \text{ gives}$$

$$\text{Rate} = kK_e[ROH][H^+]$$

$K_e k$ is a constant and the rewritten rate expression is as experimentally determined.

    (D) E1. Again E stands for elimination and 1 for unimolecular since the slow step has only one species.

144. (A) *trans*-(Major) and *cis*-(minor) 2-pentene.
    (B) 1-Methylcyclopentene.
    (C) $(CH_3)_2C{=}CHCH_3$ (major) + $CH_2{=}C(CH_3)CH_2CH_3$ (minor). Neopentyl alcohol has no β-Hs, and it cannot be dehydrated without rearrangement. The incipient 1° neopentyl cation rearranges to the more stable 3° R_3C^+ by a :Me shift from the 4° β-C^2 to the 1° $RC^1\,H_2^+$. The H^+ loss gives the product.

145. Cl is more electronegative than I, making I the E^+ that, according to the Markovnikov rule, adds to the C with the greater number of Hs. The product is 2-chloro-1-iodo-2-methylpropane, Me_2CClCH_2I.

146.

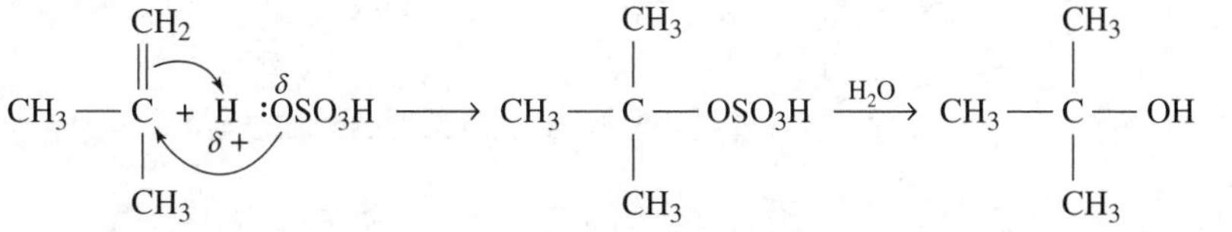

Isobutylene   *t*-Butyl hydrogen sulfate   *t*-Butyl alcohol, bp 83°C
                               A   **B**

147.

	(A)	(B)	(C)
(I)	Markovnikov	Anti-Markovnikov	Markovnikov
(II)	No clear stereospecificity	*Syn*	No clear stereospecificity
(III)	Yes	No	No

148. (A)   I.

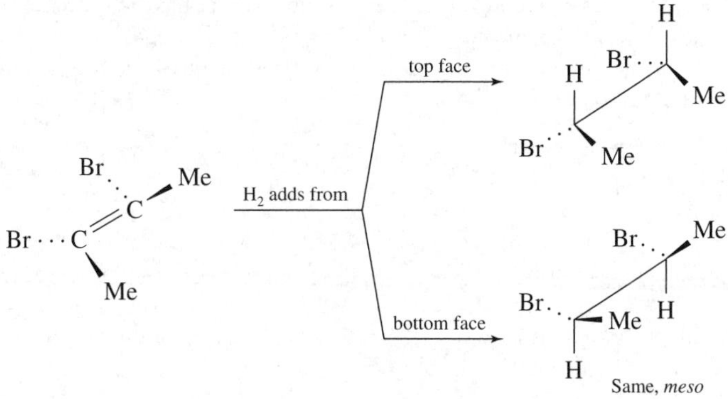

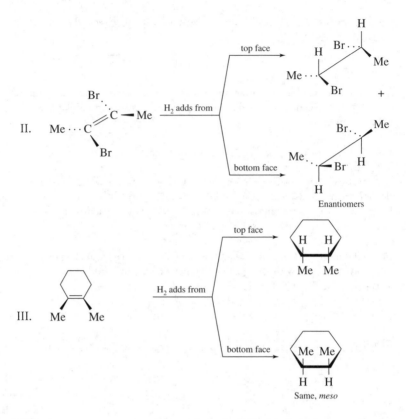

In **(I)** and **(III)**, the same *meso* product is formed whether H₂ adds from the top or bottom face of the π bond.

   (B) *Syn (cis)*.

149. A is $(CH_3CH_2CH_2)_3B$; B is $CH_3CH_2CH_3$.

150. (A) The product is a three-member ring either called an *epoxide* or *oxirane*. The epoxide has the same geometry as the alkene reactant. The epoxide can be considered as the oxygen analog of a bromonium ion without a + charge. However, it is isolable unlike the bromonium ion.

III.

$$\overset{H}{\underset{Me}{\overset{\cdots}{O}}}\overset{\cdot\cdot}{\underset{H}{\diagup}}Me$$

(B) The HO of the peroxyacid can be considered as an E^+. However, the $:Nu^-$ portion, $RCOO^-$, removes the H from OH as the O bonds to the $C=C$, giving the epoxide directly.

151. (A) The formation of a single carbonyl compound signals a symmetrical alkene. Write twice the structural formula of the ketone with the $C=O$ groups facing each other. Omit the Os and join the Cs with a double bond.

$$\underset{CH_3CH_2C=O}{\overset{CH_3}{|}} \quad \underset{O=CCH_2CH_3}{\overset{CH_3}{|}} \longleftarrow \underset{CH_3CH_2C=CCH_2CH_3}{\overset{H_3C\quad CH_3}{|\quad\;\;|}} \;(cis \text{ or } trans)$$

(B) Two different carbonyl compounds means the alkene is unsymmetrical.

$$H_2C=O \quad O=CHCH(CH_3)CH(CH_3)_2 \longleftarrow H_2C=CHCH(CH_3)CH(CH_3)_2$$

(C) The presence of two $C = Os$ in the same product indicates a cycloalkene, in this case cyclopentene.

$$\underset{H_2C}{\overset{HC=O}{|}}\qquad \underset{CH_2}{\overset{O=CH}{|}} \longleftarrow \bigcirc$$
$$\underset{CH_2}{}$$

(D) A total of four $C=Os$ in the products indicates a diene, a compound with two $C=Cs$.

$$(C_2H_5)_2C=O + O=CHCH=O + O=CHCH_2CH_3 \longleftarrow (C_2H_5)_2C=CHCH=CHCH_2CH_3$$
$$(cis \text{ or } trans)$$

(E) Two moles of a dicarbonyl compound signal a symmetrical cycloalkadiene

$$\underset{HC=O}{\overset{HC=O}{}}\quad \underset{O=CH}{\overset{O=CH}{}} \longleftarrow \bigcirc$$

152. Just as an electrophile adds to $C=C$ to give the more stable R^+, a radical adds to give the more stable $\cdot R$. Since the order of stability of radicals is $3° > 2° > 1° > CH_3$, Br· adds to the less substituted C to give the radical intermediate with the more substituted C.

153. (A) $Me_3C-CH=CMe_2$ (minor) (**A**); $Mc_3C-CH_2C(Me)=CH_2$ (major) (**B**)

(B) The reaction is called dimerization.

(C) The expected Saytzeff product **A** is sterically hindered because the bulky *t*-butyl group is *cis* to a Me.

(D)

Step 1.　　$Me_2C=CH_2 + H^+ \longrightarrow Me_3C^+$

Step 2.　　$Me_2C^+ + \quad H_2C=CMe_2 \quad \longrightarrow Me_3C-CH-\overset{+}{C}-CH_2$

"Tail"　　　"Head"

Electrophile　Nucleophile

below the product:

H	Me	H

$3°$ Dimeric R^+

Step 3.　　$R^+ \xrightarrow{\ -H^+\ } A$ and $R^+ \xrightarrow{\ -H^+\ } B$

Step 2 is a Markovnikov addition of an electrophile. Attack at the tail gives the $3°$ R^+; attack at the head would give the much less stable $1°$ carbocation $Me_3C-CMe_2CH_2^+$.

(E) The acid catalyst must have a weakly nucleophilic conjugate base to avoid addition of HX to C=C. Cl^-, Br^-, and I^-, the conjugate bases of HCl, HBr, and HI, respectively, are good nucleophiles that bind to R^+.

154. (A) A radical initiator, RO· from decomposition of ROOR, adds according to Markovnikov's rule as shown with $MeCH=CH_2$.

$RO· + H_2C=CHMe \longrightarrow H_2C-\overset{·}{C}H \xrightarrow{H_2C=CHMe} H_2C-CH-CH_2\overset{·}{C}H$

with substituents RO, Me below first; RO, Me, Me below second.

This process continues with thousands of monomeric molecules The polymerization chain terminates when two long-chain intermediate radicals either combine, $R·+R· \rightarrow R-R$, or disproportionate.

(B) Anions such as $R:^-$, generated from organometallics or $:NH_2^-$ (from $LiNH_2$), initiate the polymerization by adding to one end of the monomer.

$R:^- + H_2C=CHX \longrightarrow \left[RCH_2\overset{··}{C}H \atop X \right]^- \xrightarrow{H_2C=CHX} \left[RCH_2CH-CH_2\overset{··}{C}H \atop \quad X \qquad\quad X \right]^-$

(C) Since ordinary alkenes do not undergo nucleophilic addition, the alkene must have a functional group, such as $-C\equiv N$ or $O\equiv COR$, on C=C that can stabilize the

negative charge by delocalization. These polymers show the controllable stereochemistry.

155. All three reactions are allylic substitutions.

(A) and **(B)** 3-Chlorocyclohexene. **(C)** 3-Bromocyclohexcne.

156. For each synthesis dehydrate PrOH with conc. H_2SO_4 to $CH_3CH=CH_2$ (**B**).

(**A**) $B \xrightarrow{Me_3COCl/peroxide} ClCH_2CH=CH_2 \xrightarrow{Cl_2} ClCH_2CHClCH_2Cl$

(**B**) $B \xrightarrow{NBS} BrCH_2CH=CH_2 \xrightarrow{BrCl} BrCH_2CHClCH_2Br$

(**C**) $BrCH_2CH=CH_2 \xrightarrow{ICl} BrCH_2CHClCH_2I$

(**D**) $B \xrightarrow{Br_2} BrCH_2CHBrCH_3 \xrightarrow{alc.\ KOH} BrCH=CHCH_3 \xrightarrow{Br_2}$
$Br_2CHCHBrCH_3$

Little $H_2C=CBrCH_3$ is formed because (1) the 1° H of $-CH_2Br$ is more acidic and more easily removed by OH^- than the 2° H of $-CHBr$, (2) the 1° H is less sterically hindered, and (3) there is twice as much of a chance to remove a 1° H, since there are twice as many of them. Little allyl bromide is formed because (1) the 1° H of CH_3 is less acidic than $\underline{H}-C-Br$ and (2) the vinyl bromide is more stable by virtue of delocalization of e^-s from Br to C=C.

(**E**) $BrCH_2CH=CH_2 + Cl_2/H_2O \longrightarrow BrCH_2CHOHCH_2Cl$

157. The unknown compound has 4° of unsaturation coming from three C=Cs and one cyclohexane ring. A comes from a terminal $=CH_2$ group that must be outside of the ring. The Mes must also be outside the ring; one is attached to C^4, the other is part of the i-Pr group on C^1. The terminal $=CH_2$ cannot be the precursor of Me in the reduced product and must also be part of the i-Pr skeleton. This is shown by merging **A** to **B** and pointing the remaining C=Os toward those of **C**:

Merging **A**, **B**, and **C**

tells us the unknown is

Chapter 8: Alkyl Halides

158. (**A**) They are classified by the type of C to which X is bonded: *primary* (1°), *secondary* (2°), or *tertiary* (3°). Their definitions and corresponding general formulas are as follows:

    I. Primary: C is bonded to only one C; RCH_2X.

    II. Secondary: C is bonded to two Cs; R_2CHX.

    III. Tertiary: C is bonded to three Cs; R_3CX.

CH_3X is unique because the C is bonded only to Hs. It is simply called a *methyl halide*.

(B) The prefix *gem* (geminal) is used for two Xs on the same C and *vic* (vicinal) for two Xs on adjacent Cs; CH_3CHBr_2 is a *gem*-dibromide, and $BrCH_2CH_2Br$ is a *vic*-dibromide.

159. First write the isomeric parent hydrocarbons, and then replace one of each type of equivalent H by X. Duplication of isomers is avoided by assigning IUPAC names.

    (A) The three isomeric pentanes showing their numbers of different kinds of equivalent Hs are

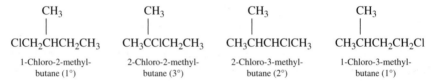

        Pentane (3)   Isopentane (4)   Neopentane (1)

Three isomers have the pentane skeleton:

$ClCH_2CH_2CH_2CH_2CH_3$ $CH_3CHClCH_2CH_2CH_3$ $CH_3CH_2CHClCH_2CH_3$

  1-Chloropentane (1°)   2-Chloropentane (2°)   3-Chloropentane (2°)

Four isomers have the isopentane skeleton:

CH_3	CH_3	CH_3	CH_3
|	|	|	|
$ClCH_2CHCH_2CH_3$	$CH_3CClCH_2CH_3$	$CH_3CHCHClCH_3$	$CH_3CHCH_2CH_2Cl$
1-Chloro-2-methyl-butane (1°)	2-Chloro-2-methyl-butane (3°)	2-Chloro-3-methyl-butane (2°)	1-Chloro-3-methyl-butane (1°)

One isomer has the neopentane skeleton: $(CH_3)_3CCH_2Cl$, 1-chloro-2,2-dimeihylpropane (1°).

    (B) Dihalogenated *n*-butanes and isobutanes are derived by systematically first placing the two Fs on the same C and then on different Cs. *n*-Butane affords two *gem*-difluoro isomers:

           $F_2CHCH_2CH_2CH_3$ $CH_3CF_2CH_2CH_3$,

            1,1-Difluorobutane   2,2-Difluorobutane

There are four isomers with two Fs on different Cs:

           $FCH_2CHFCH_2CH_3$ $FCH_2CH_2CHFCH_3$

      1,2-Difluorobutane (*vic*)   1,3-Difluorobutane

           $FCH_2CH_2CH_2CH_2F$ $CH_3CHFCHFCH_3$

        1,4-Difluorobutane   2,3-Difluorobutane (*vic*)

The isobutane skeleton affords three difluoro isomers:

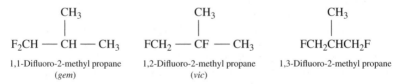

  1,1-Difluoro-2-methyl propane   1,2-Difluoro-2-methyl propane   1,3-Difluoro-2-methyl propane
        (*gem*)   (*vic*)

160. **(A)** (I) CH_2Br_2, dibromomethane; (II) $CHCl_3$, trichloromethane; (III) H_2C=CH—CH_2Br, 3-bromo-1-propene; (IV) $(CH_3)_2CClCH_2CH_3$, 2-chloro-2-methylbutane; and (V) $(CH_3)_3CCH_2Br$, 1-bromo-2,2-dimethyl-propane.

    (B) The "form" method is used for the HCX_3 type of compounds: HCF_3, fluoroform; $HCCl_3$, chloroform; $HCBr_3$, bromoform; HCl_3, iodoform; $HC(NO_2)_3$, nitroform.

161. **(A)**

$$CH_3\overset{\overset{\displaystyle C_2H_5}{\displaystyle |}}{C}HCCH_2CH_2CH_2CH_3$$
$$\underset{\text{Br Br}}{|\ |}$$

(B)

CH$_2$Cl

Br

(C)

I

Br

(D)

H

Cl

(E)

Cl
H
H
Cl

162. **(A)** (1) The van der Waals (London) forces of attraction depend on the overall shapes and sizes of molecules and on their molecular weights. Linear molecules have more surface contact and enhanced attraction than branched-chain molecules, while spherically shaped molecules have very slight tangential contacts. (2) Dipole-dipole attraction is a significant factor for RXs, but not at all for alkanes.

    (B) (I) All alkyl halides boil at a higher temperature than the parent alkane. In this sequence the increases in molecular weight and size lead to increasing bp's. At the same time, dipole-dipole attractions decrease, and this change should decrease the bp's. Clearly the effect of increasing van der Waals forces of attraction dwarfs the effect of decreasing dipole-dipole attraction. (II) As with alkanes (Problem 78), branched C chains are more spherical-like, and their smaller surface area results in lower boiling points. (III) Accumulation of Cls on CH_4 increases the molecular weight and size, causing the bp to increase. Notice that the Δbp gets smaller as more Cls are introduced, a fact that may be due to an increase in the spherical nature of the molecule. (IV) The perfluoroalkane, a fluorocarbon, is predicted to have the higher bp because it has the larger molecular weight. What is surprising is the small difference in bp, a result due to F being only slightly larger than H and having a low polarizability.

163. (A) $Me_2C{=}CMe_2 \xrightarrow{Br_2} Me_2CBr{-}CBrMe_2$

(B)

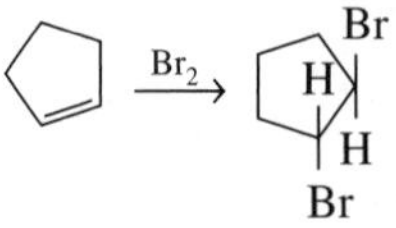

$$\text{(C)} \quad H_2C = \underset{\underset{Me}{|}}{C}CH_2CH_2CH_3 \xrightarrow{IBr} ICH_2CBrCH_2CH_2CH_3$$

(D) $H_2C{=}CBrCH_2CH_3 \xrightarrow{HBr} CH_3CBr_2CH_2CH_3$

(E) $cis\text{-}CH_3CH = CHCH_3 + CHCl_3 + (CH_3)_3CO^-K^+ \longrightarrow cis\text{-}CH_3CH \underset{\underset{CCl_2}{\diagup}}{\overset{\diagdown}{\quad}} CHCH_3$

(F) $H_2C{=}CHCH_2Br \xrightarrow[ROOR]{HBr} BrCH_2CH_2CH_2Br$

164. (A) $CH_3CH_2CH_2CH_2Br$
(B) $(CH_3)_3CCl$
(C) $CH_3CHBrCH_2CH_2CH_3$
(D) $CH_3CH_2CH_2I$
(E) Me_2CHCH_2Cl

165. (A) (I) $H_2C{=}CH_2$ (elimination of *vic* Xs), (II) cyclopropane (see Problem 107), (III) $BrMg(CH_2)_4MgBr$.
  (B) Unlike compound (II), compound (III) does not react intramolecularly because a four-member ring does not form as readily as does a three-member ring.
  (C) $CBr_4 + MeLi \xrightarrow[\text{exchange}]{\text{halogen-metal}} [Br_3CLi] + MeBr; \quad Br_3CLi \longrightarrow \underset{\text{Dibromocarbene}}{Br_2C:} + LiBr$

The carbene then adds to the alkene in the typical fashion, giving

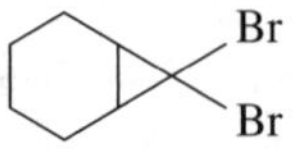

7,7-Dibromo[4.1.0]-bicycloheptane

166. (A) $CH_3C{\equiv}C{-}CH_2CH_2CH_3$
  (B) $(CH_3)_2CHO{-}CH_2CH_2CH_3$

(C) $CH_3CH(OH)CH_2CH_3$. Aqueous NaOH gives mainly displacement; alc. KOH gives mainly elimination.

(D) Iodocyclopentane

(E) Me_2CHSEt

(F) $EtMeNH_2^+I^-$

(G) $Et_2MeNH^+I^-$

(H) $[CH_3CH_2CH_2SMe_2]^+Br^-$

167. The nucleophiles in (A), (B), and (C) are ambident since they each have more than one reactive site. In each case, the more nuclcophilic atom reacts even though the other atom may bear a more negative charge.

(A) $n\text{-}PrNO_2$

(B) $i\text{-}PrSCN$

(C) $[EtSSO_3]^-$ (with its cation it is called a Bünte salt)

(D) $ClCH_2CH_2CH_2CN$. I^- is a better leaving group than Cl^-.

(E)  . When the nucleophilic and leaving groups are part of the same molecule, an intramolecular displacement occurs if a three-, a five-, or a six-member ring can form.

168. (A) Doubling the molar concentrations of either reactant doubles the rate. Doubling the concentration of both reactants quadruples the rate, which therefore is directly related to each reactant: rate $= k[RX][Nu\!:^-]$.

(B) It is a second-order reaction, first order in each reactant. Of the two possible pathways available for displacement on C, (3) is the only one that has both reactants in the rate-controlling step; hence it is a bimolecular reaction.

(C) Very small samples of the reaction mixture, kept at constant temperature, are removed periodically, quenched to stop the reaction, and quantitatively analyzed. The increasing concentration of Cl^- is determined by a standard method. In the other method, the decreasing concentration of OH^- is detected by standard acid-base titrations. The samples removed and analyzed are so very small that the only significant change in the concentrations of the reactants is due to the reaction itself.

169. These S_N2 reactions invert configuration.

(A) $(S)\text{-}CH_3CH(OMe)CH_2CH_3$

(B) $(R)\text{-}CH_3CH(OMe)CH_2CH_3$

(C) *rac*, trans-4-Ethylcyclohexanol

(D) (S)- EtOC $\overset{\displaystyle CH_3}{\underset{\displaystyle\underset{O}{\|}\ H}{\overset{\displaystyle |}{\underline{\qquad}}}}$ CN

Although inversion occurs, the priority order changes and the product is (S).

170. (A) The fugicity (leavability) of X; the more weakly basic is X^-, the more reactive is RX. Therefore, RI > RBr > RCl.

(B) The stability of the intermediate R^+; the more stable is R^+, the more reactive is RX. Therefore, the order of reactivity of RX is 3° > 2° > 1°. Note this order is the reverse of that in S_N2 reactions.

171. (A) S_N2 gives complete inversion of configuration of the attacked C. If a free R^+ were to form in the S_N1 reaction, it would be achiral because it would possess a plane of symmetry incorporating its three σ bonds. Its p AO could be attacked equally well at either of its faces, giving a completely racemic product.

(B) The actual mechanism does not involve a free R^+. It is believed that as X leaves and the bond angles open up from 109° to 120° there is room for a solvent molecule (HS) to approach from the rear. The anion is also solvated by H-bonding as it leaves R.

$$\text{HS:} ---\overset{\overset{\displaystyle |}{\delta+}}{C}---\overset{\delta-}{X}-\overset{\overset{\displaystyle \text{H-bond}}{\diagup}}{\vert}- \text{HS:}$$

Solvent-assisted S_N1 TS

This TS passes on to a di-solvated *intimate ion-pair* intermediate: $HS---R^+X^----HS$. If the solvation bond to C gets stronger and X^- leaves completely, an inverted product is obtained. In addition, some of these intermediate species can react with solvent to give a *solvent separated ion-pair*:

$$\underset{\text{Backside}}{HS} --- R^+ --- \underset{\text{Frontside}}{SH} --- X^- --- HS \quad \text{often simply written as} \quad R^+ \parallel X^-$$

(C) From this intermediate, bonding by the backside solvent molecule causes inversion, while bonding by the frontside solvent molecule causes retention. The stages of intermediates in the ionization and dissociation of 3° RX free of participating solvent molecules are

RX Substrate	$\underset{}{\overset{\text{ionization}}{\rightleftharpoons}}$	R^+X^- Intimate ion-pair	$\underset{\text{–HS}}{\overset{\text{HS}}{\rightleftharpoons}}$	$R^+\|X^-$ Solvent-separated ion-pair	$\overset{\text{dissociation}}{\rightleftharpoons}$	$R^+ + X^-$ Dissociated (free) ions

Note that each step is reversible. Each intermediate would have its own TS.

172. During an S_N1 solvolysis, ionization produces an intermediate 2° R^+ which rearranges, here by a hydride shift, to a more stable 3° R^+ that reacts with H_2O to form the 3° ROH.

$$CH_3-CH(Br)-C(CH_3)(H)-CH_3 \xrightarrow[\text{slow}]{-Br^-} CH_3-\overset{+}{CH}-C(CH_3)(\ddot{H})-CH_3 \xrightarrow{\sim :H}$$

2°

$$CH_3-CH(H)-\overset{+}{C}(CH_3)-CH_3 \xrightarrow[\text{fast}]{+H_2O \\ -H^+} CH_3-CH(H)-C(CH_3)(OH)-CH_3$$

3°

173. See Table 8-1.

Table 8-1

	S_N1	S_N2
Number of steps	Two*: (1) R:L $\xrightarrow{\text{slow}}$ R$^+$+:L$^-$ (2) R$^+$+ :NuH $\xrightarrow{\text{fast}}$ R:Nu + H$^+$	One: R : L + Nu$^-$ → R:Nu+:L$^-$ or R:L + NuH → R:NuH$^+$+:L$^-$
Reaction rate and order	Rate = k_1[RL]; first order	Rate = k_2[RL][:Nu$^-$]; second order
Molecularity	Unimolecular	Bimolecular
TS of slow step	HNu: $---$ C$^{\delta+}$ $---$ $^\delta{}^-$L$---$HNu:	δ^-Nu:$---$C$---$:L$^\delta$ (with :Nu$^-$) δ^+HNu:$---$C$---$:L$^\delta$ (with HNu:)
Stereo-chemistry	Inversion and retention	Inversion (backside attack)
Reacting nucleophile	Nucleophilic solvent; stable R$^+$may react with added nucleophile	Added nucleophile

*The simplified mechanism has two steps; the ion-pair concept has more steps.

174. (A) For any type of reaction, whenever the rate-determining TS involves breaking of the C—X bond (S_N2,E2), the rate is directly related to the leavability of X$^-$ which, in turn, is indirectly related to its basicity. The weakest base is the best leaving group: I$^-$ > Br$^-$ > Cl$^-$ > F$^-$. The order of reactivity is RI > RBr > RCl > RF.

(B) If E1$_{cb}$ prevails, expulsion of X$^-$ occurs in the fast second step, and the rate of the overall reaction is independent of the leavability of X—all RXs should then react at about the same rate. In E2, expulsion of X$^-$ occurs in the rate-determining step and the nature of X influences the rate.

175. See Table 8-2.

Table 8-2

	E1	E2
Steps	1. H—C—C—X ⟶ H—C—C⁺ + X⁻ 2. H—C—C⁺ $\xrightarrow{-H^+}$ C=C	1. B:⁻ + H—C—C—X ⟶ 2. B:H + C=C + :X⁻
Transition state	1. H—C—C$^{\delta+}$ --- X$^{\delta-}$ --- HS: 2. HS:$^{\delta+}$ --- H --- C $\,\cdots\,$ C$^{\delta+}$	B:$^{\delta-}$--- H --- C $\cdots$ C --- X$^{\delta-}$ --- HS:
Kinetics	First-order, unimolecular Rate = k_1 [RX]; rate of ionization	Second-order, bimolecular Rate = k_2 [RX][:B⁻]
Driving force	Ionization of R—X	Attack by B:⁻ on H
Stereo-specificity	Nonstereospecific	*anti* Elimination but *syn* if *anti* not possible (both coplanar)
Effect of R	Stability of R⁺; 3°>2°>1° 3°>2°>1° RX	Alkene stability (Saytzeff rule)
Rearrangement	Common	None, except for allylic (S_N2')
H/D isotope effect	None	Observed
Competing reaction	S_N1, S_N2	S_N2
Regio-selectivity	Saytzeff	Usually Saytzeff, but Hofmann with bulky bases <Me3CO⁻)

176. (A) $CH_3CHOHCH_2CH_3 \xrightarrow{H_2SO_4} CH_3CH{=}CHCH_3$

(D) $\xrightarrow{2NBS} BrCH_2CH{=}CHCH_2Br^* \xrightarrow{2I^-}$

$ICH_2CH{=}CHCH_2I \xrightarrow{H_2NNH_2/O_2} ICH_2CH_2CH_2CH_2I^{**}$

*Little or no *gem*-dibromide is formed because Br deactivates —CHBr.
**Allylic halides undergo hydrogenolysis (C—X → C—H) with H_2/Pd.

(B) (D) $\xrightarrow{NBS} BrCH_2CH{=}CHCH_3 \xrightarrow[-HBr]{MeSH}$

$CH_3CH{=}CHCH_2SMe \xrightarrow{H_2NNH_2/O_2} CH_3CH_2CH_2CH_2SMe^{***}$

***C—S bonds undergo catalytic hydrogenolysis.

(C) $CH_3CHOHCH_2CH_3 \xrightarrow{HBr} CH_3CHBrCH_2CH_3 \xrightarrow{Me_3CO^-K^+}$

$H_2C{=}CHCH_2CH_3 \xrightarrow{NBS}$

$H_2C{=}CHCHBrCH_3 \xrightarrow{Br_2} H_2CBrCHBrCHBrCH_3 \textbf{(E)}$

E has two different stereocenters and exists as two racemates.

177. (A) E1, E2, S_N1; **(B)** S_N2; **(C)** S_N1; **(D)** E2, S_N2; **(E)** S_N1, very little E1; **(F)** E2; **(G)** S_N1, E1; **(H)** mainly S_N2, little E2; **(I)** S_N2, E2; **(J)** S_N2, E2; **(K)** E1 (E2 does with small base but not with bulky base); **(L)** E1, S_N1; **(M)** all; **(N)** S_N1, E1; **(O)** S_N2 and E2, S_N2 and E1; **(P)** E1, S_N1; **(Q)** E1, S_N1.

178. (A)

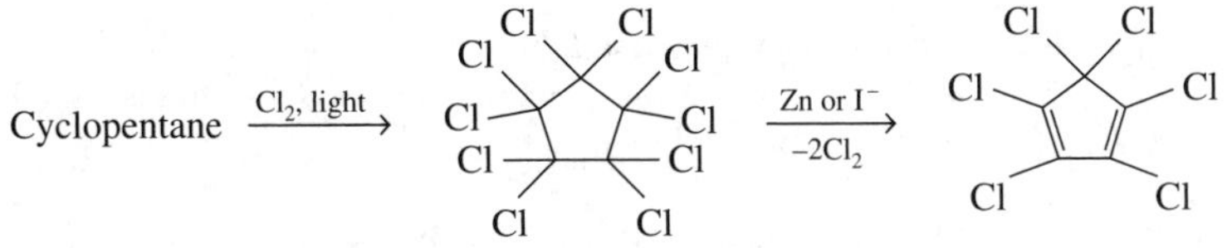

A

(B) **B** and **C** are prepared using Diels–Alder reactions.

I.

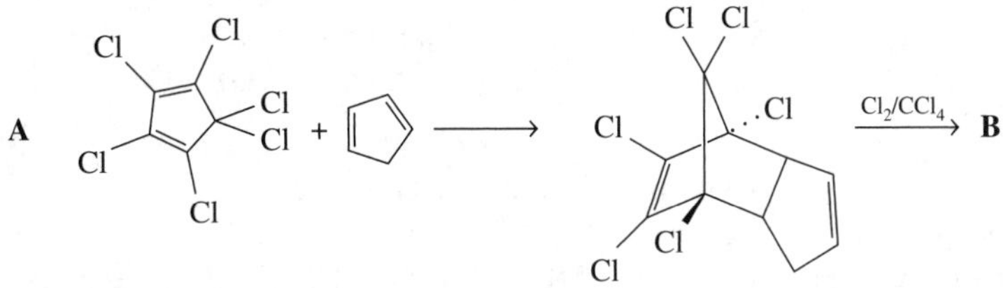

II.

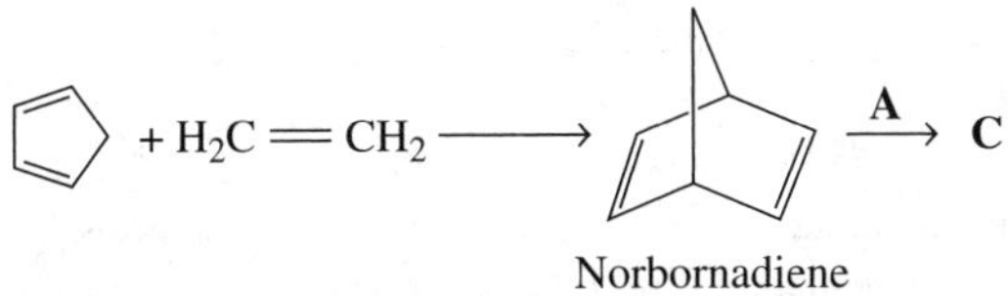

Norbornadiene

Chapter 9: Alkynes, Dienes, and Orbital Symmetry

179. The triple bond is shorter and stronger than the double bond. The C atoms of $C{\equiv}C$ are shielded by six e^-s (from three bonds), whereas the Cs of $C{=}C$ are shielded by four e^-s (from two bonds). With more shielding e^-s present, the triply bonded Cs can get closer to each other (shorter bond length) to give greater orbital overlap (stronger bond).

180. (A) 2-Butyne
(B) 2-Pentyne $C{=}C$ has priority over $C{\equiv}C$ and gets the smaller number.
(C) 2,2,5-Trimethyl-3-hexyne
(D) 1-Penten-4-yne
(E) 4-Chloro-1-butyne

181. **(A)** $HC\equiv C-C\equiv CH$

(B) $(NO_2)CH_2C\equiv CCH(CH_3)_2$

(C)
$$\begin{array}{c}CH_3\\ \diagdown\\ C=C\\ H\diagup\diagdown\\ C\equiv CH\end{array}$$

with H on upper right of the $C=C$

(D)
$$\begin{array}{c}CH_3\\ \diagdown\\ C=C\\ H\diagup\diagdown\\ H\end{array}$$

with $C\equiv C-C\equiv CH$

182. **(A)** Cyclopentylethyne

(B) *cis*-1-Methyl-2-(1-propynyl)cyclohexane

(C) Cyclobutylcyclopropylethyne (note that numbers are not necessary)

(D) 5-(2-Propynyl)-1,3-cyclohexediene

183. The order of decreasing acidities is: alkyne > alkene > alkane.

184. **(A)** $HC\equiv CH \xrightarrow{\text{NaNH}_2} HC\equiv C^- \xrightarrow{\text{D}_2\text{O}} HC\equiv CD$

(B) $HC\equiv CH + 2Na \rightarrow \ ^-:C\equiv C:^- \xrightarrow{\text{D}_2\text{O}} DC\equiv CD$

185. **(A)** $CaO + 3C \longrightarrow CaC_2 + CO; \ CaC_2 + 2H_2O \longrightarrow HC\equiv CH + Ca(OH)_2$

(B) $(:C\equiv C:)^{2-} + 2H_2O \longrightarrow HC\equiv CH + 2OH^-$

$\qquad\qquad$ Base$_1$ $\quad$ Acid$_1$ $\qquad\qquad$ Acid$_1$ $\quad$ Base$_2$

$\qquad$ (Ca^{2+} is the spectator ion and is omitted.)

186. **(A)** $CH_3CH_2CH_2CH_2CHBr_2 \xrightarrow[200°C]{\text{KOH(s)}} CH_3CH_2C\equiv CCH_3$

(B) $CH_3CH_2CH_2CH_2CHBr_2 \xrightarrow{\text{NaNH}_2} CH_3CH_2CH_2C\equiv C^- \xrightarrow{\text{H}_3\text{O}^+}$
$CH_3CH_2CH_2C\equiv CH$

187. The derived acetylene name tells you which R groups, originating from RXs, are on the $C\equiv C$. In this case they are ethyl (1°) and cyclohexyl (2°). Since the alkylating RX must be an unbranched 1° halide, CH_3CH_2Br is the choice rather than cyclohexylbromide.

$$\text{cyclohexyl}-C\equiv CH \xrightarrow[\text{2. CH}_3\text{CH}_2\text{Br}]{\text{1. NaNH}_2} \text{cyclohexyl}-C\equiv CCH_2CH_3$$

188. $CH_3C\equiv CCH_3 \xrightarrow{\text{H}_2/\text{Pt}} CH_3C=CCH_3 \xrightarrow{\text{H}_2/\text{Pt}} CH_3CH_2CH_2CH_3$

with H, H below the double bond

(Z)-2-Butene

189. **(A)** $CH_3CH_2CBr=CH_2$ $\qquad$ a Markovnikov electrophilic addition

(B) $CH_3CH_2CH=CHBr$ $\qquad$ an anti-Markovnikov radical addition

(C) $CH_3CH_2CBr=CHBr$ $\qquad$ an electrophilic addition

190. $CH_3C \equiv CH + H_2O \xrightarrow{HgSO_4,\ H_2SO_4} [CH_3C = CH_2] \longrightarrow CH_3CCH_3$

$$\underset{\substack{\text{A vinyl alcohol (enol)} \\ \text{unstable}}}{\overset{\displaystyle |}{\underset{\displaystyle OH}{}}} \qquad \underset{\substack{\text{Acetone (a ketone)} \\ \text{stable}}}{\overset{\displaystyle \|}{\underset{\displaystyle O}{}}}$$

The Markovnikov addition of H_2O gives an unstable vinyl alcohol that rearranges, as shown, to the more stable ketone.

191. (A) Methyl ketones, $CH_3C = O$, are best made from terminal alkynes; use $(CH_3)_2CHC \equiv CH$.
$$\overset{\displaystyle |}{\underset{\displaystyle R}{}}$$

(B) Use the symmetrical internal alkyne $CH_3CH_2C \equiv CCH_2CH_3$ rather than the unsymmetrical $CH_3C \equiv CCH_2CH_2CH_3$, which also gives $CH_3\underset{\displaystyle \underset{O}{\|}}{C}CH_2CH_2CH_2CH_3$.

(C) — C ≡ C —

192. (A) With CuCl under mildly acid conditions (NH_4^+), acetylene adds to itself (couples) to form the dimer, $H_2C=CHC \equiv CH$, butenyne (or vinylacetylene) (note that numbers are superfluous). Note that under basic conditions (NH_3) the copper acetylide is formed.

(B) Under oxidative conditions, the dimer formed is $HC \equiv C - C \equiv CH$, butadiyne.

193. By retrosynthetic analysis the target compounds are each prepared from the alkyne which in turn is made from the corresponding alkene.

(A)

$CH_3CH_2CHBrCH_3 \xrightarrow{\text{alc. KOH}} CH_3CH = CHCH_3 \xrightarrow{Br_2}$

$CH_3CHBrCHBrCH_3 \xrightarrow[\text{heat}]{\text{KOH(s)}} CH_3C \equiv CCH_3 \xrightarrow{\text{Na, EtOH}}$

(E)-2-Butene

The double dehydrogenation is effected with hot solid KOH, rather than $NaNH_2$, to prevent isomerization to 1-butyne.

(B) $CH_3C \equiv CCH_3$ or

H$_2$, Lindlar's catalyst

BH_3, then CH_3COOH

(Z)-2-Butene

194. The precursor of this stereospecific alkene is the corresponding alkyne made by alkylating 1-propyne with 1-bromo-1-deuteropropane. Since this S_N2 alkylation goes with inversion but without change in priorities at the stereocenter, the R enantiomer of the halide must be used. The alkyne is reduced with Na/EtOH.

$$*CH_3C\equiv C^- + (R)\text{-}Br \overset{H}{\underset{D}{\mid}}Et \xrightarrow{-Br^-} (S)\text{-}Et \overset{H}{\underset{D}{\mid}}C\equiv CCH_3 \xrightarrow{Na/EtOH} (S)\text{-}(E)\text{-}Et \overset{H}{\underset{D}{\mid}}C=C\overset{H}{\underset{H}{\mid}}CH_3$$

*From $CH_3C\equiv CH + NaNH_2$.

195. (A) $H_2C=C=CHCH_2CH_3$, 1,2-pentadiene
(B) $H_2C=CH-CH=CHCH_3$, 1,3-pentadiene, Z and E
(C) $H_2C=CHCH_2CH=CH_2$, 1,4-pentadiene
(D) $CH_3CH=C=CHCH_3$, 2,3-pentadiene

196. $2HC\equiv CH \xrightarrow[NH_4Cl]{CuCl} H_2C=CHC\equiv CH \xrightarrow[(BaSO_4)]{H_2/Pt} H_2C=CHCH=CH_2$

197.

3-Bromo-cyclohexene

198. D has 3° of unsaturation, one of which is a ring, because only 2 eq of H_2 is consumed ($C_7H_{10} + 2H_2 \rightarrow C_7H_{14}$). **D** is not an alkyne (no reaction with H_2, Ni/B) and must be a diene. Since the oxidation product has only six Cs, the seventh C was lost as CO_2, indicating the presence of a terminal $=CH_2$ group. The open-chain oxidation product **E** had to come from a cycloalkene. Had both $C=C$ groups in **D** been *exocyclic* (outside the ring), **E** would have been a cyclic compound. One of the three Cs in **E** with an oxygen-containing functional group has to be bonded to the exocyclic $=CH_2$; the other two come from cleavage of the *endocyclic* (internal) $C=C$. If C^1 and C^6 are the Cs of the endo $C=C$ and C^4 is part of the exo $C=C$, then **D** has the structure **D-1**. If C^1 and C^4 come from the endo bond and C^6 from the exo bond, the compound is **D-2**. The third possibility has C^4 and C^6 from the endo bond and C^1 from the exo bond with the structure **D-3**.

D-1   **D-2**   **D-3**

It is noteworthy that **D-3** has a high enthalpy because it has a very high ring strain.

199. (A) Cyclobutene.

(B) Electrocyclic; a single molecule undergoes ring closure or opening.

(C) One double bond is lost and a single bond is formed.

(D) In electrocyclic reactions only the HOMO is considered, and its terminal p AOs must rotate so that their lobes with like signs point toward each other.

      I. Thermally, the HOMO of butadiene is π_2 with $(+\ -)$ symmetry. The rotation of the terminal orbitals must be in the *same* direction (i.e, both counterclockwise or both clockwise), called *conrotatory*, so that a proper match is achieved as shown in Figure A9-1(A).

      II. Since UV light causes electron excitation, the HOMO is now π_3^*. Now the proper match is achieved when the terminal p's rotate in opposite directions (one clockwise and one counterclockwise), called *disrotatory*, as shown in Figure A9-1(B).

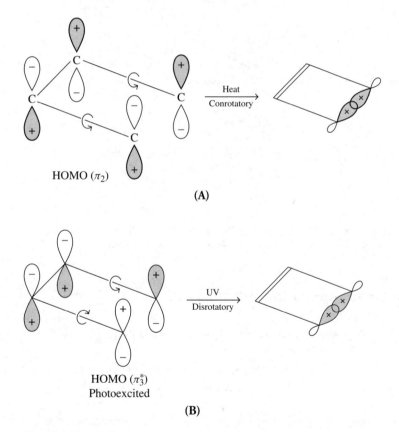

HOMO (π_2)

(A)

HOMO (π_3^*)
Photoexcited

(B)

Figure A9-1

200. **(A)** At 45°C, 1,4-addition is the dominant pathway, giving two possible products:

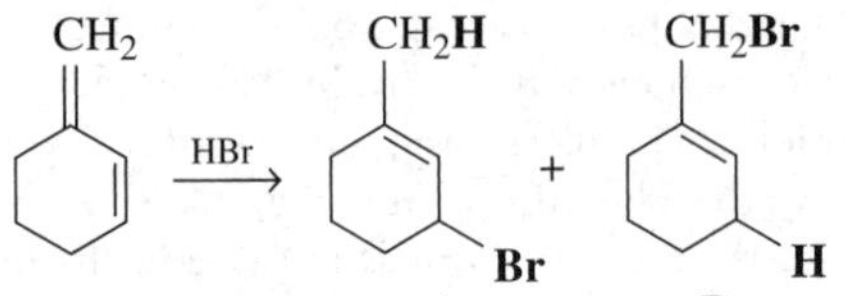

A B

(B) Addition of **H**$^+$ to the methylene group gives **C**.

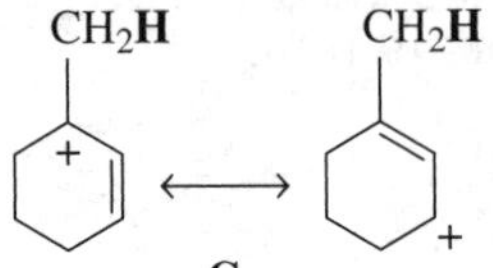

C

This allylic R$^+$ has a positive charge on a 3° and 2°C. Addition of H$^+$ to the ring C=C gives an allylic R$^+$ **(D)** having a positive charge on a 2° and 1°C:

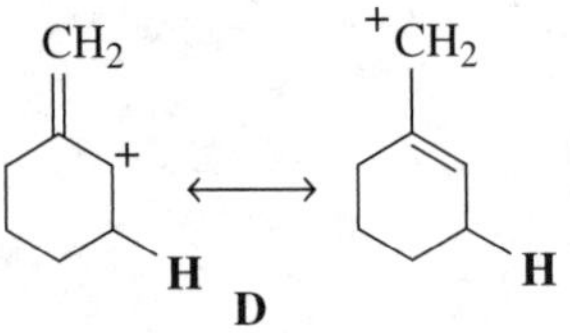

D

In **C** the positive charge is dispersed to more substituted Cs. Thus **C** is the more stable R$^+$.
(C) **Br**$^-$ adds to **C**, the dominant R$^+$, to give the 1,4-trisubstituted adduct **A**.

Chapter 10: Aromaticity and Benzene

201. **(A)** $C_6H_6 + \frac{15}{2}O_2 \rightarrow 6CO_2 + 3H_2O$
(B) The contribution is calculated for each bond and then totaled for the molecule.

$$\begin{aligned} \text{Six C—H bonds} &= 6(-54.0) = -324.0 \text{ kcal/mol} \\ \text{Three C—C bonds} &= 3(-49.3) = -147.9 \\ \text{Three C=C bonds} &= 3(-117.7) = \underline{-353.1} \\ \text{Calculated value} &= -825.0 \text{ kcal/mol} \end{aligned}$$

The difference [$-789.1 - (-825.0) = 35.9$ kcal/mol] is a measure of the resonance energy, the energy that benzene does *not* have.

202. The ring (skeleton) is comprised of six sp^2 hybridized Cs, each σ-bonded to two Cs and an H (Figure A10-1). Each C also has a p AO with one e⁻; the AOs project above and below the plane of the ring which is a nodal plane. Rather than form three localized alternating double bonds (cyclohexatriene), these p AOs overlap laterally to form an extended π system in which the e⁻s are symmetrically delocalized over all six Cs, making the Cs equivalent (Figure A10-2). Delocalization results in less electron repulsion, greater stabilization, and lower energy.

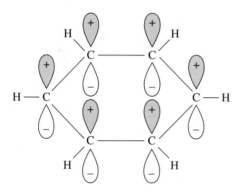

Figure A10-1

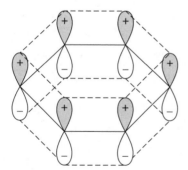

Figure A10-2

203. Six p AOs, one from each C, yield six π molecular orbitals—three bonding and three antibonding. Each p AO has an e⁻, and the six e⁻s completely fill the three bonding MOs with two e⁻s in each, accounting for the extraordinary stability of benzene. The π*'s are empty. Since benzene is cyclic, instead of nodal points there are nodal planes (shown as lines) that are perpendicular to the plane of the ring (Figure A10-3).

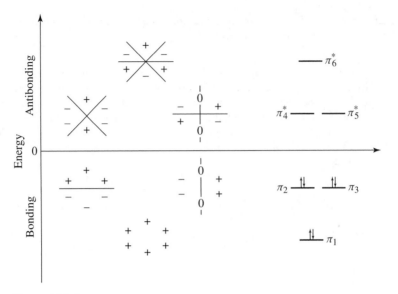

Figure A10-3

204. (A) There are three isomers:

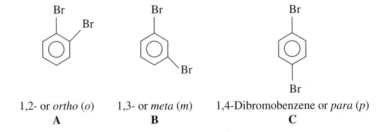

| 1,2- or *ortho* (*o*) | 1,3- or *meta* (*m*) | 1,4-Dibromobenzene or *para* (*p*) |
| A | B | C |

(B) There are three isomers:

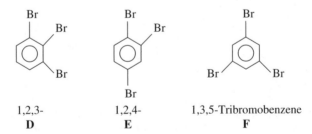

| 1,2,3- | 1,2,4- | 1,3,5-Tribromobenzene |
| D | E | F |

205. (A) $C_6H_5^+$ is a vinyl carbocation and is less stable than $C_6H_{11}^+$, a 2° carbocation.
(B) In $C_6H_5:^-$ the electron pair is an sp^2 HO. This carbanion has more *s* character and is more stable than $C_6H_{11}:^-$ whose unshared pair is in an sp^3 HO.

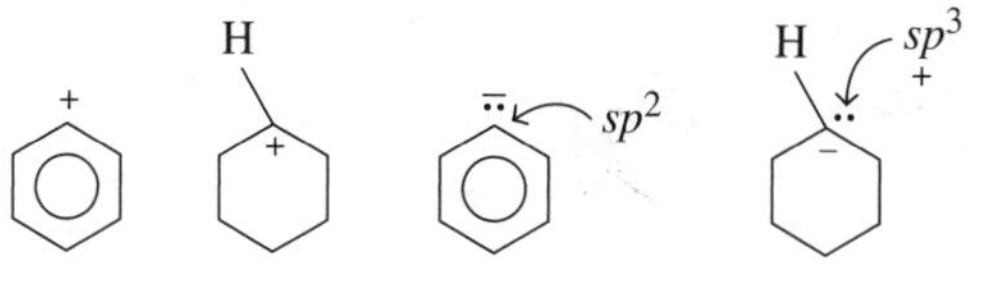

$$C_6H_5^+ \qquad C_6H_{11}^+ \qquad C_6H_5\!:^- \qquad C_6H_{11}\!:^-$$

206. (A) (I) A strongly electron-withdrawing substituent such as $-\overset{+}{N}=\overset{..}{\underset{..}{O}}:$ on the adjacent ring C. (The positive formal charge on N makes $-NO_2$ an even better electron-withdrawer than $-NO_2$.) (II) An electron-donating substituent such as methyl or any R group on the adjacent ring C.

(B)

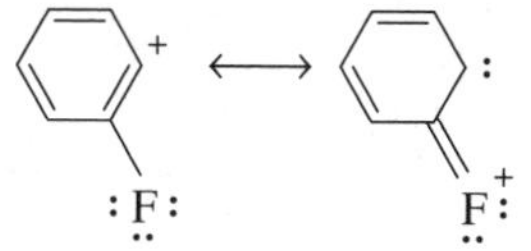

The contributing structure with the carbene makes a meager contribution because it no longer has the stable aromatic ring.

207. (A) I.

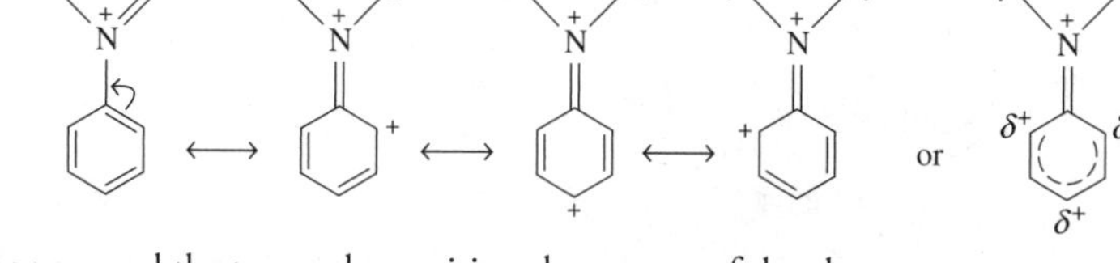

II.

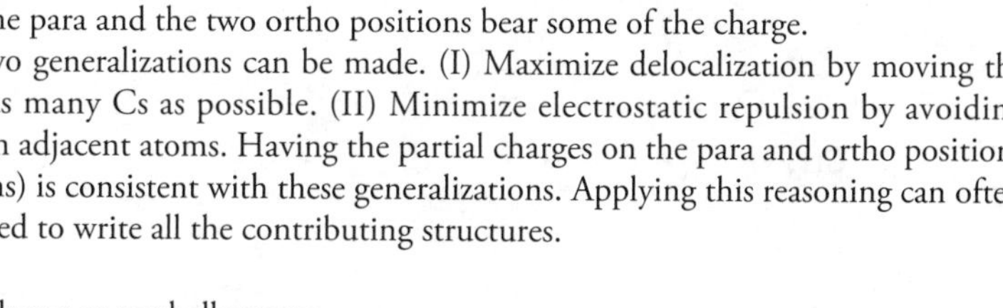

In each case the para and the two ortho positions bear some of the charge.

(B) Two generalizations can be made. (I) Maximize delocalization by moving the charge onto as many Cs as possible. (II) Minimize electrostatic repulsion by avoiding like charges on adjacent atoms. Having the partial charges on the para and ortho positions (three positions) is consistent with these generalizations. Applying this reasoning can often obviate the need to write all the contributing structures.

208. (A) Toluene or methylbenzene
(B) styrene or ethenylbenzene (vinylbenzene)
(C) 1, 4-dimethylbenzene or *p*-xylene
(D) 1-bromo-3-nitrobenzene or *m*-bromonitrobenzene
(E) 2,4-dinitrophenol
(F) *o*-chloroaniline

209. **(A)** 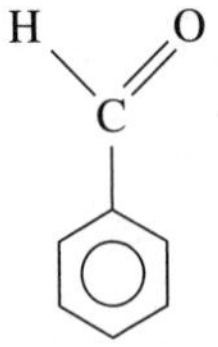

(B) 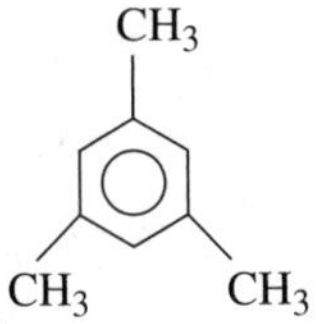

(C) 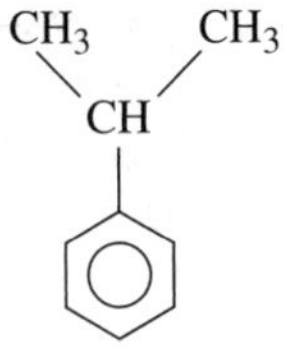

(D) 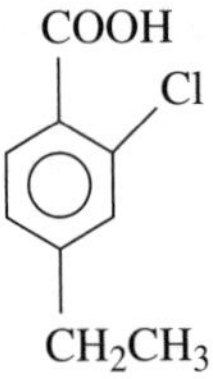

(E) 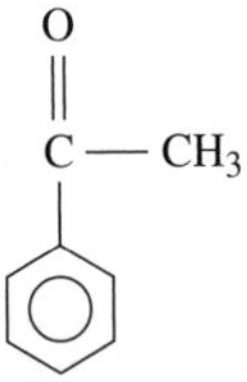

(F) 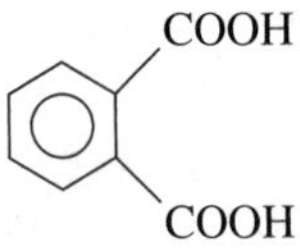

(G) 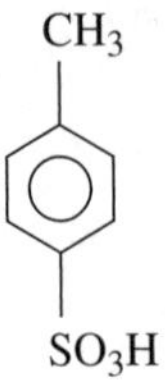

210. **(A)**

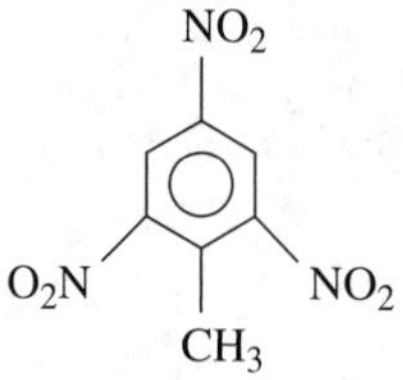

2,4,6-Trinitrotoluene

(B)

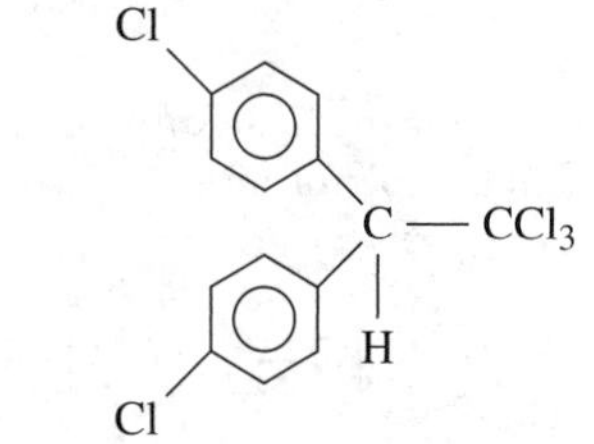

4,4′-Dichlorodiphenyltrichloroethane

(C)

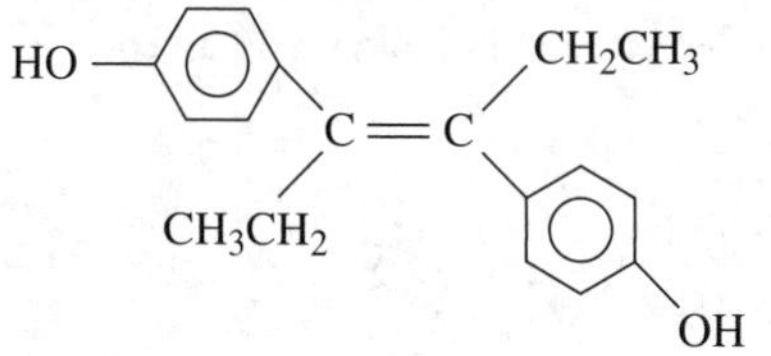

(E)-3,4-(4,4′-Dihydroxyphenyl)-3-hexene

(D)

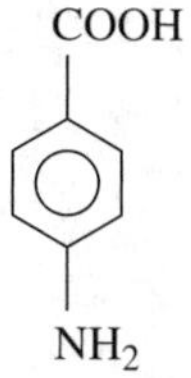

p-Aminobenzoic acid

211. Hückel's rule applies to flat, carbocyclic molecules, where each C in the ring is capable of being sp or sp^2 hybridized, thus providing a p orbital for extended π bonding. To be aromatic, such a molecule must have $(4n + 2)$ π electrons, where n equals zero or a whole number. Some *Hückel numbers* are 2, 6, 10, 14, and 18.

212. Aromatic > nonaromatic > antiaromatic.

213. **(A)**

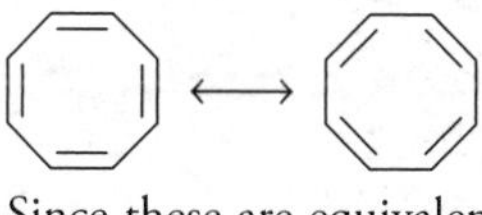

(B) Since these are equivalent energy resonance forms like those for benzene, we predict **A** to be aromatic.

(C) There is little or no π electron delocalization (resonance). If there were, ΔH_h for cyclooctatetraene would be lower, indicating lower energy and greater stability.

(D) No. MO theory, including Hückel's rule, is the best method for predicting aromaticity.

214. (A) $3HC\equiv CH \xrightarrow[\Delta]{\text{Ni or Co complex}} $ benzene

This trimerization, a [2. 2. 2] cycloaddition, requires passage through a hot tube.

(B) $CH_3(CH_2)_4CH_3 \xrightarrow[450-550°C]{CrO_3} $ benzene

This type of reaction is used to produce mixtures of aromatic hydrocarbons by cyclization and dehydrogenation of aliphatic hydrocarbons found in petroleum.

215. $HC\equiv CH + CH_2 = CHCH = CH_2 \longrightarrow$ $\xrightarrow[\Delta]{Pd}$ $+ H_2$

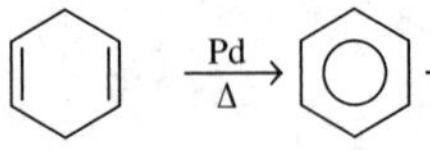

1,4-Cyclohexadiene

216. This *Birch reduction* is related to the reduction of alkynes to alkenes. The product is 1, 4-cyclohexadiene.

$$C_6H_6 + 2M + 2EtOH \xrightarrow{\text{liq. NH}_3}$$ $+ 2(M^+EtO^-)$ where M = Li, Na

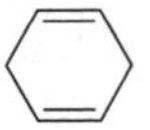

217. (A)

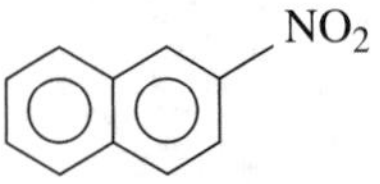

(B)

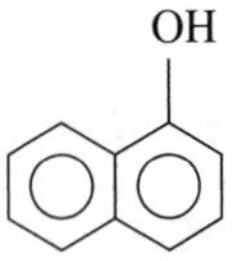

(C)

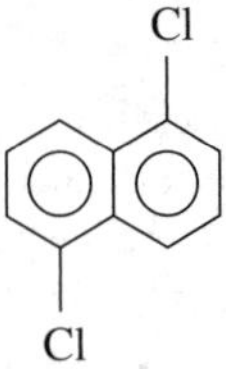

(D)

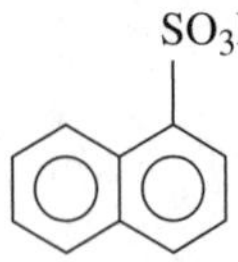

(E)

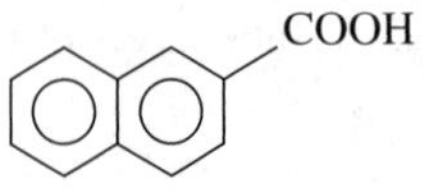

218. **(A)** 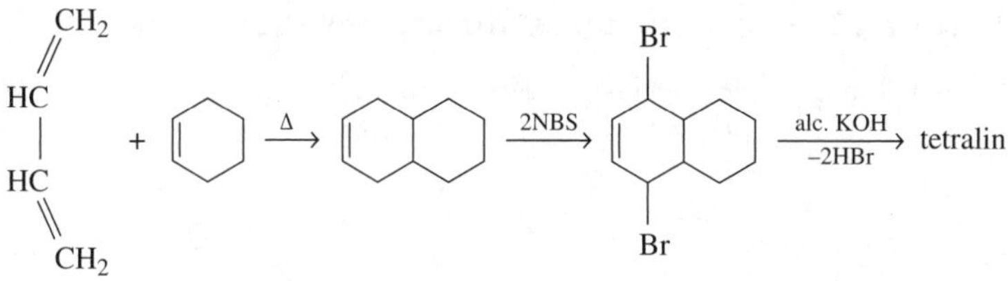

(B) Tetralin is dehydrogenated with S or Pd to give naphthalene.

219. In each case two Hs add individually to C^9 and C^{10}. The products are

(A) 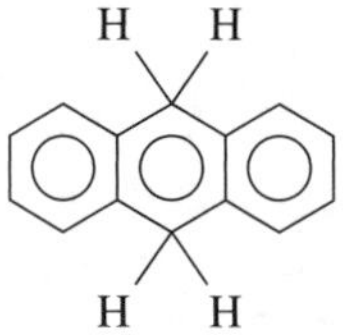

9,10-Dihydroanthracene

(B) 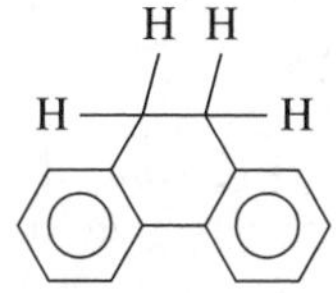

9,10-Dihydrophenanthrene

220. The molecular formula of completely hydrogenated **F** reveals the presence of two rings. The formation of phthalic acid shows that one of the rings is phenyl and that the remaining three Cs must be part of a five-member ring system fused to two adjacent Cs in the ring.

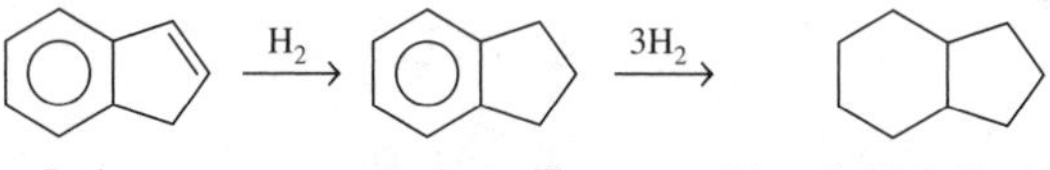

Indene   Indane, **E**   Bicyclo[4.3.0]octane, **F**

The C═C in the five-member ring is not part of an aromatic system; it behaves as a typical C═C.

221. Add Br_2/CCl_4 to each of the three liquids. Cyclohexene, which undergoes addition, instantaneously decolorizes the red-brown color of Br_2. In presence of light, cyclohexane slowly decolorizes Br_2 but with the evolution of HBr gas, which is detected by its formation of a white cloud when in contact with moist breath. Cyclohexane, a typical alkane, undergoes free radical substitution. Benzene is unreactive under these conditions.

Chapter 11: Aromatic Substitution, Arenes

222. **(A)** Electrophilic reagents or Lewis acids.
(B) An H is replaced by an electrophilic group, E, preserving the aromatic system.

223. **(A)** I.

Contributing structures

II.

Delocalized (hybrid) structure

(B) The benzenonium ion is a stable allylic carbocation. The C attacked by E^+ becomes sp^3 hybridized. The other five Cs are sp^2 hybridized, and their remaining p AOs overlap laterally to form a delocalized π electron cloud.

224. Formation of the intermediate arenium cation is usually slow and rate-determining. Elimination of H^+ is fast since it restores aromaticity—it has no effect on the overall reaction rate.

225. The catalyst makes the reagent more electrophilic, thereby raising the H_{GS}, lessening the $\Delta H^{\ddagger}$ of TS_1, and enabling the substitution to proceed at a faster rate. The catalyst plays this role by either actually forming the electrophile or by polarizing the reagent.

226. **(A)** $HOCl + H^+ \longrightarrow H_2OCl^+ \longrightarrow Cl^+(E) + H_2O$ (B)
(B) $2HONO_2 \longrightarrow NO_3^- + H_2ONO_2^+ \longrightarrow NO_2^+(E) + H_2O$ (B)
(C) $2I-Cl + ZnCl_2 \longrightarrow 2I^+(E) + ZnCl_4^{2-}$ (B) (I^+ is more stable than Cl^+.)
(D) $HONO + H^+ \longrightarrow H_2ONO \longrightarrow NO^+(E) + H_2O$ (B)

227. **(A)** I, II. $PhCOCH_2CH_2CH_3$
(B) $RCOCl + AlCl_3 \longrightarrow \left[R-C\equiv\overset{+}{O}: \longleftrightarrow R-\overset{+}{C}=\ddot{O}: \right] + AlCl_4^-$

A   An acylium ion   B

A is the main contributing resonance structure for the *acylium ion* (the electrophile) because both C and O have an octet. The anhydride gives the same acylium ion and $[AlCl_3OAc]^-$.
(C) The acylium ion is much more stable than any alkyl carbocation, and so it cannot rearrange to a more stable cation.
(D) The ketone prepared in **(A)** reduced to the hydrocarbon:

$$PhCOCH_2CH_2CH_3 \xrightarrow[\text{or } H_2NNH_2, OH^- \text{ (Wolff–kishner)}]{\text{Zn/Hg, HCl(Clemmensen)}} PhCH_2CH_2CH_2CH_3$$

228. **(A)** Acylation:

$$Ph-H + R-C\equiv O^+ \longrightarrow \longrightarrow PhCR + HAlCl_4$$

(B) Both require a Lewis acid of the type MX_n, most commonly $AlCl_3$, but also BF_3, $FeCl_3$, $ZnCl_2$. In acylation, a 1:1 complex of $RCOCl$ and catalyst forms, which then dissociates into the acylium ion:

$$R \underset{\delta+}{-} \overset{\displaystyle O}{\underset{\displaystyle \|}{C}} --- Cl --- \overset{\delta-}{AlCl_3} \longrightarrow R - C \equiv O^+ + AlCl_4^-$$

Acylations require more than one equivalent of catalyst because the ketonic product also complexes with $AlCl_3$:

$$\overset{\delta+}{:O:} --- \overset{\delta-}{AlCl_3}$$

$$\underset{Ph \quad\quad R}{\overset{\displaystyle \|}{C}}$$

229. (A) $PhCH(CH_3)_2$

(B)

(C) $Ph - \overset{\displaystyle O}{\overset{\displaystyle \|}{C}} - CHMe_2$

(D) $PhCH_2CH{=}CH_2$

230. (A) Such Gs affect the electrophilic aromatic substitution in two ways:

I. *Reactivity* or rate of reaction. Those more reactive than benzene are *activating*, those less reactive are *deactivating*.

II. *Orientation*—whether E enters *ortho, meta*, or *para*.

(B) There are three classes of substituent groups:

I. All activating groups direct E to the *ortho* and *para* positions.

II. Most deactivating groups direct E to the *meta* positions.

III. A few deactivating groups, e.g., halogen, differ from (II) in being *ortho-* and *para*-directing.

231. The electronegative halogens inductively withdraw e⁻s from all ring Cs of the σ complex, and the *o-, p-,* and *m*-benzenonium ions each have a higher $\Delta H^{\ddagger}$ than that of the cation from benzene. The halogens have unshared electrons and can delocalize electron density to the *o-* and *p*-Cs. Halogens are said to be π -donating but σ -withdrawing.

232. (A) The order of activation is $-O^->-OH>-OCOCH_3$. The $-O^-$, with a full negative charge, is best able to donate electrons, thereby giving the very stable uncharged intermediate

In $\begin{matrix} O \\ \| \\ -OCCH_3, \end{matrix}$ the C of the $\overset{\delta+}{C} = \overset{\delta-}{O}$ has a positive charge and makes demands

on the $-\overset{..}{\underset{..}{O}}-$ for electron density. This *cross-conjugation* diminishes the ability of the

$-\overset{..}{\underset{..}{O}}-$ to donate e^-s to the arenonium ion.

   (B) The order is $-NH_2 > -NHCOCH_3$ because of cross-conjugation in the amide,

$$Ar - \underset{\underset{H}{|}}{N} = \underset{\underset{:\overset{..}{\underset{..}{O}}:^-}{|}}{C} - CH_3.$$

233. (A) p-$O_2NC_6H_4NHCOCH_3$ **(F)**
   (B) m-$BrC_6H_4CBr_3$ **(S)**
   (C) p-$ClC_6H_4CCMe_3$ **(F)**
   (D) p-$O_2NC_6H_4Ph$ **(F)** (Ph is an activating o, p group)
   (E) m-$O_2NC_6H_4COOMe$ **(S)**
   (F) p-$HSO_3C_6H_4CHMe_2$ **(F)**
   (G) m-$O_2NC_6H_4CN$ **(S)**
   (H) p-BrC_6H_4I **(S)**

234. In **E**, Me directs E^+ *ortho* and *para* to C^4 and C^6, positions that are also *meta* to NO_2—the substituents reinforce each other. In **F**, the orientation is in opposition. The *o*, *p*-director controls the orientation, but somehow E^+ enters mostly *ortho*, not *para*, to the *meta*-directing NO_2. Both Gs are reinforcing in **G**, and E^+ is directed *ortho*, on to C^2.

235. (A) The α position.
   (B) Attack at the α position has a lower $\Delta H^\ddagger$ because the intermediate σ complex **A** and its TS_1 are more stable than the σ complex **B** and its TS_1 from β-attack. They both have an intact benzene ring, but **A** is an allylic R^+ and **B** is not. Thus, the $+$ charge in **A** is better delocalized.

An allylic R^+
α-substitution

Not an allylic R^+
β-substitution

A

B

(In both **A** and **B** the intact aromatic ring has the same effect on stabilizing the $+$ charge.)

236. Rule 1. α-Substitution always dominates.
   Rule 2.   When one ring has a deactivating G on it, further substitution occurs in the unsubstituted ring at an α position, if available.

Rule 3. When one ring has an activating α-G, further substitution occurs in the same ring at position 4, and to a smaller extent at position 2. An activating β-G orients E⁺ to position 1.

237. (A)

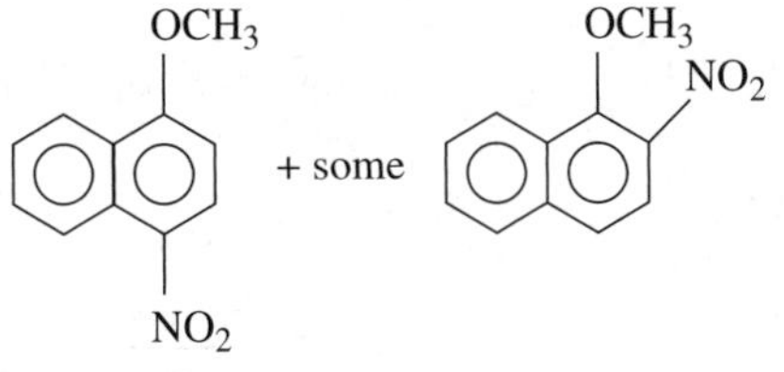

+ some

(B)

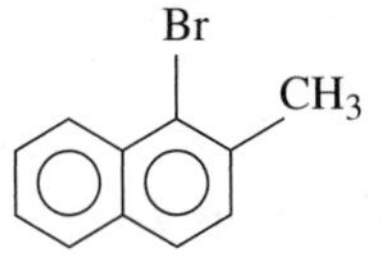

In **(B)** the activated ring has no available *p* position so substitution occurs at the more reactive *ortho* (α) position.

238. (A) Acylation introduces a deactivating group (—COR) that prevents further acylation from occurring. Introduction of an activating-R group induces polyalkylations.
   (B) (I) 1-Acetylnaphthalene and (II) 2-acetylnaphthalene.
   (C) $PhNO_2$ may form a bulky complex with $RCOCl$—$AlCl_3$ that can only attack the more spacious 2 position.

239. (A) (I) $PhNH_2 + KCl$ and (II) $PhOH + NaCl$.
   (B) *m*- and *p*-Hydroxytoluene + NaCl.
   (C) (1) The halogen is not activated by electron-withdrawing Gs. (2) The base is much stronger ($:NH_2^-$) or the temperature is elevated (340°C). (3) The entering group does not always occupy the vacated position (called *cine substitution*).

240. (A) The *meta*-directing NO_2 is introduced first:

$$C_6H_6 \xrightarrow[H_2SO_4]{HNO_3} C_6H_5NO_2 \xrightarrow[FeCl_3]{Cl_2} m\text{-}ClC_6H_5NO_2$$

(B) The *para*-directing Cl is introduced first:

$$C_6H_6 \xrightarrow[FeCl_3]{Cl_2} C_6H_5Cl \xrightarrow[H_2SO_4]{HNO_3} p\text{-}ClC_6H_4NO_2$$

(C) The *para* is first blocked so that NO_2 goes exclusively to the *ortho* position:

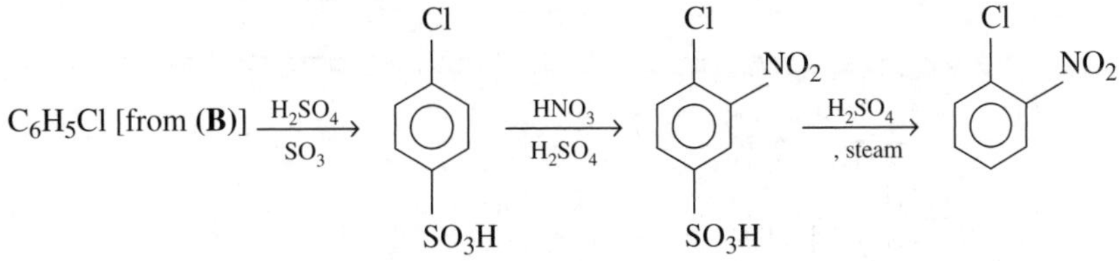

$$C_6H_5Cl \text{ [from (B)]} \xrightarrow[SO_3]{H_2SO_4} \cdots \xrightarrow[H_2SO_4]{HNO_3} \cdots \xrightarrow[\text{, steam}]{H_2SO_4} \cdots$$

241. (A) Bromination of toluene is more efficient than alkylation of bromobenzene, with Br deactivating.

$$C_6H_6 \xrightarrow[AlCl_3]{CH_3Cl} C_6H_5CH_3 \xrightarrow[Fe]{Br_2} p\text{-}CH_3C_6H_4Br \xrightarrow{hot\ KMnO_4^*} p\text{-}HOOCC_6H_4Br$$

(B) The *para* position of PhMe is blocked by Sulfonation, followed by bromination.

(C) The —COOH is introduced first to direct the —Br to the *meta* position.

$$C_6H_6 \xrightarrow[AlCl_3]{CH_3Cl} C_6H_5CH_3 \xrightarrow{*hot\ KMnO_4} C_6H_5COOH \xrightarrow[Fe]{Br_2} m\text{-}BrC_6H_4COOH$$

*These two-phase oxidations are best done with phase-transfer catalysts.

242. (A) $p\text{-}BrC_6H_4COOH$ [from Problem 241(A)] $\xrightarrow[H_2SO_4]{HNO_3}$ A

(B) $CH_3C_6H_5 \xrightarrow[SO_3]{H_2SO_4} p\text{-}CH_3C_6H_4SO_3H \xrightarrow[H_2SO_4]{HNO_3}$

$o\text{-}O_2NC_6H_4CH_3 \xrightarrow{Br_2,\ Fe}$

$\xrightarrow{hot\ KMnO_4}$ B

(C) $CH_3C_6H_5 \xrightarrow[H_2SO_4]{HNO_3} p\text{-}CH_3C_6H_4NO_2 \xrightarrow[Fe]{Br_2} 2\text{-}Br\text{-}4\text{-}NO_2C_6H_3CH_3 \xrightarrow[\Delta]{KMnO_4} C$

(D) Nitration of a ring with two deactivating groups is difficult and requires more vigorous conditions.

$$CH_3C_6H_5 \xrightarrow{hot\ KMnO_4} C_6H_5COOH \xrightarrow[H_2SO_4]{HNO_3} m\text{-}NO_2C_6H_4COOH \xrightarrow[H_2SO_4,\Delta]{fuming\ HNO_3} D$$

243. (A) Friedel–Crafts alkylation of benzene with
    I. CH_3CH_2X, $AlCl_3$
    II. $CH_2{=}CH_2$, HF
    III. CH_3CH_2OH, BF_3 or conc. H_2SO_4

(B) Friedel–Crafts acylation with CH_3COCl or $(CH_3CO)_2O$, $AlCl_3$ giving $PhCOCH_3$; followed by reduction of the C=O to CH_2 (Problem 227).

(C) Corey–House reaction of $Ph_2CuLi + CH_3CH_2Br$.

244. It is usually impossible to stop these reactions after the addition of one equivalent of these polychloromethanes. The products are

(A) Ph_2CH_2

(B) Ph_3CH

(C) Ph_3CCl. In **(C)**, the reaction stops after three rings have been substituted, mainly because of steric hindrance toward having four Phs on a single C

245. (A) $2Ph_3CCl + 2Ag(\text{or } Zn) \longrightarrow [2Ph_3C \cdot \rightleftharpoons (Ph_3C)_2] + 2AgCl(\text{or } ZnCl_2)$

$$\underset{\text{radical}}{\underset{\text{Yellow}}{}} \qquad \text{Dimer}$$

(B) I. $2Ph_3C \cdot + O_2 \xrightarrow{0\degree C} Ph_3C\!-\!O\!-\!O\!-\!CPh_3$

$$\underset{\text{radical}}{\underset{\text{Triphenylmethyl}}{}} \qquad \text{A colorless peroxide}$$

II. $Ph_3C \cdot \xrightarrow[0\degree C]{I_2} Ph_3C\!-\!I$

$$\text{Colorless}$$
$$\text{triphenyliodomethane}$$

(C)

The dimer is in equilibrium with the triphenylmethyl radical.

(D) Hexaphenylethane is unstable relative to the radical because (I) the crowding of the six aromatic rings weakens the C—C bond and (II) the radical has considerable delocalization energy.

246. A has 6° of unsaturation, four of which often signal the presence of a benzene ring, as confirmed by isolation of phthalic acid on vigorous oxidation. Reaction with Br_2 and one eq. of H_2 indicates there is a C=C. Addition of three more eq. of H_2 further indicates the presence of a benzene ring. So far 5° of unsaturation have been accounted for—the sixth degree resists reduction and must be a ring with C=C. Oxidation to the *ortho*-dicarboxylic acid indicates the ring is fused to the benzene ring. The structure is indene.

Phthalic acid   Indene, **A**   Indane, **B**   Bicyclo[4.3.0] nonane

Chapter 12: Spectroscopy and Structure Proof

247. (A) I. The *period* (T) is the time required to complete one full cycle; the unit is s/cycle.

II. The *frequency* (v) is the number of cycles that occur per second. It is also the number of waves passing through a given point in a second; the unit is cycles/s (s^{-1}) or hertz (Hz). When referring to λ, T, and v, the word *cycle* is understood and often dropped.

(B) $v\lambda = c$, where $c =$ speed of light in vacuum $= 3.0 \times 10^8$ m/s; the longer the wavelength, the smaller is the frequency, and vice versa.

248. (A) Frequency and energy of a wave are related by the equation $E = hv$, where $h (= 6.63 \times 10^{-34}$ J·s/particle) is *Planck's constant*. (In this context, the particle is a photon.) Thus, the greater the frequency, the higher is the energy of the radiation.

(B) Since wavelength and frequency are inversely related, the longer the wavelength, the smaller is the energy: $E = hc/\lambda$.

249. The wavelengths are substituted into the equation $v = c/\lambda$ (see Problem 247). Thus

Violet: $\quad v = \dfrac{3.0 \times 10^8 \text{ m/s}}{(400 \text{ nm})(10^{-9} \text{ m/1 nm})} = 7.5 \times 10^{14} \text{ s}^{-1} = 750 \text{ THz}$

Red: $\quad v = \dfrac{3.0 \times 10^8 \text{ m/s}}{(750 \text{ nm})(10^{-9} \text{ m/1 nm})} = 4.0 \times 10^{14} \text{ s}^{-1} = 400 \text{ THz}$

where 1 THz $= 10^{12}$ Hz. Violet light has the shorter wavelength and higher frequency.

250. Those with double bonds have excitations to a π *, and those with unshared pairs have excitations from an n MO. All have $\sigma \to \sigma$ *. In addition,

(A) $n \to \sigma$ *

(B) $n \to \pi$*, $\pi \to \pi$*, $\sigma \to \pi$*, $n \to \sigma$*, $\pi \to \sigma$ *

(C) $\pi \to \pi$*, $\sigma \to \pi$*, $\pi \to \sigma$ *

(D) $n \to \sigma$ *

251. (A) λ_{max} is a discernable wavelength at which an electronic transition occurs.

(B) At λ_{max}, the absorbance A (optical density), which is a measure of the light absorbed through the solution, follows an exponential law (Beer–Lambert) of the form

$$A = \log(I_0/I) = \epsilon \, Cl$$

where I_0 is the intensity of the incident light, I is the intensity of the emergent light, ϵ is the *molar extinction coefficient* (also called *molar absorptivity*), C is the molarity, and l is the path length. At λ_{max}, the molar extinction coefficient is expressed as ϵ_{max}.

(C) ϵ_{max} is related to the molecule's probability of absorbing a photon at λ_{max}, or to the intensity of excited molecules. Values for $\epsilon \geq 10^4$ are termed *high-intensity absorptions*, while values $< 10^3$ are *low-intensity absorptions*. (Units for ϵ_{max} are customarily omitted.)

(D) Transmittance $T = I/I_0$, and it is often given as a percentage, i.e., $\% T = I/I_0 \times 100$.

252. It is usually taken on a very dilute solution (10^{-5} to $10^{-6}\,M$), the solvent being transparent above 200 nm. The solution is placed in a 1-cm-wide silica cell (cuvette) that permits light to pass through. Alongside the solution cell is a matched cell (same value of 1) containing pure solvent (the reference cell). The beam of uv or visible light, whose wavelength is continuously changing, is split into two beams, one passing through the sample solution and the other through the reference cell. The spectrum is automatically recorded on a chart, usually as a plot of A vs. wavelength. Peaks occur at wavelengths, λ_{max}, at which light is absorbed. Actually, absorption peaks are typically broad. In most cases, only the λ_{max}'s and corresponding ϵ_{max}'s are reported. These, like a melting point, are inherent physical properties of a compound. Most instruments have two light sources, one for uv (H_2 lamp) and the other for white visible light (tungsten lamp), which have to be interchanged for a complete scan over both ranges.

253. **(A)** The chromophore is $\diagdown C = O$. The transitions are: $n \to \sigma^*$ (154 nm), $\pi \to \pi^*$ (190 nm), and $n \to \pi^*$ (280 nm).
   (B) 154 nm. The $\pi \to \pi^*$ (190 nm) is at the low observable limit of ordinary uv spectrometers.

254. Functional groups with a single O are alcohols (ROH), ethers (ROR), and carbonyl compounds (aldehydes, $RCH=O$, and ketones, $R_2C=O$). The formula lacks four Hs from being saturated—there are 2° of unsaturation. This means there may be two rings, one double bond and one ring, two double bonds, or one triple bond. The absorption peaks signal an unconjugated $C=O$. The possibilities are cyclic carbonyl compounds as shown:

   Cyclobutanone   Methylcyclopropanone   Cyclopropylcarboxaldehyde
and the unconjugated 3-butenal, $H_2C=CHCH_2CH=O$.

255. Use uv spectroscopy to measure in **(A)** the decline in the absorbance of the $C=O$ group, **(D)** the increase in absorbance of $C=O$, **(E)** the decrease in absorbance of the conjugated diene system, and **(F)** the loss of their absorbance of anthracene. Reactions **(B)** and **(C)** cannot be studied by uv because neither their reactants nor their products have detectable absorptions.

256. **(A)** They dissolve the NaCl used for cell windows, causing fogging. (All solutes and solvents must be carefully dried before use.) In addition, they both absorb strongly in several regions, they H-bond with many solutes, and they may form dipole interactions with polar solutes, possibly shifting peaks. Water may be used if the sealed cells are constructed from water-insoluble salts such as AgCl.
   (B) $CHCl_3$, CCl_4.

257. When ir light impinges on a molecule, only certain frequencies—those corresponding to vibrational frequencies—are absorbed; the process is quantized. The absorption excites the molecule to a higher-energy *vibrational* state where the amplitude of that vibration is increased. The *fundamental absorption peak* is a result of the transition from the ground state to the first excited state. Radiation in the energy range of 2–11 kcal/mol corresponds to the range encompassing stretching and bending frequencies in most covalent molecules.

258. (A) Excitation of stretching vibrations requires more energy and takes place at higher frequencies (4000 to 1250 cm^{-1}) than bending frequencies (between 1400 and 675 cm^{-1}).

(B) Because of the variety and complexity of the bending modes, the region below 1250 cm^{-1} has peaks that are characteristic of the particular molecule. This region is therefore called the *fingerprint region* and is very useful in determining whether two samples are chemically identical.

259. It is extremely difficult and impractical to attempt an interpretation of each band in an ir spectrum. Only characteristic absorptions will be identified. Peak **A** below 3000 cm^{-1}, at about 2900 cm^{-1}, is due to H—C$_{sp^3}$ stretching. Peak **B** at 1750 cm^{-1} is due to the characteristic C=O stretch. The bands at 1380 and 1500 cm^{-1}, labeled **C**, are due to C—H bending, and the bands labeled **D** at 1050 and 1240 cm^{-1} are due to the C—O stretching.

260. The C=O bond of all carbonyl compounds has a very high-intensity peak between 1750 and 1680 cm^{-1}, present in all three spectra. The distinguishing feature of the aldehyde is the C—H doublet at 2820 and 2715 cm^{-1}, shown in **Figure 12-2(A)**. The acid is identified in **Figure 12-2(B)** because of the very broad absorption from 3500 to 2500 cm^{-1}. By elimination, the spectrum in **Figure 12-2(C)** with neither of these features is the ketone.

261. Both would show OH stretching in the 3450–3200 cm^{-1} range, with the phenol in the lower region. Phenol, however, would show the typical Ar—H absorption above 3000 cm^{-1} and no C—H below 3000 cm^{-1}. This situation is reversed in cyclohexanol, which has C$_{sp^3}$—H below 3000 cm^{-1}, but no C$_{sp^2}$—H. Phenol would also absorb in the 1000–650 cm^{-1} range due to aromatic C—H bending.

262. (A) ClCH$_2$CH$_2$Cl; the isomeric 1,1-dichloroethane has two kinds of Hs.

(B) A saturated hydrocarbon with eight Cs must have only equivalent branched CH$_3$s: (CH$_3$)$_3$C —C(CH$_3$)$_3$.

(C) Four degrees of unsaturation points to a substituted benzene: 1,3,5-trimethylbenzene, mesitylene.

(D) One C=C is present; all Hs must be in Mes: (CH$_3$)$_2$C=C(CH$_3$)$_2$.

(E) CH$_3$CH$_2$CH$_2$Cl; the incorrect isomer, 2-chloropropane, has only two kinds of Hs.

263. The single H^a splits H^b into a doublet integrating for three Hs. H^a appears as a *quartet* ($n = 3$) due to the following spinning pattern for the three Hs:

$$↑↑↑ \{↑↑↓, ↑↓↑, ↓↑↑\} \{↓↓↑, ↓↑↓, ↑↓↓\} ↓↓↓$$

Relative intensities:　1　:　　3　　:　　3　:　1

The entire quartet integrates for one H.

264. Splitting is not observed in **(A)** or **(D)**, which each have only equivalent Hs, or in **(C)**, which has no nonequivalent Hs on *adjacent* Cs. The Hs of CH$_2$ in **(B)** are nonequivalent, and each is split into a triplet ($n = 2$; $2 + 1 = 3$). In **(E)** the two Hs are not equivalent, and each is split into a doublet. The vinylic Hs in **(F)** are nonequivalent since one is *cis* to Cl and the other is *cis* to **I**. Each is split into a doublet. In this case the interacting Hs are on the same C. Compound **(G)** gives a singlet for the four equivalent uncoupled aromatic Hs, a quartet for the Hs of the two equivalent CH$_2$ groups coupled with CH$_3$, and a triplet for the two equivalent CH$_3$ groups coupled with CH$_2$.

265. The three possible structures are

$$CH_2^a-\underset{\underset{Cl}{|}}{CH^c}-\underset{\underset{CH_3^b}{|}}{CH_2^d}-CH^e-CH_3^f \quad \underset{CH_3^f}{|}$$

1-Chloro-2,4-dimethylpentane (**A**)

$$CH_3^a-\underset{\underset{CH_3^a}{|}}{CH^b}-\underset{\underset{Cl}{|}}{CH^c}-CH^b-CH_3^a \quad \underset{CH_3^a}{|}$$

3-ChIoro-2,4-dimethylpentane (**B**)

$$CH_3^a-\underset{\underset{Cl}{|}}{\underset{\underset{CH_3^a}{|}}{C}}-CH_2^b-CH^c-CH_3^d \quad \underset{CH_3^d}{|}$$

2-Chloro-2,4-dimethylpentane (**C**)

The best clues come from the splitting pattern and integration of the most downfield signal, arising from the Hs closest to Cl. In spectrum (**B**) this is a triplet, for one H, clearly due to H^c of **B**. In addition, the most upfield signal is a doublet, integrating for the 12 H^as of the four Mes, split by the methine H^bs. In spectrum (**A**) the signal with the highest δ value is a *doublet*, integrating for two Hs, that corresponds only to $ClCH_2^a$ of structure **A**. This is confirmed by the complex multiplet due to the nine Hs (H^b and H^f) of the three Mes that are most upfield and the four Hs (H^c, H^d, and H^e) with signals between these. This leaves C for spectrum (**C**). The most downfield group of irregular signals, integrating for three Hs, comes from H^b and H^c, respectively. The most upfield doublet, integrating for the six H^ds, arises from the two equivalent Mes split by H^c. The six H^as give rise to the singlet at δ = 1.6 ppm.

266. (**A**) False. The chance of finding a **D** in a molecule is miniscule because its natural abundance is only 0.016%.

(**B**) True. The natural abundance of ^{13}C is 1.08%, and its presence in a parent molecule is detectable by the mass spectrometer.

(**C**) True. The natural abundance of ^{18}O is 0.20%, and its presence is detectable.

(**D**) True. The natural abundance of ^{15}N is 0.38%, and its presence is detectable.

(**E**) False. The chances of having one of each of these isotopes in the same molecule is practically nil (1.08% × 0.38%).

267. (**A**) Divide the given values by 12 to get the number of Cs; the remainder is the mass due to the Hs:

I. $C_2H_5^+$

II. $C_4H_3^+$

III. $C_7H_7^+$

(B) I. If one N is present, subtracting 14 leaves a mass of 15, enough for one **C** and three Hs. The formula is CH_3N^+.

II. One, two, or three Ns can be present, giving three cations: $C_3H_7N^+$, $C_2H_5N_2^+$, or $CH_3N_3^+$.

268. A peak at $m/z = 15$ suggests a CH_3. Because $43 - 15 = 28$, the mass of $C{=}O$, the m/z value of 43 may be due to an acetyl, CH_3CO, group in the compound. The highest value, 148, gives the molecular weight. Cleaving an acetyl group ($m/z = 43$) from 148 gives 105, which is an observed peak. Next below 105 is 91, a difference of 14; this suggests a CH_2 attached to CH_3CO. So far we have CH_3COCH_2 adding up to 57, leaving $148 - 57 = 91$ to be accounted for. This peak is likely to be $[C_7H_7]^+$, whose precursor is the stable benzyl cation, $C_6H_5CH_2$. The structure is $CH_3 \overset{\displaystyle \|}{\underset{\displaystyle O}{-\!\!-\!\!- C -\!\!-\!\!-}} CH_2 -\!\!-\!\!- CH_2 -\!\!-\!\!- C_6H_5$.

269. (A) Peaks for parent cations of aromatic compounds usually appear in mass spectra. The parent has a molecular weight of 134 and a molecular formula of $C_{10}H_{14}$. The base peak at 91 is typically $C_6H_5CH_2^+$, indicating that the compound is a monosubstituted benzene with a CH_2 attached to the ring. Two compounds, $C_6H_5CH_2CH_2CH_2CH_3$ and $C_6H_5CH_2CH(CH_3)_2$, can give this fragment.

(B) A ^{13}C nmr spectrum would help, as *n*-butylbenzene would give eight signals, and *i*-butylbenzene would give seven signals. A pmr spectrum would show the characteristic heptet for the 3°H.

270. (A) Conjugation

(B) functional groups

(C) environment of Hs in a molecule and consequently its molecular skeleton including the Hs

(D) carbon skeleton

(E) molecular weight of the parent and major structural features from the fragmentation pattern

271. (A) I. Like IR, Raman is a type of vibrational spectroscopy. In IR spectra all of the absorbed energy causes excitation of vibrational states, but in Raman only some of it does. The unabsorbed energy is scattered, and its changed wavelength is detected and plotted in wave numbers vs. intensity on chart paper. Unlike IR, Raman can detect vibrational absorptions even though there is no change in the dipole moment. Thus, a comparison of IR and Raman spectra affords useful information about molecular symmetry. For example the $C{=}C$ stretch in tetrachloroethene is intense in Raman but absent in IR.

II. The esr spectroscopy utilizes the fact that an odd e^- has two-spin states just as does an ^1H nucleus. In a magnetic field the e^--spin states have two different energies, and excitation from the lower to the higher is affected by lower frequency microwave radiation. The same situation prevails for NMR spectroscopy except that *radiowaues* are used to excite the *nuclear* states. The ESR spectroscopy is used to study the structures of free radicals.

(B) Absorption in the microwave region causes excitation of the quantized *rotational* states of molecules. The rotational levels of a molecule are related to the nuclei masses and the internuclear distances. Microwave spectroscopy is used. to obtain bond angles and bond distances in simple molecules. For example, it can detect the relative amounts of *anti* and *gauche* conformations of 1-iodopropane. (In microwave cooking, the very rapid switching back and forth of the excited rotational states of H_2O molecules in the food results in heating the food.)

Chapter 13: Alcohols and Thiols

272. (A) 2-Methyl-3-heptanol, 2°
(B) 2,2-dimethyl-1-propanol, 1°
(C) 2-phenyl-2-propanol, 3°
(D) 5-bromo-2,2-dimethyl-3-pentanol, 2°
(E) 3-buten-2-ol, 2°
(F) phenylmethanol, 1°
(G) 4-phenyl-1-butanol, 1°

273. (A) $CH_3CH(OH)CH_2CH_3$
(B) $Ph—CH=CHCH_2OH$
(C) $CH_3CHClCH(CH_3)CH_2OH$

(D) 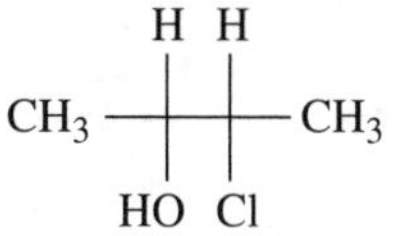
$$CH_3 \underset{\underset{HO}{|} \; \underset{Cl}{|}}{\overset{\overset{H}{|} \; \overset{H}{|}}{———}} CH_3$$

(E)

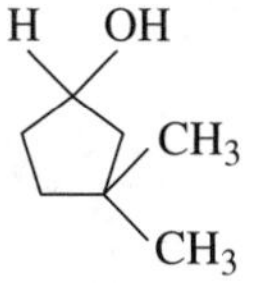

(F)

274. Markovnikov addition to a double bond can be accomplished by hydration in the presence of dilute H_2SO_4 or by oxymercuration with $Hg(OAc)_2/H_2O$ followed by reduction with $NaBH_4$ in preparing (A), (B), and (E). BH_3-THF followed by oxidation with H_2O_2 in aq. OH^- gives the anti-Markovnikov addition for the synthesis of (C) and (D). The starting materials are:

(A) $CH_3CH=CHCH_3$ or $CH_3CH_2CH=CH_2$

(B)

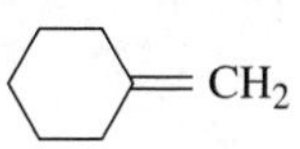

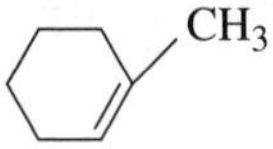

(C) $(CH_3)_2C=CH_2$

(D)

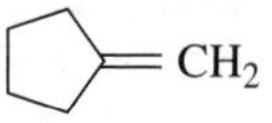

(E) $(CH_3)_2C=CHCH_3$ or $H_2C=\overset{\overset{CH_3}{|}}{C}CH_2CH_3$

275. (A) $CH_3CH_2CH_3 \xrightarrow[hv]{Cl_2} CH_3CHClCH_3 \xrightarrow{aq.\ OH^-} CH_3CH(OH)CH_3$

or $\xrightarrow{alc.\ KOH} CH_3CH = CH_2 \xrightarrow{H_3O^+}$

(B)

$H-C\equiv C-H \xrightarrow{1\ mol\ H_2} H_2C=CH_2 \xrightarrow{HBr} CH_3CH_2Br(A)$

$\downarrow NaNH_2$

$H-C\equiv C^- \xrightarrow{A} H-C\equiv C-CH_2CH_3 \xrightarrow[2.BH_3/H_2O_2,OH^-]{1.1\ mol\ H_2} HOH_2CCH_2CH_2CH_3$

(C) From (A),

$CH_3CH=CH_2 \xrightarrow{NBS} H_2BrCCH=CH_2 \xrightarrow{aq.\ OH^-} HOH_2CCH=CH_2$

(D) $(CH_3)_3CCl + H_2O \longrightarrow (CH_3)_3COH$ (S_N1 solvolysis of a 3° halide)

276. (A) $CH_3CH_2MgX + H_2CO$ or $CH_3MgX + H_2C\overset{O}{\overset{\triangle}{-}}CH_2$
(B) $CH_3CH_2CH_2MgX + (CH_3)_2CO$ or $CH_3CH_2CH_2COCH_3 + CH_3MgX$
(C) $PhCH_2MgX + CH_3CHO$ or $PhCH_2CHO + CH_3MgX$
(D) $PhCOCH_3 + CH_3CH_2MgX$ or $CH_3CH_2COCH_3 + PhMgX$ or $PhCOCH_2CH_3 + CH_3MgX$

(E) $O= \langle\text{hexagon}\rangle + (CH_3)_2CHMgX$

(F) $H_2C=O + \langle\text{cyclopentane}\rangle\overset{H}{\underset{MgX}{}}$

(G) $H_2C\overset{O}{\overset{\triangle}{-}}CH_2 + (CH_3)_2CHMgX$ or $H_2CO + (CH_3)_2CHCH_2MgX$

277. The electron-withdrawing Cl delocalizes the negative charge of $ClCH_2CH_2O^-$ by induction, making it a weaker base than $CH_3CH_2O^-$. Hence, 2-chloroethanol is more acidic.

278. (A) $(CH_3CH_2)_2CH(OH) + PBr_3 \longrightarrow CH_3CH_2CHBrCH_2CH_3$
(B) The OH group is first converted into a *tosylate ester* by reaction with *p*-toluenesulfonyl chloride (called *tosyl chloride*, often abbreviated TsCl). The tosyl group, a good leaving group, is then easily displaced by reaction with Br^- in an S_N2 reaction.

$(CH_3CH_2)_2\,CH(OH) + ClSO_2-\langle\text{ring}\rangle-CH_3 \xrightarrow{-HCl} (CH_3CH_2)_2\,CHOSO_2-\langle\text{ring}\rangle-CH_3$

TsCl $\qquad\qquad\qquad\downarrow Br^-$ Tosylate ester, ROTs

$(CH_3CH_2)_2\,CHBr + {}^-OSO_2-\langle\text{ring}\rangle-CH_3$

Tosylate ion

279. (A) $3ROH + PBr_3 \longrightarrow (RO)_3P + 3HBr \longrightarrow 3RBr + H_3PO_3$

Trialkyl phosphite

(B) The phosphite ester undergoes an S_N2 attack by Br^-, protonated phosphite being the leaving group. The overall reaction occurs with inversion when ROH is 1° or 2°.

$$\overset{\frown}{Br^- + R} - \overset{+}{\underset{H}{O}} - P(OR)_2 \longrightarrow Br - R + HOP(OR)_2$$

280. (A) The *Lucas* reagent, conc. HCl with $ZnCl_2$, converts alcohols to the corresponding alkyl chlorides, which are insoluble in the reaction mixture and appear as a cloudiness or a second denser layer. A 3° ROH reacts immediately, a 2° ROH reacts within 5 min, and a 1° ROH does not react at all at room temperature.

(B) $ZnCl_2$, a strong Lewis acid, encourages an S_N1 pathway for formation of the alkyl chlorides. Thus, the rate of reaction of the alcohols is: 3° > 2° > 1°.

(C) Initially, the alcohol must be soluble in the reagent. Alcohols having more than six Cs are not soluble, so two layers are present at the start.

281. (A) The *Jones* reagent is a chromic acid in aqueous acetone solution.

(B) The Jones reagent is sufficiently mild that it oxidizes alcohols without oxidizing or rearranging double bonds. The products are (I) $CH_3CH{=}CHCOCH_3$ and

(II)

282. In acid, 1° ROH → RCOOH; 2°ROH → $R_2C{=}O$; 3° ROH is not oxidized. In base, the only difference is the formation of carboxylate ion, $RCOO^-$. RCOOH is isolated by adding H^+. In base, $KMnO_4$ is reduced to MnO_2, which precipitates as a brown sludge.

283. A, cyclohexanol; **B**, cyclohexene; **C**, $HOOC(CH_2)_4COOH$, adipic acid.

284. (A) The higher-frequency band is due to O—H stretch of a "free" unassociated ROH, and the lower-frequency band is due to $O-H---O$ of H-bonded ROH.

(B) In a concentrated solution, or neat, with molecules close to one another, the spectrum shows the strong $O-H---O$ stretching frequencies. With increasing dilution, the ROH molecules move farther apart, decreasing the intermolecular H-bonding.

285. Add I_2 in aq. KOH (the iodoform test). 2-Pentanol, having the $-CH(OH)CH_3$ group, reacts, giving a yellow precipitate of CHI_3. The 3-pentanol does not react.

286. (A) Add acid $Cr_2O_7^{2-}$ (orange). The 1° *n*-butyl alcohol is oxidized; its solution changes color to green Cr(III). The 3° *t*-butyl alcohol is unchanged. Alternately, when Lucas reagent (HCl + $ZnCl_2$) is added, the 3° ROH quickly reacts to form the insoluble *t*-butyl chloride that appears as a second (lower) layer or a cloudiness. The 1° ROH does not react and remains dissolved in the reagent.

(B) Add I_2 in OH^- until the I_2 color persists. A pale yellow precipitate of CHI_3 appears, indicating that ethyl alcohol is oxidized. *n*-Propyl alcohol does not have the —$CH(OH)CH_3$ group and is not oxidized.

(C) Add Br_2 in CCl_4; as the Br_2 adds to the $C{=}C$ of the colorless allyl alcohol, its orange color disappears. The orange color persists in the unreactive *n*-propyl alcohol.

(D) Add acid CrO_7^{2-}. It oxidizes the alcohol, and the color changes to green. The ether is unreactive. Alternately, if the two compounds are absolutely dry, add a small piece of Na (caution, use hood and wear goggles!) to each. H_2 is released from the alcohol; the ether does not react.

(E) The simplest test is to add conc. H_2SO_4 to each dry compound. There will be only one layer as the alcohol dissolves, evolving some heat. Two layers will be discernable for the chloride, which is not soluble in H_2SO_4.

287. These compounds are called *thiols*, or, occasionally, *mercaptans*.
    (A) 1-Propanethiol
    (B) 2-melhyl-3-pentane-thiol
    (C) 3-butene-1-thiol
    (D) benzyl mercaptan (phenylmethanethiol)
    (E) 1-methylcyclopentanethiol
    (F) *cis*-2-ethylcyclohexanethiol

288. (A) $(CH_3)_3CSH$
    (B) $(CH_3)_3CCH_2SH$

(C)

(D)

    (E) $CH_2{=}CHCH_2SH$
    (F) $PhCH_2CH(SH)CH_3$
    (G) $HSCH_2CH_2CH_2OH$

289. (A) RS^-. Anions, being charged, have a higher electron density and are stronger nucleophiles than their uncharged conjugate acids.

(B) RS^-. In a protic solvent, the nucleophilicity of anions increases, going down a group in the periodic table. The electron cloud on the larger S is more easily polarized or distorted, which makes it easier for it to attack an electrophile. Furthermore, the smaller RO^- has a higher electron density on O per unit surface area, causing it to form strong H-bonds with protic solvents and thereby diminishing the availability of its electron pairs in displacement reactions.

290. Thiols have very distinct, unpleasant odors. 1-Butanethiol is a component of the skunk spray, and a trace of thiol is often added to heating gas by the supplier as an aid in the detection of gas leaks.

291. (A) The thiol gives a precipitate with heavy metal cations such as Hg^{2+}, and Pb^{2+}, and Cu^{2+}.

(B) The thiol dissolves in aqueous NaOH, forming $RS^- Na^+$.

(C) The 2° ROH gives a yellow precipitate of CHI_3 with I_2/OH^- (the iodoform test).

(D) The 2° ROH is oxidized by a Cr(VI) reagent, thus changing its color from orange to green.

Chapter 14: Ethers, Epoxides, Glycols, and Thioethers

292. The common name is comprised of the names of the groups as separate words with the word *ether*. The groups are listed alphabetically.

(A) Diethyl ether or more commonly ethyl ether, because with simple ethers the prefix *di* is often omitted.

(B) *sec*-Butyl isopropyl ether.

(C) β-Chloroethyl methyl ether.

(D) Methyl phenyl ether, usually called anisole.

(E) Ethyl *p*-nitrophenyl ether, usually called *p*-nitrophenetole.

(F) Cyclohexyl *n*-propyl ether.

(G) Benzyl vinyl ether.

293. (A)

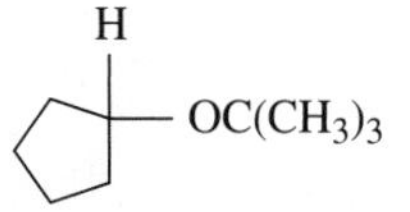

(B)

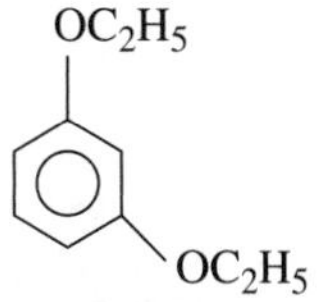

(C) $CH_3CHCH_2CH_2CH_2OCH_3$
$\qquad\quad |$
$\qquad\;\; OH$

(D)

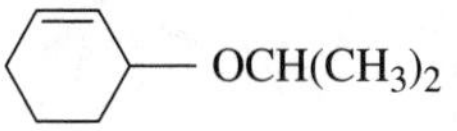

(E) $PhCH_2OCH_2Ph$

(F)

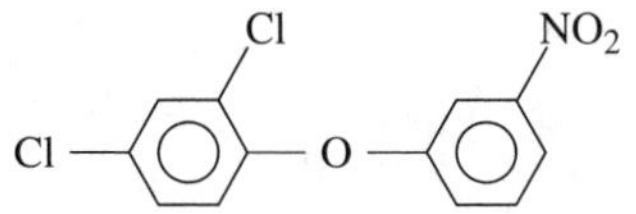

294. (A) (I) 1,2-Dimethoxyethane, commonly called *glyme* and (II) bis-β-methoxyethyl ether (*diglyme*).

(B) The *oxa method* pretends that the O of the longest chain or ring is a C, and it is so counted to determine either the longest carbon parent chain or the parent ring. Its presence is indicated by the prefix *oxa-* and a number to designate its position in the chain or ring. (I) The two Os and four Cs are taken as six Cs, and the parent is hexane; thus, 2,5-dioxahexane. (II) 2,5,8-Trioxanonane.

295. Three-member cyclic ethers may be considered as being oxides of the parent alkene whose common name is used.

   (A) The common name is ethylene oxide. This type of ring is also called an *epoxide*.
   (B) 1,2-Butene oxide or 1,2-epoxybutane.
   (C) Styrene oxide or phenylethylene oxide.
   (D) *trans*-3-Methylcyclohexene oxide or *trans*-1, 2-epoxy-3-methylcyclohexane. *Trans* refers to the relationship of the oxide ring, which must always be *cis*, and the Me group.
   (E) Methylenecyclohexane oxide.
   (F) *cis*-2,3-Butene oxide or (*Z*)-2,3-epoxybutane.

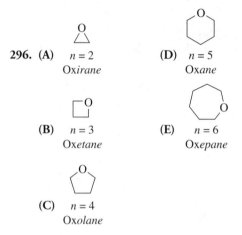

296. **(A)** $n = 2$
          Ox*irane*

(D) $n = 5$
          Ox*ane*

(B) $n = 3$
          Ox*etane*

(E) $n = 6$
          Ox*epane*

(C) $n = 4$
          Ox*olane*

The italicized portions of these names are the suffixes used to represent the size of saturated heterocyclic rings other than those with N atoms.

297. **(A)** 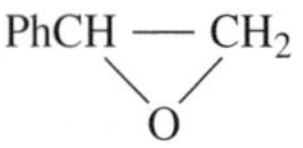   PhCH —— CH$_2$
                    \ /
                     O

   (B) 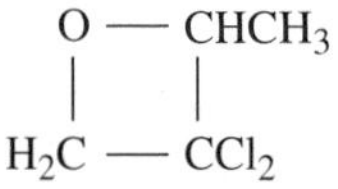   O — CHCH$_3$
             | |
            H$_2$C — CCl$_2$

   (C)   [structure with H, Et, O, Cl, H]

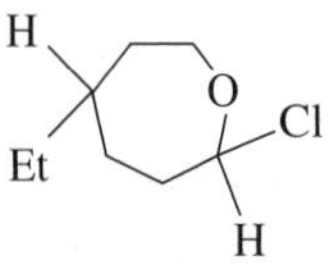

   (D) 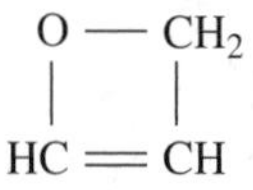   O — CH$_2$
             | |
            HC ═══ CH

298. (A) Because ethers are weakly polar, their intermolecular forces of attraction are about as weak as are those of the hydrocarbons. Hence, the bp's are about the same: for ether 34.6°C and for n-pentane 36°C.

(B) Ethers are much more soluble in H_2O because of H-bonding between the **O** of ethers and the **H** of water. Hydrocarbons do not participate in H-bonding.

H-bond

299. (A) $n\text{-PrOH} \xrightarrow{\text{Na}} n\text{-PrO}^- \xrightarrow{n\text{-PrBr}} \textbf{A}$

(B) $\text{MeOH} \xrightarrow{\text{Na}} \text{MeO}^- \xrightarrow{\text{PhCH}_2\text{Br}} \textbf{B}$

(C) $\text{PhOH} \xrightarrow{\text{NaOH}} \text{PhO}^- \xrightarrow{\text{EtBr}} \textbf{C}$

(D) $t\text{-BuOH} \xrightarrow{\text{Na}} t\text{-BuO}^- \xrightarrow{\text{EtBr}} \textbf{D}$ (This reaction produces a poor yield because of the bulkiness of $t\text{-BuO}^-$.)

300. B, allylic, > **D**, a bromide, > **C**, a chloride, > **A**, neopentyl, too hindered.

301. (A) The S_N2 reaction to prepare cyclic ethers must be intramolecular. The number of Cs separating **X** and **OH** in the chain is the number in the ring. In this case enough alkoxide ion can be formed by adding NaOH to the alcohol.

4-Chlorobutanol   An alkoxide intermediate   Tetrahydrofuran

The alkoxide intermediate may not be completely formed. The incipient anion can begin to displace Cl^- as it forms, a one-step reaction.

(B) As shown in the equation in **(A)**, the substrate must be in the highest energy-eclipsed conformation.

(C) $\text{HOCH}_2\text{CH}_2\text{CH}_2\text{CH}_2\text{OH}$.

(D) Formation of the diol is a bimolecular displacement, which is slower than the intramolecular ring closure.

302. (A)

$$\text{H}_2\text{C}=\text{CHCH}_3 \xrightarrow[\text{2. H}_2\text{O}_2,\, \text{OH}^-]{\text{1. BH}_3,\, \text{THF}} \text{HOCH}_2\text{CH}_2\text{CH}_3 \xrightarrow{\text{BuLi}} {}^-\text{OCH}_2\text{CH}_2\text{CH}_3 (\textbf{D})$$

$\downarrow \text{NBS}$

$$\text{H}_2\text{C}=\text{CHCH}_2\text{Br} \xrightarrow{\text{Br}_2} \text{H}_2\text{CBrCHBrCH}_2\text{Br} \xrightarrow{\text{alc. KOH}} \text{BrCH}=\text{CHCH}_2\text{Br} (\textbf{E})$$

$$\textbf{D} + \textbf{E} \text{ (allylic, not vinylic Br reacts)} \longrightarrow \textbf{A}$$

(B)

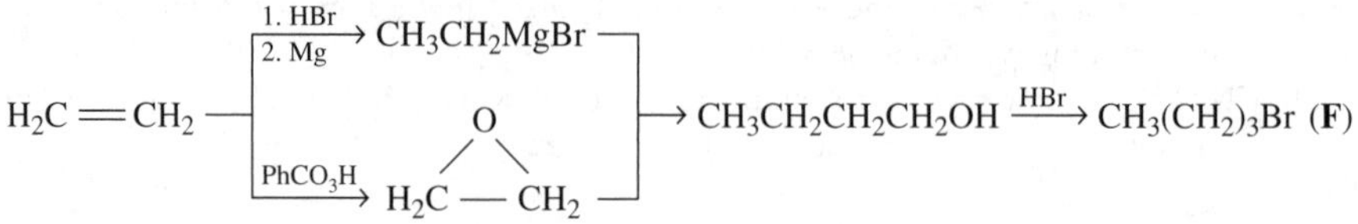

$$H_2C=CH_2 \begin{cases} \xrightarrow[\text{2. Mg}]{\text{1. HBr}} CH_3CH_2MgBr \\[2mm] \xrightarrow{PhCO_3H} \underset{H_2C-CH_2}{\overset{O}{\triangle}} \end{cases} \longrightarrow CH_3CH_2CH_2CH_2OH \xrightarrow{HBr} CH_3(CH_2)_3Br \ (\textbf{F})$$

(C)

$$PhH + CH_3CH_2Cl \xrightarrow{AlCl_3} PhCH_2CH_3 \xrightarrow{NBS} PhCHBrCH_3 \xrightarrow{\text{alc. KOH}} PhCH=CH_2$$

$$\swarrow_{\text{aq. OH}^-}$$

$$PhCH(OH)CH_3 + PhCH=CH_2 \xrightarrow[\text{2. NaBH}_4]{\text{1. Hg(OCOCF}_3)_2} C$$

Although the ether is symmetrical, dehydration of $PhCH(OH)CH_3$ cannot be used because it would readily undergo intermolecular dehydration to give the stable conjugated alkene, $PhCH=CH_2$.

303. (A) Formation of tetrahydropyranyl ethers:

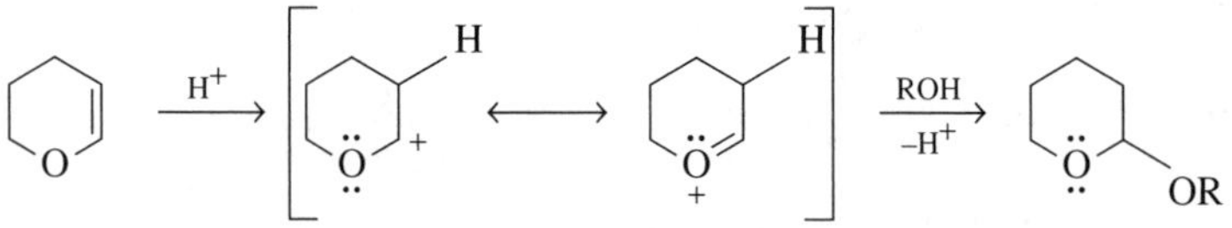

2,3-Dihydro-4H-
pyran (DHP)

A tetrahydropyranyl
ether (ROTHP)

followed by hydrolysis in aqueous acid: $ROTHP + H_2O \xrightarrow{H^+} ROH + DHP$.

(B) Formation of benzyl ethers (benzylation):

$$ROH + C_6H_5CH_2Br \xrightarrow{Ag_2O} C_6H_5CH_2OR \text{(a benzyl ether)}$$

followed by catalytic hydrogenolysis: $C_6H_5CH_2OR \xrightarrow{H_2/Pd} C_6H_5CH_3 + ROH$.

(C) Formation of silyl ethers

$$Me_3Si{-}Cl + ROH \xrightarrow{\text{amine base}} Me_3Si{-}OR$$

Chlorotrimethylsilane   A silyl ether

followed by hydrolysis with mild acid: $Me_3Si{-}OR \xrightarrow{\text{mild H}^+} ROH + Me_3Si{-}OH$.

304. (A) Add a peroxy acid, $R\overset{O}{\overset{\|}{C}}{-}OOH$ to $CH_3CH=CH_2$ any of the following—F_3CCO_3H, $PhCO_3H$, CH_3CO_3H, $m\text{-}Cl{-}C_6H_4CO_3H$ (m-chloroperoxybenzoic acid, MCPBA)—are suitable.

(B) $CH_3CH=CH_2 \xrightarrow{Cl_2, H_2O} CH_3CH(OH)CH_2Cl \xrightarrow{\text{aq. NaOH}} \text{product}$

305. The precursor of a *cis*-alkene is an alkyne. Acetylides add to epoxides by an S_N2 pathway.

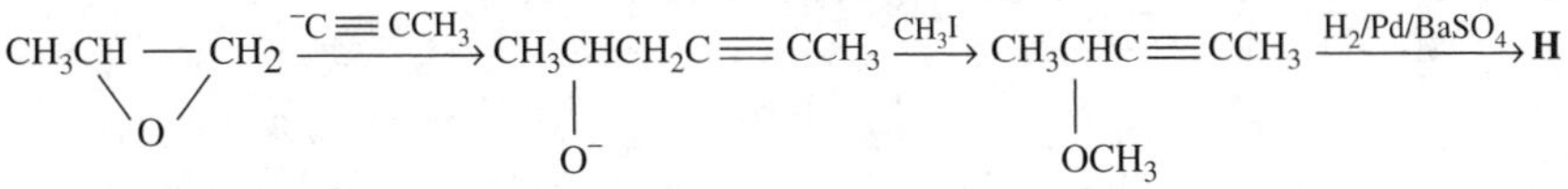

$$CH_3CH \overset{}{\underset{O}{\diagdown}} CH_2 \xrightarrow{\ ^-C\equiv CCH_3\ } CH_3CHCH_2C\equiv CCH_3 \xrightarrow{CH_3I} CH_3CHC\equiv CCH_3 \xrightarrow{H_2/Pd/BaSO_4} H$$

with O^- below the first product and OCH_3 below the second product.

306. (A) $CH_3CH(OH)CH_2OH$,

   (B) $HOCH_2CH(OH)CH_2OH$,

   (C) $HOCH_2(CHOH)_4CH_2OH$, and

   (D) $C(CH_2OH)_4$.

307. (A) See Figure A14-1.

   (B) **E**, because the two **OH** groups are diaxial and point away from each other.

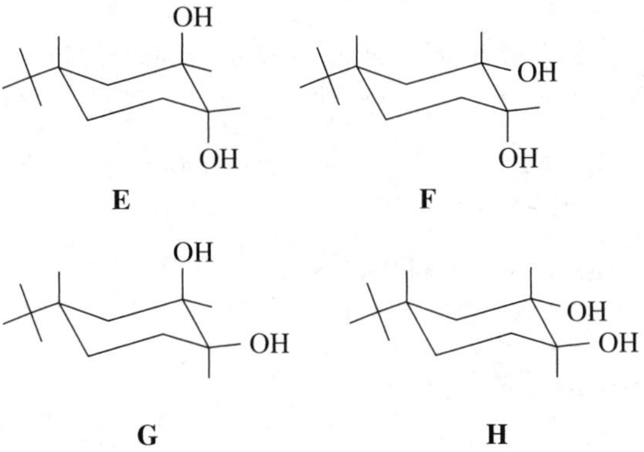

Figure A14-1

308. (A) Oxidation with cold aq. $KMnO_4$.

   (B) Dehydration with conc. H_2SO_4, followed by oxidation as in (A).

   (C) Hydrolysis with H_3O^+.

   (D) Alkaline hydrolysis with aq. OH^-.

309. (A) The common name as a sulfide (similar to naming an ether) is *n*-butyl isopropyl thioether; as an alkylthioalkane, the IUPAC name is 1-isopropylthiobutane; the *thia* method, like the oxa method for ethers (see Problem 294), gives 2-methyl-3-thiaheptane.

   (B) (I) 3-Methylthio-1-propanol (OH has priority). (II) Ethyl phenyl sulfide or ethylthiobenzene or thiophenetole. (III) Bis(2-chloroethyl) sulfide, commonly called mustard gas, a powerful vesicant used as a poisonous gas. (IV) 3-Methyl-2,4-dithiapentane. The thia method is best used for compounds with more than one sulfide linkage. (V) Phenyl *p*-tolyl sulfide. (VI) Ethylene episulfide or thirane. (VII) Tetrahydrothiophene or thiolane or thiacyclopentane (see Problem 296).

310. (A) $A = CH_3CH_2CH_2S—SCH_2CH_2CH_3$, dipropyl disulfide; $B = CH_3CH_2CH_2SH$, propanethiol (disulfides are reduced to thiols); $C = A$ (thiols are oxidized to disulfides);

D = CH₃CH₂CH₂SCl, propylsulfenyl chloride; **E** = CH₃CH₂CH₂SSCH₂CH₃, ethyl propyl disulfide (a preferred method to produce mixed disulfide).

$D = CH_3CH_2CH_2SCl$, propylsulfenyl chloride; $E = CH_3CH_2CH_2SSCH_2CH_3$, ethyl propyl disulfide (a preferred method to produce mixed disulfide).

   (B) **F** = $CH_3CH \overset{\displaystyle\diagdown\,\diagup}{\underset{S}{}} CH_2$,   propylene episulfide; **G** = $CH_3CH(SH)CH_2Ph$, 1-phenyl-2-propanethiol;

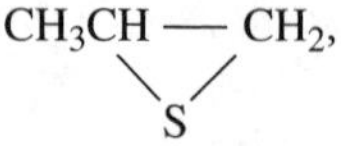

      H = $CH_3CH(SH)CH_3$,   2-propanethiol. (Episulfides and epoxides undergo ring openings in the same manner.)

   (C)

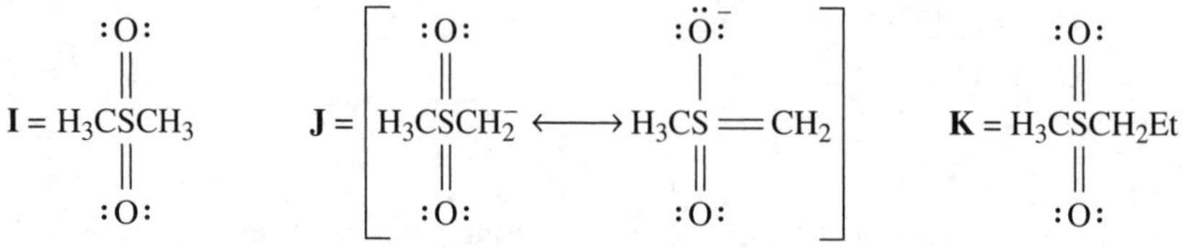

$$I = H_3CSCH_3 \qquad J = \left[H_3CSCH_2^- \longleftrightarrow H_3CS = CH_2 \right] \qquad K = H_3CSCH_2Et$$

(with $:O:$ above and $:O:$ below each sulfur, double-bonded)

Demethyl sulfone   A carbanion of dimethyl sulfone   Methyl propyl sulfone

The carbanion is stabilized by delocalization of the negative charge from the C to each **O**. One of several possible resonance structures shows the delocalization to one of the **O** atoms.

311. (A) The ether dissolves in conc. H_2SO_4; the halide does not. Alternatively, AgBr precipitates when alc. $AgNO_3$ is added to the halide.
   (B) Br_2 (in CCl_4) is decolorized by (reacts with) the alkene.
   (C) The *dry* alcohol liberates H_2 gas on addition of K.
   (D) The chloromethyl ether with $AgNO_3$ gives a precipiiate of AgCl.

Chapter 15: Aldehydes and Ketones

312. (A) Acetaldehyde
   (B) α-chloropropionaldehyde
   (C) isobutyraldehyde
   (D) acrolein,
   (E) β-hydroxyvaleraldehyde
   (F) trans-crotonaldehyde

313. (A) Ethanal
   (B) 2-chloropropanal
   (C) methylpropanal
   (D) propenal
   (E) 3-hydroxypentanal
   (F) (*E*)-2-butenal

314. (A)

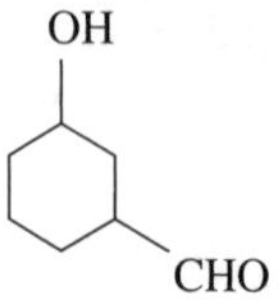

(cyclohexane ring with OH and CHO substituents)

   (B) $PhCOCH_2CH_2CH_2Br$

(C)

(D)

Me   Me

315. Carbonyl Cs absorb more downfield than any other type of C (about 200 ppm from TMS) because (I) sp^2-hybridized Cs resonate more downfield from sp^3-hybridized Cs and (II) the polar nature of $C=O$ causes additional diminished shielding. These effects diminish for Cs farther away from the $C=O$.

316. Stretching of the polar $C=O$ bond causes a large change in the dipole moment, resulting in a strong band at about 1725 cm^{-1} for RCHOs and 1715 cm^{-1} for R'CORs. In cyclic ketones, as the size of the ring decreases from 7 to 3, the frequency increases from 1705 to 1850 cm^{-1}. Conjugation shifts the carbonyl absorption to lower frequencies. Aldehydes also have a characteristic C—H stretching absorption doublet at 2720 and 2820 cm^{-1}.

317. (A) $CH_3OH + O_2 \xrightarrow[Ag]{600°C} H_2CO$

(B) $PhCH_3 \xrightarrow[\Delta]{Cl_2} PhCHCl_2 \xrightarrow[OH^-]{H_2O} PhCHO$

(C) $HC\equiv CH \xrightarrow[H_3O^+]{HgSO_4} CH_3CHO$

or $H_2C=CH_2 + O_2 \xrightarrow[H_2O]{PdCl_2,CuCl_2} CH_3CHO$ (Wacker process)

318. (A)

$CH_3CH_2CH_2OH$ —
$\xrightarrow[ZnCl_2]{HCl} CH_3CH_2CH_2Cl \xrightarrow{Mg/ether} CH_3CH_2CH_2MgCl(A)$
$\xrightarrow[Py]{CrO_3} CH_3CH_2CHO(B) \xrightarrow{A} CH_3CH_2CHCH_2CH_2CH_3 \xrightarrow[OH^-]{KMnO_4} CH_3CH_2CCH_2CH_2CH_3$
$\quad\quad\quad\quad\quad\quad\quad\quad\quad\quad |OH \quad\quad\quad\quad\quad\quad\quad\quad ||O$

(B) $HC\equiv CH \xrightarrow[liq.NH_3]{NaNH_2} HC\equiv C:^- \xrightarrow{CH_3CH_2CH_2Cl}$
$CH_3CH_2CH_2C\equiv CH \xrightarrow[2.H_2O_2,OH^-]{1.Sia_2BH} CH_3CH_2CH_2CH_2CHO$

(C) $(CH_3)_2CHOH \xrightarrow{SOCl_2} (CH_3)_2CHCl \xrightarrow{Mg/ether} (CH_3)_2CHMgCl \xrightarrow{+B}$
$(CH_3)_2CHCHOHCH_2CH_3 \xrightarrow[H^+]{Cr_2O_7^{2-}} (CH_3)_2CHCOCH_2CH_3$

319. Reduction of RCOOR' with LiAlH$_4$ gives RCH$_2$OH, since the intermediate aldehyde RCHO is generally susceptible to further reduction. If one equivalent of the *less* reactive $(i\text{-}C_4H_9)_2$ AlH, diisobutylaluminum hydride (DBAH), is used at $-70°C$ followed by hydrolysis, RCHO is obtained in good yield.

320. (A) $A = C_6H_5CH(OCOCH_3)_2$, $B = C_6H_5CHO$
(B) $C = p\text{-}CH_3C_6H_4CHO$
(C) $D = C_6H_5CH_2CHO$. In **A**, the formation of the acetal ester prevents oxidation of the intermediate aldehyde to —COOH.

321. 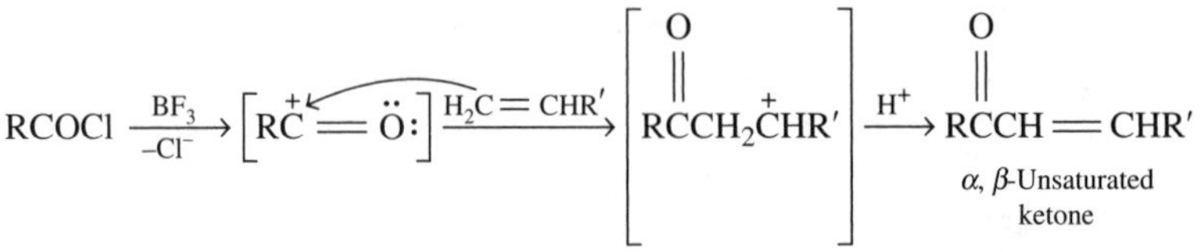 $RCOCl \xrightarrow[-Cl^-]{BF_3} \left[R\overset{+}{C} = \overset{\cdot\cdot}{O}: \right] \xrightarrow{H_2C=CHR'} \left[\underset{\text{O}}{\overset{\text{O}}{\parallel}} RCCH_2\overset{+}{C}HR' \right] \xrightarrow{H^+} \underset{\substack{\alpha,\ \beta\text{-Unsaturated} \\ \text{ketone}}}{\overset{\text{O}}{\underset{}{RCCH=CHR'}}}$

This is a Markovnikov addition initiated by the acylium ion.

322. This electrophilic aromatic substitution, a formylation, is the *Gatterman–Koch* reaction.
(A) C_6H_5CHO
(B) $p\text{-}CH_3OC_6H_4CHO$ (+ *some ortho*)

323. (A) $H_2C{=}O + H_2O \rightleftharpoons H_2C(OH)_2$

(B) $Me_2C{=}O + H_2O \rightleftharpoons Me_2C(OH)_2$

324.

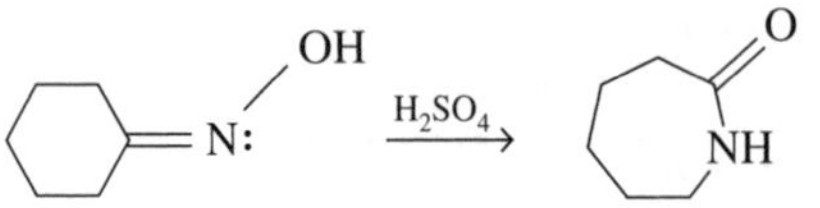

ε-Caprolactam
(a cyclic amide)

325. (A) Clemmensen reduction. Strong base causes dehydrohalogenation. $HSCH_2CH_2CH_2SH$ can displace Br^-.
  (B) and **(C)** Wolff–Kishner reduction or desulfurization. In **(B)** the 3°OH is dehydrated in acid. In **(C)** the 2°OH is easily dehydrated because the C=C formed is conjugated with the benzene ring, **(D)** None. All methods lead to opening of the epoxide ring.

326. (A) $PhCH_2OH + PhCOO^-$
(B) $Me_3CCH_2OH + Me_3CCOO^-$
(C)

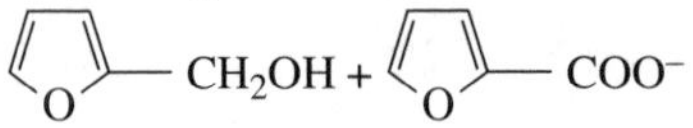

327. (A) $PhCH_2OH + HCOO^-$
(B) $Me_3CCH_2OH + HCOO^-$

328. Two chiral Cs are formed in this reaction, leading to a racemate and a *meso* structure:

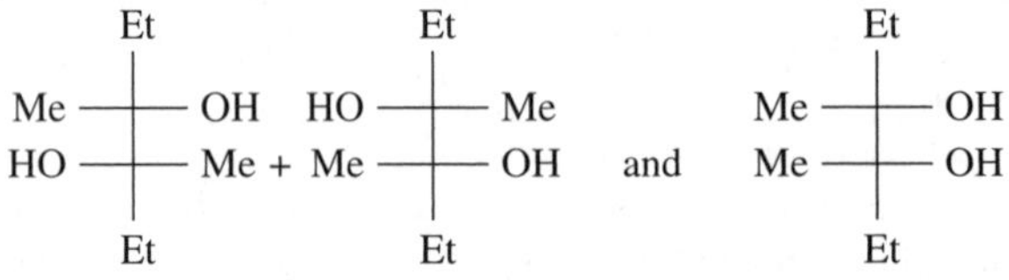

| Racemate | Mirror image | *meso* |

329. (A) $CH_3CH_2CH{=}O + RO\cdot \longrightarrow CH_3CH_2\dot{C}{=}O + ROH$

(B) $CH_3CH_2C{=}O + H_2C{=}CHCH_3 \longrightarrow CH_3CH_2C{-}CH_2CHCH_3$
$\qquad\qquad\qquad\qquad\qquad\qquad\qquad\qquad\qquad\quad \overset{\|}{O}$

(C) $CH_3CH_2\underset{\underset{O}{\|}}{C}CH_2CHCH_3 + CH_3CH_2\underset{\underset{O}{\|}}{C}{-}H \longrightarrow CH_3CH_2\underset{\underset{O}{\|}}{C}CH_2CH_2CH_3 + CH_3CH_2\underset{\underset{O}{\|}}{C}\cdot$

(A) is the initiation step; **(B)** and **(C)** propagate the chain.

330. This *benzoin condensation* competes favorably with cyanohydrin formation when aromatic aldehydes are used. The product, a dimer, is $PhCH(OH)COPh$.

331. (A) and **(B)** The aldehydes give a positive Tollen's test with $Ag(NH_3)_2^+$ (Ag mirror). Also, in **(A)** only the aldehyde gives a precipitate with either H_2NOH or $PhNHNH_2$. **(C)** Only the alcohol is oxidized by CrO_3 (color change from orange-red to green); alternatively, the ketone gives a solid oxime or phenylhydrazone with H_2NOH or $PhNHNH_2$, respectively. **(D)** Only the aldehyde gives a positive Tollen's test; only the ketone gives a positive iodoform test (precipitate of CHI_3).

332. (A) The oxidation to benzoic acid reveals that there is one side chain with the three remaining Cs. The formula reveals 5° of unsaturation, 4° for the ring and 1° in the side chain. The extra degree of unsaturation must be due to a $C{=}O$ (positive test with DNPH) and not to $C{=}C$ (negative test with Br_2). The possible structures are

$$PhCOCH_2CH_3 \qquad PhCH_2COCH_3 \qquad PhCH_2CH_2CHO \qquad PhCH(CH_3)CHO$$
$$\quad\text{I} \qquad\qquad\qquad \text{II} \qquad\qquad\qquad\quad \text{III} \qquad\qquad\qquad\quad \text{IV}$$

(B) The aldehydes, **III** and **IV**, are distinguished from the ketones by undergoing mild oxidation with cold $KMnO_4$. **II** can be distinguished from **I** by the haloform test; it gives a precipitate of the pale yellow CHI_3 when reacted with KI/OH^-. **III** and **IV** cannot be differentiated by any simple chemical tests.

Chapter 16: Carboxylic Acids

333. With common names, positions of substituents are shown by Greek letters α, β, γ, δ. The α-C is attached to the COOH group.

    (A) Chloroacetic acid. (α is not needed here because there is only one other C in the chain.)

    (B) β-Nitropropionic acid

    (C) γ-bromobutyric acid

    (D) α, α-dimethylpropionic acid

    (E) δ-formylvaleric acid. (COOH has naming priority over CHO which as a functional group is called formyl.)

    (F) α, β, γ-Tribromobutyric acid

    (G) α-fluoro-γ-hydroxybutyric acid

    (H) β-ketovaleric acid. (With common names *keto* indicates O= on a chain.)

334. The IUPAC system replaces the *-e* of the corresponding alkane with *-oic acid*. The required names are methanoic, ethanoic, propanoic, butanoic, pentanoic, and hexanoic acids.

335. **(A)** (I) 3-Phenylpropanoic acid; (II) propenoic acid (the common name is acrylic acid); (III) 2-butenoic acid, *cis* or *trans* (common name is crotonic acid); (IV) 3-formylpentanoic acid; if the CHO is not part of the longest chain, it is named as a *formyl* substituent.

    (B) Carboxy

336. Substituted phenyl carboxylic acids are named as benzoic acids.

    (A) Benzoic acid, the parent acid

    (B) *p*-nitrobenzoic acid

    (C) 3, 5-dibromobenzoic acid

    (D) *m*-formylbenzoic acid (COOH takes priority over CHO; thus it is named as an acid, not as an aldehyde)

    (E) *o*-methylbenzoic acid, commonly called *o*-toluic acid from toluene

    (F) 2- (or β-) naphthoic acid

337. **(A)** *Fatty acids* are long-chain aliphatic acids derived by hydrolysis from naturally occurring fats and oils.

    (B) (I) Palmitic or hexadecanoic acid; (II) stearic or octadecanoic acid; (III) oleic or *cis*-9-octadecenoic acid; (IV) linoleic or *cis*, *cis*-9, 12-octadecadienoic acid; (V) linolenic or *cis*, *cis*, *cis*-9, 12, 15-octadecatrienoic acid.

338. **(A)**

Benzene-1,2-
dicarboxylic acid

(B)

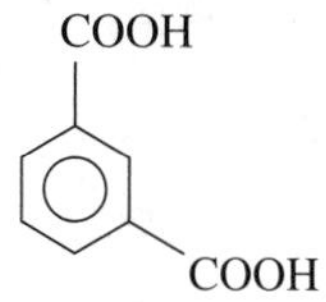

COOH

COOH

Benzene-1,3-
dicarboxylic acid

(C)

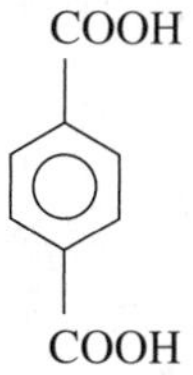

COOH

COOH

Benzene-1,4-
dicarboxylic acid

(D)

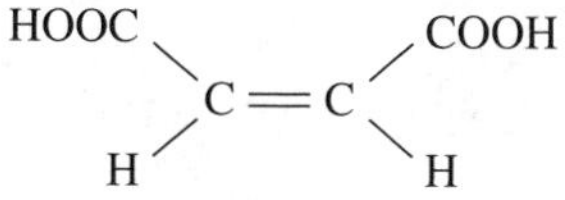

$$\begin{array}{c} HOOC \\ \diagdown \\ H \diagup \end{array} C = C \begin{array}{c} \diagup COOH \\ \diagdown H \end{array}$$

cis-Butenedioic acid

(E)

$$\begin{array}{c} HOOC \\ \diagdown \\ H \diagup \end{array} C = C \begin{array}{c} \diagup H \\ \diagdown COOH \end{array}$$

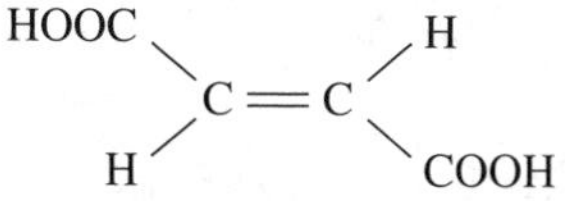

trans-Butenedioic acid

(F) HOOCCH(OH)CH(OH)COOH
    2,3-Dihydroxybutanedioic acid

(G) HOOCCH$_2$C(OH)CH$_2$COOH
                    |
                    COOH
    3-Hydroxy-1,2,3-propanetricarboxylic acid

Carboxylic acids with at least three COOHs are named as alkanepolycarboxylic acids because only two COOHs can be part of the longest chain.

339. CH$_3$COOH undergoes intermolecular H-bonding and exists as the dimer

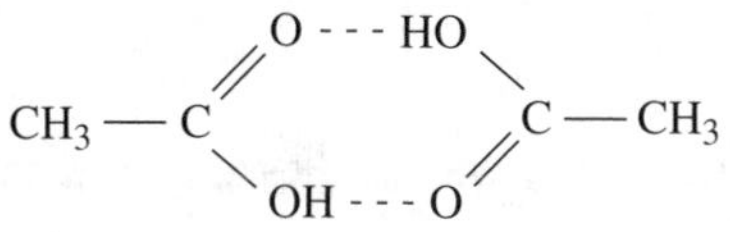

$$CH_3 - C \begin{array}{c} \diagup O - - - HO \\ \diagdown OH - - - O \end{array} C - CH_3$$

340. (A) (I), (II) In both cases the number of Cs in the precursor and in the acid is the same. This signals the need for oxidation. Acidified KMnO$_4$ can be used for both.

(B) It is necessary to first nitrate $PhCH_3$, because —COOH is a *meta* director, and then oxidize.

$$PhCH_3 \xrightarrow[H_2SO_4]{HNO_3} p\text{-}NO_2C_6H_4CH_3 \xrightarrow[H^+, \Delta]{KMnO_4} p\text{-}NO_2C_6H_4COOH$$

The presence of the electron-withdrawing NO_2 encourages the oxidation of the phenyl side chain.

(C) Adipic acid can be prepared by oxidative cleavage of cyclohexene prepared from benzene.

$$C_6H_6 \xrightarrow{H_2/Pd} \underset{\text{Cyclohexane}}{C_6H_{12}} \xrightarrow[h\nu]{Cl_2} \underset{\text{Chlorocylohexane}}{C_6H_{11}Cl}$$

$$\xrightarrow{\text{alc. KOH}} \underset{\text{Cyclohexene}}{C_6H_{10}} \xrightarrow[H^+]{KMnO_4} \underset{\text{Adipic acid}}{HOOC(CH_2)_4COOH}$$

Industrially, cyclohexane is oxidized directly.

341. (A) In the absence of an electron-withdrawing substituent, the oxidation of toluene goes in poor yields.

$$C_6H_6 \xrightarrow{Br_2/Fe} C_6H_5Br \xrightarrow[\substack{2.\,CO_2 \\ 3.\,H^+}]{1.\,Mg} C_6H_5COOH$$

(B) $CH_3C_6H_5 \xrightarrow{Br_2/Fe} p\text{-}CH_3C_6H_4Br \xrightarrow[\substack{2.\,CO_2 \\ 3.\,H^+}]{1.\,Mg} p\text{-}CH_3C_6H_4COOH$

(C) 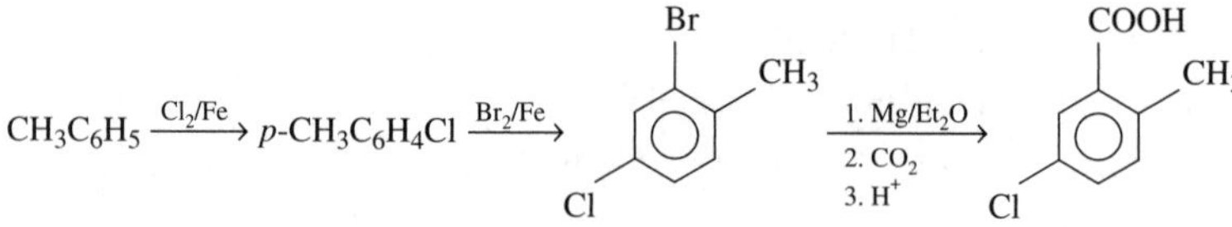 $CH_3C_6H_5 \xrightarrow{Cl_2/Fe} p\text{-}CH_3C_6H_4Cl \xrightarrow{Br_2/Fe}$

In ether, aryl chlorides are inert toward Grignard formation; aryl bromides react. In tetrahydrofuran (oxacyclopentane), ArCl reacts.

(D) $p\text{-}CH_3C_6H_4Br \xrightarrow{NBS} p\text{-}BrCH_2C_6H_4Br \xrightarrow{2Mg}$

$$p\text{-}BrMgCH_2C_6H_4MgBr \xrightarrow[2.\,H_3O^+]{1.\,2CO_2} p\text{-}HOOCC_6H_4CH_2COOH$$

(E) 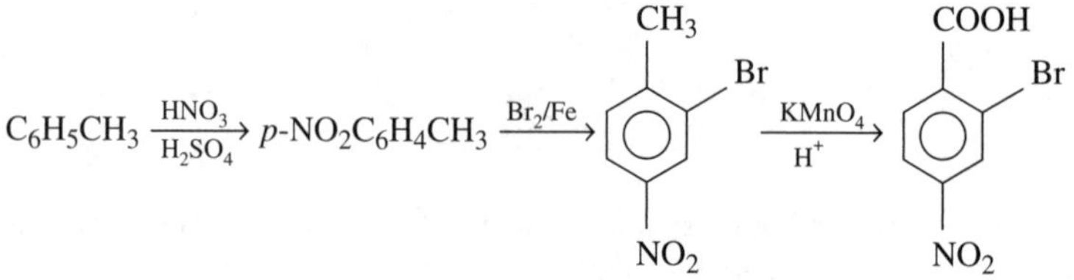 $C_6H_5CH_3 \xrightarrow[H_2SO_4]{HNO_3} p\text{-}NO_2C_6H_4CH_3 \xrightarrow{Br_2/Fe}$

(F)

$$C_6H_5CH_3 \xrightarrow{2Br_2/Fe} \quad \xrightarrow{\text{dicarbonation}} \quad \xrightarrow[H^+]{KMnO_4}$$

342. **(A)** $CH_3OH_4 + CO \xrightarrow{Rh/I_2} CH_3COOH$ (major method);

$$CH_3CHO \xrightarrow[\text{catalyst}]{O_2} CH_3COOH$$

(B) $CO + NaOH \longrightarrow HCOO^-Na^+ \xrightarrow{H_2SO_4} HCOOH$

343. When naming the anion (conjugate base) of the carboxylic acid, exchange the suffix *-ate* for *-ic* and drop *acid*.
  (A) $CH_3COOH + NaOH \longrightarrow H_2O + CH_3COO^-Na^+$, sodium acetate
  (B) $2CH_3CH_2COOH + Ca(OH)_2 \longrightarrow 2H_2O + (CH_3CH_2COO^-)_2Ca^{2+}$, calcium propionate (a food preservative)
  (C) $3CH_3(CH_2)_{16}COOH + Fe^{3+} + 3OAc^- \longrightarrow 3HOAc + [CH_3(CH_2)_{16}COO^-]_3$ Fe(s), ferric stearate. Heavy metal salts of fatty acids are insoluble in water.

344. **(A)** A soap has two distinctly different portions. The charged COO^- polar end ("head") is hydrophilic and tends to project into the water. The large alkyl portion ("tail") is hydrophobic and tends to avoid water. In a colloidal soap solution, the soap molecules form a sphere with their tails pointing inward toward each other, affording a congenial water-free environment. Their heads on the surface of the sphere, face the stabilizing water medium. The sphere-like structure, shown in cross section in Figure A16-1(A), is called a *micelle*. Solid dots represent the polar heads and the wavy lines the nonpolar tails buried in the interior.
  (B) The micelles do not coalesce because of the repulsions between their like-charged surfaces.
  (C) Most dirt is held to surfaces, such as skin and in clothing, by thin films of oil or grease which are nonpolar hydrophobic materials. When the dirty object is agitated with soap (or with other detergents), the oil is dispersed into very fine droplets that dissolve in the interiors of the micelles. The micelles with the trapped oil [see Figure A16-1(B)], still with an affinity for water because of their ionic shells, wash away.

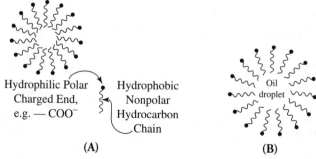

Hydrophilic Polar
Charged End,
e.g. — COO^-

Hydrophobic
Nonpolar
Hydrocarbon
Chain

Oil
droplet

(A)

(B)

Figure A16-1

345. (A) $RCOOH + H_2O \rightleftharpoons RCOO^- + H_3O^+$; $K_a = \dfrac{[RCOO^-][H_3O^+]}{[RCOOH]}$

    (B) $\Delta G° = -2.30 RT \log K_a = \Delta H° - T\Delta S°$ or $pK_a = (\Delta H° - T\Delta S°)/2.30\,RT$
A more negative $\Delta H°$ or a more positive $T\Delta S°$ makes K_a larger and pK_a smaller; the acid becomes stronger.

    (C) (I) Electronic effects such as induction, field effect, and resonance. (II) Solvation effects. The better the anion is solvated, the more the equilibrium is driven to the right and the stronger is the acid. Better solvation does not necessarily mean *more* water molecules are constrained.

    (D) H_3O^+ is present in the aqueous solutions of all acids; it is a common factor and can be disregarded.

346. *Meta* directing, deactivating substituents, such as —NO_2, are acid strengtheners. When *ortho*, *para* directing activating groups such as OH and Me are *para* to —COO^-, these acids are weaker than PhCOOH. Their effect from the *meta* position is not easily predictable.

347. (A) (I) Both, (II) BH_3/THF, (III) both, (IV) BH_3/THF, (V) $LiAlH_4$, (VI) BH_3/THF.
    (B) (I) $CH_3CH(CH_3)CH_2CH_2OH$, (II) p-$CH_3COC_6H_4CH_2OH$,

    (III) ⟨cyclohexane with H⟩— CH_2OH, (IV) m-$O_2NC_6H_4CH_2OH$,

    (V) (Z)-$CH_3CH{=}CHCH_2CH_2OH$, (VI) $Br(CH_2)_3CH_2OH$.

348. (A) $CH_3CH_2 + COOH \xrightarrow{\text{Br}_2/\text{PBr}_3}$

    $CH_3CH_2COBr \xrightarrow{\text{Br}_2} CH_3CHBrCOBr \xrightarrow{\text{H}_2\text{O}} CH_3CHBrCOOH$
       Acid bromide α-Bromoacid bromide α-Bromoacid

    (B) CH_3CBr_2COOH.
    (C) No reaction, the acid does not have an α H, necessary for the reaction.
    (D) (I) The same product and (II) 2-chloropropanoic acid. The α halogen comes from X_2.

349. (A) I. $CH_3CH_2COOH \xrightarrow{\text{CH}_3\text{MgBr}} CH_3CH_2COO^-(MgBr)^+ + CH_4$

    II. $CH_3CH_2COOH \xrightarrow[-\text{CH}_4]{\text{CH}_3\text{Li}} CH_3CH_2COO^-Li^+ \xrightarrow{\text{CH}_3\text{Li}} CH_3CH_2\overset{\displaystyle CH_3}{\overset{\displaystyle |}{C}}(O^-Li^+)_2$
                                                                   Dialkoxide of a *gem*-diol

Water converts the dianion into the diol that decomposes to the ketone, $CH_3CH_2COCH_3$, the final product.

    (B) The more electropositive the metal (M) of the R—M bond, the more ionic is the bond. Li is more electropositive than Mg. R from R—Li bears more – charge than R from R—MgX, and thus is a stronger nucleophile capable of adding to the C=O of COO^-.

350. Dehydrohalogenate 2-chlorobutanoic acid and add HCl to the product, 2-butenoic acid. H^+ adds to give a + on the β-carbon, which then bonds to Cl^-.

$$CH_3CH_2CHClCOOH \xrightarrow{\text{alc. KOH}} CH_3CH=CHCOOH \xrightarrow{H^+}$$

$$\begin{array}{cc} & H \\ & | \\ CH_3\overset{+}{C}HCHCOOH & \xrightarrow{Cl^-} \end{array}$$

$$\begin{array}{c} H \\ | \\ CH_3CHClCHCOOH \end{array}$$

The α-R^+ is not formed because its + would be next to the $C^{\delta+}$ of COOH:

$$\begin{array}{cc} H & O^{\delta-} \\ | & \| \\ CH_3CH\overset{+}{C}HC-OH \\ & {\scriptstyle \delta+} \end{array}$$

351. Stearic acid, $CH_3(CH_2)_{16}COOH$, has 18 Cs.

(A) Three Cs must be lost, two by oxidation and one by brominative decarboxylation (Hunsdiecker reaction).

$$CH_3(CH_2)_{14}CH_2CH_2COOH \xrightarrow{Br_2/PBr_3} CH_3(CH_2)_{14}CH_2CHBrCOOH \xrightarrow[2.\,H^+]{1.\,\text{alc. KOH}}$$

$$CH_3(CH_2)_{14}CH=CHCOOH \xrightarrow[\Delta]{KMnO_4} CH_3(CH_2)_{14}COOH \xrightarrow[2.\,Br_2]{1.\,Ag^+} CH_3(CH_2)_{14}Br$$

(B) This synthesis is a step up.

$$CH_3(CH_2)_{16}COOH \xrightarrow{LiAlH_4} CH_3(CH_2)_{16}CH_2OH \xrightarrow{SOCl_2}$$

$$CH_3(CH_2)_{16}CH_2Cl \xrightarrow[\substack{2.\,CO_2 \\ 3.\,H^+}]{1.\,Mg}$$

$$CH_3(CH_2)_{16}CH_2COOH \xrightarrow{LiAlH_4} CH_3(CH_2)_{18}OH$$

352. (A) (I) Consider a Cl in place of —COOH and —OH in place of =O. Then

$$\text{Cyclopentanol} \xrightarrow{H_2SO_4} \text{cyclopentene} \xrightarrow{Cl_2/H_2O}$$

$$\text{2-chlorocyclopentanol} \xrightarrow{CN^-} \text{2-cyanocyclopentanol} \xrightarrow{H_3O^+}$$

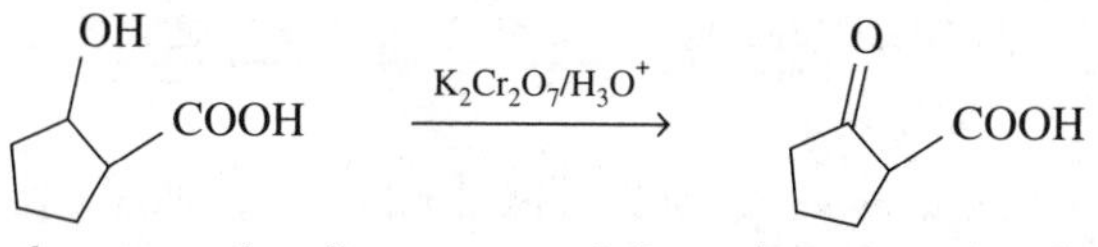

2-Hydroxycyclopentanecarboxylic acid

$$\xrightarrow{K_2Cr_2O_7/H_3O^+}$$

2-Oxocyclopentanecarboxylic acid

(II)

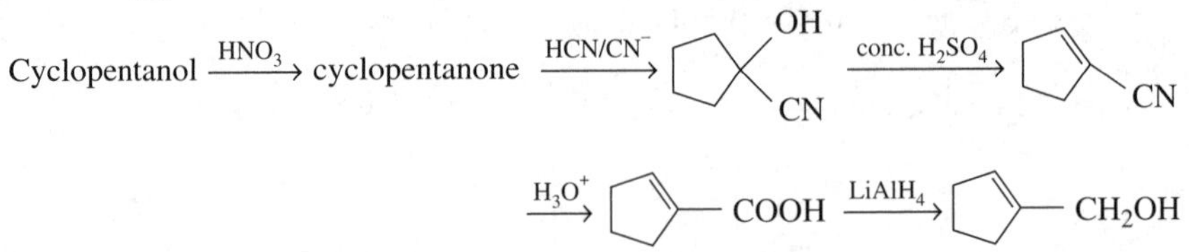

Cyclopentanol $\xrightarrow{HNO_3}$ cyclopentanone $\xrightarrow{HCN/CN^-}$ OH / CN $\xrightarrow{conc.\ H_2SO_4}$ CN

$\xrightarrow{H_3O^+}$ COOH $\xrightarrow{LiAlH_4}$ CH$_2$OH

1-Cyclopentenylmethanol

Were the hydroxyacid made first, an attempt to dehydrate it in conc. H_2SO_4 would lead to some decarbomonoxylation.

(B) Use the Diels–Alder reaction to make the cyclohexane ring. To get *cis* COOHs, use maleic acid as the dienophile with 1, 3-butadiene as the diene.

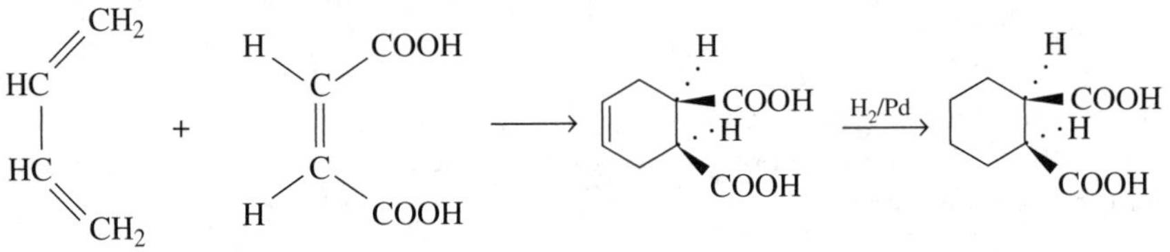

353. (A) The *neutralization equivalent* (NE) is the equivalent weight (g/eq) of an acid as determined by titration with standardized NaOH.

(B) The number of ionizable Hs of an acid is the number of equivalents per mole, and it is equal to MW/NE. Here the number of equivalents (number of ionizable Hs) = (210 g/mol)/ (70 g/eq) = 3 eq/mol. The number of equivalents of NaOH equals the number of ionizable Hs, in this case 3 eq/mol.

(C) The neutralization equivalent of mellitic acid is

$$NE = \frac{MW}{\text{number of ionizable H's}} = \frac{342\ g/mol}{6\ eq/mol} = 57\ g/eq$$

354. A is $CH_3(CH_2)_{14}CH_2OH$, B is $CH_3(CH_2)_{14}CH_2Cl$, C is $CH_3(CH_2)_{16}CH_2OH$, and D is $CH_3(CH_2)_{16}COOH$ (stearic acid).

Chapter 17: Acid Derivatives

355. Replace *-ic acid* by *-yl halide*.

(A) (I) Propanoyl chloride, (II) 3, 3-dimethylbutanoyl chloride, (III) 2-bromopentanoyl bromide, (IV) 3-hexenoyl chloride, and (V) 2-cyclopentanecarbonyl chloride.

(B) (I) Propionyl chloride, (II) β, β-dimethylbutyryl chloride, and (III) α -bromovaleryl bromide.

356. Name the acid or acids, if it is a mixed anhydride, followed by the word *anhydride*.

(A) Benzoic anhydride

(B) acetic benzoic anhydride

(C) α-chloropropionic anhydride
(D) hexanoic (or caproic) propionic anhydride
(E) 4-nitrophthalic anhydride
(F) maleic anhydride

357. First name the group bonded to —O—; then replace *-ic acid* by *-ate.*
(A) (I) *n*-Propyl acetate, (II) methyl cyclopentanecarboxylate, (III) isopropyl β-bromobutyrate, (IV) di-*n*-propylmalonate, (V) ethyl hydrogen oxalate, (VI) *sec*-butyl acrylate (or propenoate).
(B) (I) Propyl ethanoate, (II) same name, (III) isopropyl 3-bromobutanoate, (IV) dipropyl propanedioate.

358. In general, change *-ic acid* to *-amide.* Amides of $PhNH_2$ are named as anilides. Amides with Rs on N are named by writing N before the name of the R group.
(A) Propionamide
(B) acetanilide
(C) *p*-toluamide
(D) glutaramide
(E) N-ethylisobutyramide
(F) cyclobutanecarboxamide

359. (A) PhCONHPh
(B) *n*-C₄H₉OCO(CH₂)₄COOC₄H₉-*n*
(C) CH₃CO(CH₂)₃COBr

(D)

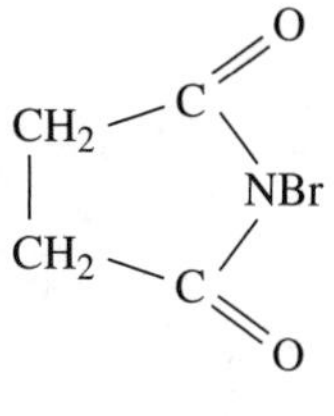

(E)

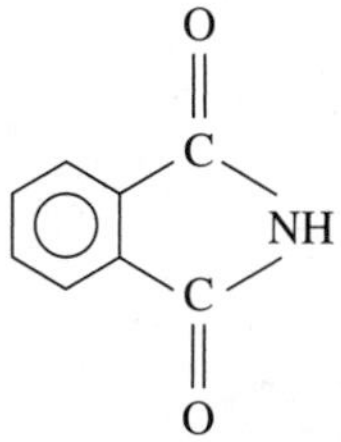

(F)

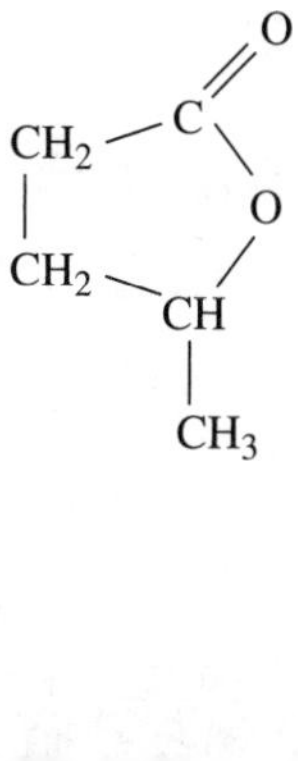

(G)

$$\overset{\displaystyle O}{\underset{\displaystyle \|}{}}$$
COMe
Br

(H)

$$\underset{H}{\overset{Ph}{}}C = C \underset{H}{\overset{CCl}{\overset{O}{\|}}}$$

360. (A) (I) $RCONHNH_2$, (II) $RCON_3$, (III) $RCOSH$, (IV) $RCOSR$; (V) $RCONHOH$.

(B) The acyl group $R-\overset{O}{\underset{\|}{C}}-$ is bonded to a heteroatom, N, in (I), (II), and (V), and S in (III) and (IV).

361. (A)

$$R-\overset{:O:}{\underset{\|}{C}}-G: \longleftrightarrow R-\overset{:\overset{..}{O}:^{-}}{\underset{|}{\overset{}{C}}}-G: \longleftrightarrow R-\overset{:\overset{..}{O}:^{-}}{\underset{|}{C}}=G^{+} \quad or \quad \left[R-\overset{O^{\delta^{-}}}{\underset{\delta^{+}}{\overset{|}{C}}} \cdots G^{\delta^{+}} \right]$$

A   **B**   **C**   Hybrid

(B) Electron release from G to O stabilizes C=O by diminishing the electrophilic character of C.

362. (A) Because of the delocalization of e^-s in the ester, the + on C of C=O is more spread out, resulting in a smaller dipole moment and weaker dipole-dipole attraction than in ketones,

(B) Acids have strong intermolecular H-bonds, lacking in esters.

363. (A)

$$R-\overset{:O:}{\underset{\|}{C}}-G+:Nu^{-} \underset{slow}{\rightleftharpoons} R-\underset{\underset{Nu}{|}}{\overset{:\overset{..}{O}:^{-}}{\underset{|}{C}}}-G \underset{fast}{\rightleftharpoons} R-\overset{:O:}{\underset{\|}{C}}-Nu+:G^{-}$$

Unstable intermediate

(B)

$$R-\overset{:O:}{\underset{\|}{C}}-G \underset{}{\overset{H^{+}}{\rightleftharpoons}} R-\overset{^{+}:OH}{\underset{\|}{C}}-G \underset{HNu:, slow}{\rightleftharpoons} R-\underset{\underset{HNu^{+}}{|}}{\overset{:\overset{..}{O}H}{\underset{|}{C}}}-G \underset{-HG, fast}{\rightleftharpoons} R-\overset{^{+}:OH}{\underset{\|}{C}}-Nu \underset{-H^{+}}{\rightleftharpoons} R-\overset{:O:}{\underset{\|}{C}}-Nu$$

Unstable intermediate

364. (A) PCl_3, $SOCl_2$, and PCl_5. **(B)** $SOCl_2$, because the by-products of the reaction are the gases SO_2 and HCl, which are easily separated from the product:

$$RCOOH + SOCl_2 \longrightarrow RCOCl + SO_2(g) + HCl(g)$$

(C) (I) PBr_3, (II) NaF + anhydrous HF.

365. (A) Transesterification is the reaction of an ester with an alcohol, different from the one in the ester, to give a new ester:

$$RCOOR' + R''OH \rightleftharpoons RCOOR'' + R'OH$$

(B) $CH_3COOC_5H_{11}$ and CH_3CH_2OH. In this case, the lower boiling ethanol is distilled off as it forms, driving the equilibrium to the right and making the conversion feasible.

366. (A) **A** is $HOOCCH_2CH_2COOMe$; **B** is $ClCOCH_2CH_2COOMe$; **C** is $MeNHCOCH_2CH_2COOMe$.

(B) **D** is

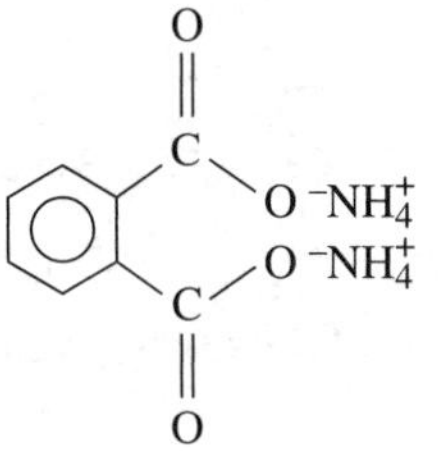

E is

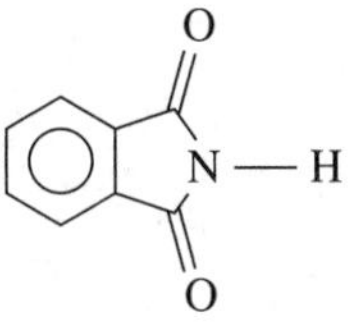

Ammonium phthalate   Phthalimide (a cyclic imide)

(C) **F** is

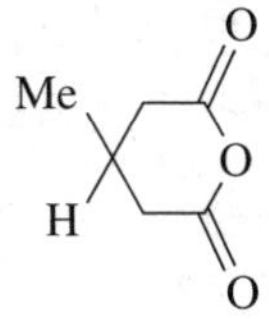

β-Methylglutaric anhydride

367. (A) RCls are much less reactive than RCOCls because (I) of the tendency of the O of C=O to attract e⁻s makes the C more positive and electrophilic; (II) the TS of the acid derivative leading to the tetrahedral intermediate is less sterically hindered than the TS with pentavalent C in the S_N2 reaction of RX; (III) a σ bond must be partially broken to form the alkyl TS, and a weaker π bond is broken in the acyl case.

(B) In each case, the addition step leads to a tetrahedral intermediate. However, the intermediate from the carbonyl compound would have to eliminate the very strong bases H:⁻ or R:⁻ from RCHO and RCOR', respectively, to restore the C=O. Instead, the intermediate alkoxide accepts an H⁺ to give the adduct. The intermediate from the acyl derivative easily eliminates G:⁻ (or GH).

368. (A) Pd/C, poisoned with quinoline and S (Rosenmund reaction) or LBAH.
 (B) NH_3 to form amide, followed by $LiAlH_4$.
 (C) $LiAlH_4$.
 (D) $PhCH_2OH$ from **(C)**, H^+.
 (E) Aq. NaOH to form $PhCOO^-Na^+$, followed by reaction with PhCOCl or heat with $(CH_3CO)_2O$.
 (F) $PhCH_2NH_2$ from **(B)**.

369. (A) **A** is $PhCOCH_2CH_3$
 (B) **B** is $(i\text{-}Bu)_2CuLi$, **C** is $PhCOCH_2CH(CH_3)_2$
 (C) **D** is $PhCOCH_3$
 (D) **E** is $PhCH_2C(OH)(n\text{-}C_4H_9)_2$
 (E) **F** is $H_2C{=}CHCH_2COPh$

370. (A) $RCONH_2 + HONO \longrightarrow RCOOH + N_2 + H_2O$

 (B) $\underset{\substack{\| \\ O}}{R - C} - NHR' + HONO \longrightarrow R - \underset{\substack{\| \\ O}}{C} - \underset{\substack{| \\ R'}}{N} - N{=}O$ (an N-nitrosoamide)

 (C) $RCONR'2$ does not react.

371. (A) $\mathbf{A} = CH_3CH_2CON_3$; $\mathbf{B} = CH_3CH_2NCO$; $\mathbf{C} = CH_3CH_2NH_2$. This *Curtius* rearrangement occurs with loss of CO_2.
 (B) $\mathbf{D} = CH_3CH_2CONHOH$. In this *Lossen* reaction, the hydroxamic acid rearranges to give the isocyanate **B**, which forms the amine **C** on reacting with H_2O.

372. (A) (I) A *lipid* is a water-insoluble substance extracted from cells by nonpolar organic solvents, (II) A triglyceride, also called *triacylglycerol,* is a triacylated ester of glycerol. (III) *Fat* is a triglyceride that is solid at room temperature. It is usually derived from animal fats such as beef fat or butter. (IV) *Oil* is a triglyceride that is liquid at room temperature, and is extracted from plants (such as corn or peanuts) or cold-blooded animals (fish). (V) *Wax* is an ester made up of a long-chain fatty acid ($\geq C_{16}$) or a long-chain alcohol ($\geq C_{16}$), e.g., beeswax.
 (B) The carboxylate parts of an oil usually have one or more *cis*-oriented double bonds, whereas those of fats have little or no unsaturation.
 (C) Steroids, such as cholesterol and terpenes.

373. (A) (I) $O{=}P(OMe)_3$ (II) $EtP(OMe)_2$ (III)

 (B) $3ROH + O{=}PCl_3 \longrightarrow (RO)_3P{=}O + 3HCl$

374. (A) (I) MeCONHMe, (II) MeCONHPh, (III) PhCONHMe, (IV)

(B) PCl_5 or acid converts the OH of the oxime into a better leaving group by forming —Cl, $—OH_2^+$, or $—OSO_2Ar$. An internal S_N2-type reaction follows.

The products of the rearrangement of the *syn* and *anti* oximes in (II) and (III) of **(A)** indicate that the group that migrates is *anti* to OH.

375. F is a saturated monoester with MW = 186 (no Br_2 reaction). We can logically determine the number of Cs and the molecular formula by subtracting the mass of the two Os and dividing the remainder by 14, the mass of CH_2: $(186 - 32)/14 = 11$. To complete the mass there must be 22 Hs. The molecular formula is $C_{11}H_{22}O_2$. The acid **G** has one more C than the alcohol **H** because it is degraded by one C in the Hunsdiecker reaction $(RCOO^-Ag^+ + Br_2)$ to **J** which is also made from **H** with no change in C content. **H** is a methyl carbinol, $CH_3CH(OH)R$, because it gives a positive iodoform reaction and, in order to be chiral, must have at least four Cs. However, **H** has five Cs because the alkene, **I**, obtained on dehydration (warm conc. H_2SO_4), must have two Mes on one of the doubly bonded Cs to avoid *cis-trans* isomerism. **I** is $CH_3CH{=}C(CH_3)_2$ with five Cs and **G** had six Cs. **H** is $CH_3CHOHCH(CH_3)_2$ and is converted to **J**, $CH_3CHBrCH(CH_3)_2$, through the

$$CH_3\overset{\displaystyle OTs}{\underset{\displaystyle |}{C}}HCH(CH_3)_2,$$

tosylate, $CH_3\overset{|}{C}HCH(CH_3)_2$, with no change in configuration, by an S_N2 reaction with Br^-. Consequently, **H** and **J** have inverted configurations. The skeleton of the alkyl group of **G** is the same as **H**. Replacing Br of **J** by COOH gives the structure of **G**, $(CH_3)_2CHCH(CH_3)$ COOH. **F** is one of the four possible enantiomers of

Chapter 18: Carbanion-Enolates and Enols

376. (A) The conjugate bases of $HC(NO_2)_3$ and $HC(CN)_3$ are extremely weak (stable) because their negative charges are delocalized by extended *p-p* π-bonding to electronegative atoms in each of three groups. Hence the acids are strong. Typically, *p-d* π delocalization, as in $Cl_3C{:}^-$, is far less significant than *p-p* π bonding. The overlap is less effective because of the longer bond length and difference in size of the 2*p* and 3*d* orbitals.
(B) *p-d* π bonding in $^-{:}CH_2SO_2CH_3$ is less effective for the same reason.

377. (A)

$$RCH_2 - \overset{\overset{\displaystyle O}{\|}}{C} - H \underset{-H^+}{\overset{+H^+}{\rightleftharpoons}} \left[R\overset{..}{C}H - \overset{\overset{\displaystyle :\overset{..}{O}}{\|}}{C} - H \leftrightarrow RCH = \overset{\overset{\displaystyle :\overset{..}{O}:^-}{|}}{C} - H \right] \underset{-H^+}{\overset{+H^+}{\rightleftharpoons}} RCH = \overset{\overset{\displaystyle OH}{|}}{C} - H$$

Keto form   Carbanion-enolate anion   Enol form

(B) The keto and enol isomers are called *tautomers*, and the equilibrium is called *tautomerism*.

378. The structural unit needed for tautomerism is encircled in each case.

(A)

$$\boxed{H - \overset{\overset{\displaystyle H}{|}}{\underset{\underset{\displaystyle H}{|}}{C}} - \overset{\overset{\displaystyle \\ }{}}{\underset{\underset{\displaystyle H}{|}}{C}} = O} \rightleftharpoons \overset{H}{\underset{H}{>}} \boxed{C = C - OH}$$

Keto   Enol

(B)

$$C_6H_5 - \boxed{\overset{\overset{\displaystyle H}{|}}{\underset{\underset{\displaystyle O}{\|}}{C}} - \overset{\overset{\displaystyle \\ }{}}{\underset{\underset{\displaystyle H}{|}}{C}}} - H \rightleftharpoons C_6H_5 - \boxed{\overset{\overset{\displaystyle \\ }{}}{\underset{\underset{\displaystyle OH}{|}}{C}} = C \overset{H}{\underset{H}{<}}}$$

Keto   Enol

(C)

$$\boxed{H - \overset{\overset{\displaystyle H}{|}}{\underset{\underset{\displaystyle H}{|}}{C}} - \overset{\overset{\displaystyle \\ }{}}{\underset{\underset{\displaystyle O^-}{|}}{N^+}} = O} \rightleftharpoons \overset{H}{\underset{H}{>}} \boxed{C = N^+ - O - H}$$
$$\underset{\underset{\displaystyle O^-}{|}}{}$$

Nitro form   *Aci* form

(D) $Me_2 \boxed{C = N - O - H} \rightleftharpoons Me_2 \boxed{C - N = O}$

Oxime   Nitroso

(E)

$$\boxed{H - \overset{\overset{\displaystyle H}{|}}{\underset{\underset{\displaystyle H}{|}}{C}} - \overset{\overset{\displaystyle \\ }{}}{\underset{\underset{\displaystyle CH_3}{|}}{C}} = N} \rightleftharpoons \overset{H}{\underset{H}{>}} \boxed{C = C - N - H}$$

Imine   Enamine

379. (A)

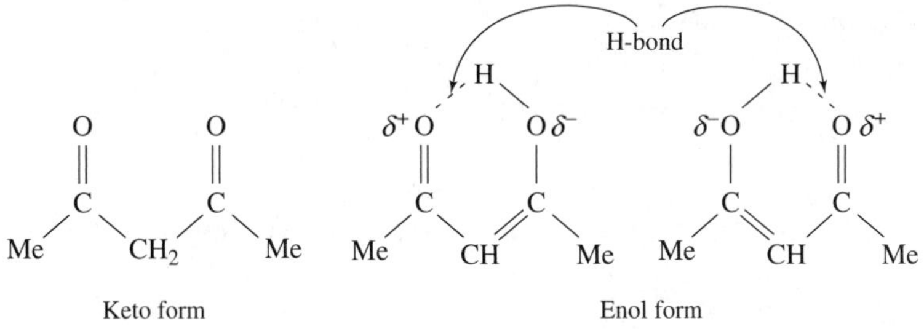

Keto form   Enol form

(B) This enol is more stable because it has a conjugated $(C{=}C{-}C{=}O)\pi$ system and intramolecular H-bonding (chelation).

(C) Water forms H-bonds with the $C{=}O$s, thereby inhibiting the intramolecular H-bonding that helps stabilize the enol.

(D) The enol decolorizes a solution of Br_2 in CCl_4. The more volatile enol tautomer is separated by careful distillation of the mixture in a fused quartz apparatus (eliminates base from glass).

380. The keto form has only three types of Hs while the enol has four types. In the solvent used for pmr spectroscopy, the enol is the almost exclusive tautomer.

381. A three-step α-C halogenation, proceeding through carbanion-enolate intermediates, results in the intermediate $PhCOCl_3$.

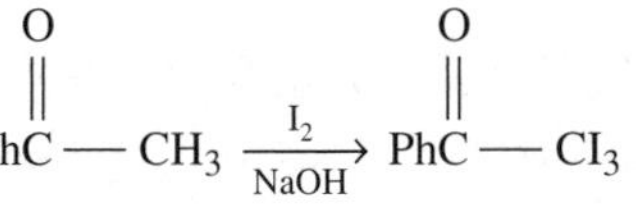

Then, OH^- adds to the carbonyl group, and $I_3C:^-$ is eliminated because this anion is stabilized by electron withdrawal by the three Is. Finally, H^+-exchange occurs.

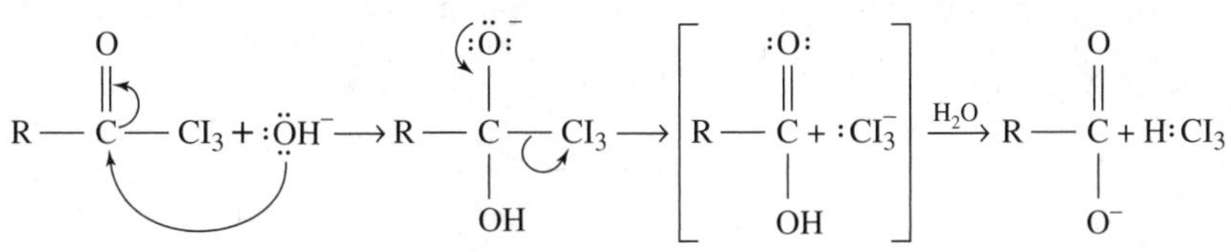

382. A is the carbanion-enolate;

$$\left[R\overset{..}{C}H - \underset{|}{C} = \overset{..}{O}: \longleftrightarrow RCH = \underset{|}{C} - \overset{..}{\underset{..}{O}}: \right]$$

B is $(i\text{-}Pr)_2NH$; **C** is the C-alkylated product, $RCHR'\underset{|}{C}{=}O$; **D** is the O-alkylated product, an enol ether, $RCH{=}\underset{|}{C}{-}OR'$.

383. (A)

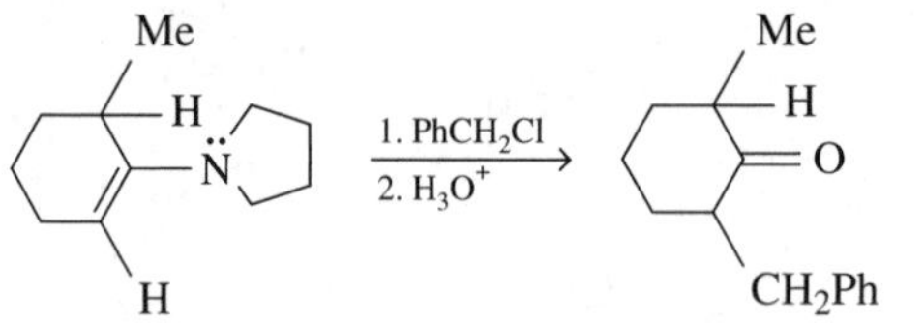

Enamine **A**   2-Benzyl-6-methylcyclohexanone, **A**

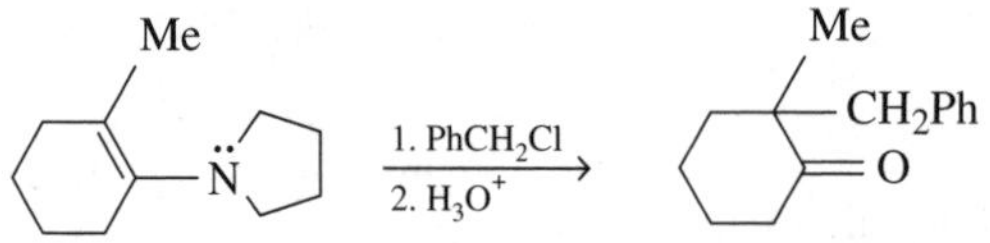

Enamine **B**   2-Benzyl-2-methylcyclohexanone, **B**

(B) We might expect **B′** with Me on C=C to be more stable because it is more substituted and should go to **B**. However, this does not does not happen because **B** is more sterically hindered and **A′** affords the major product, **A**, instead.

384.

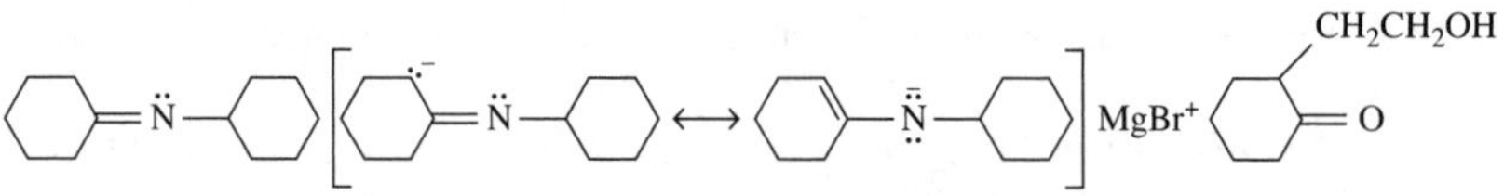

A   B   C

385. (A) $(EtOOC)_2CH_2 \xrightarrow[RX]{NaOEt} (EtOOC)_2CHR \xrightarrow[2.\,H_3O^+]{1.\,OH^-} RCH_2COOH + CO_2$

DEM $NaOEt \downarrow R'X^*$

$(EtOOC)_2CRR' \xrightarrow[2.\,H_3O^+]{1.\,OH^-} RR'CHCOOH + CO_2$

*If RX is used again, the product is $R_2CHCOOH$.

(B) The methylene Hs have appreciable acidity because they are flanked by two C=Os. EtO$^-$ removes one of these Hs, leaving a stable carbanion

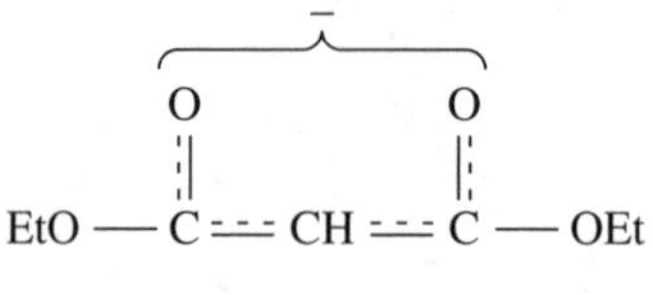

that acts as a nucleophile in an S_N2 reaction with RX (or ROTs). The process can be repeated to from a dialkylated derivative. The mono or dialkylated malonic ester is then hydrolyzed to the corresponding intermediate malonic acid which readily loses CO_2 to given the substituted acetic acid.

(C) DEM has only two replaceable α Hs. The α H in the dialkylated acetic acid product arises from decarboxylation of $HOOCCR_2COOH$.

386. In each case, analyze the origin of the different pieces of the product acid (the parts derived from the halide are shown in boldface):

$$R(R')\!-\!\boxed{CHCOOH} \longleftarrow \text{from malonic ester}$$

↑ ⎣— from alkyl halides

(A) In $Me_2CH\!-\!CH_2COOH$, there is a single R, Me_2CH, coming from RX which must be Me_2CHCl.

$$CH_2(COOEt)_2 \xrightarrow[\text{2.Me}_2\text{CHCl}]{\text{1.NaOEt}} Me_2CHCH(COOEt)_2 \xrightarrow[\text{2.H}_3\text{O}^+]{\text{1.OH}^-,\,\Delta}$$

$$\left[Me_2CHCH(COOH)_2\right] \xrightarrow{-CO_2} Me_2CHCH_2COOH$$

(B) In $(CH_3CH_2)_2CHCOOH$, there are two Ets attached to the α C, indicating the need for two sequential alkylations with EtBr.

$$CH_2(COOEt)_2 \xrightarrow[\text{2.EtBr}]{\text{1.NaOEt}} EtCH(COOEt)_2 \xrightarrow[\text{2.EtBr}]{\text{1.NaOEt}}$$

$$Et_2C(COOEt)_2 \xrightarrow[\text{2.H}_2\text{O}^+,\,\Delta]{\text{1.OH}^-} Et_2CHCOOH$$

(C) $CH_3CH_2CH(CH_3)COOH$ has Et and Me bonded to the α C, signaling the need for dialkylation with MeI and EtBr. (These halides are used because they are liquids that are easier to handle than gases such as MeCl and EtCl.) The larger R is introduced first to minimize steric hindrance in the second alkylation step.

$$CH_2(COOEt)_2 \xrightarrow[\text{2.EtBr}]{\text{1.NaOEt}} EtCH(COOEt)_2 \xrightarrow[\text{2. MeI}]{\text{1. NaOEt}}$$

$$EtCHMe(COOEt)_2 \xrightarrow[\text{2. H}_3\text{O}^+,\,\Delta]{\text{1. OH}^-} EtCHMeCOOH$$

387. (A) $CH_3CCH_2COEt \xrightarrow{OEt^-} \left[CH_3C \,\text{---}\, CH \,\text{---}\, COEt\right] \xrightarrow{RX} CH_3CCHRCOEt \xrightarrow[\text{2. H}_3\text{O}^+]{\text{1. OH}^-} CH_3CCH_2R$

with carbonyls ($\|\;\|$ / O O) shown, bracketed resonance form, and final products.

AAE

$\downarrow$ NaOEt | R'X

$$CH_3COCRR\;COOEt \xrightarrow[\text{2. H}_3\text{O}^+,]{\text{1. OH}^-} CH_3COCHRR$$

(B) The chemistry is the same as that for DEM (Problem 385).

(C) The ^3C of the ketonic product must have at least one H which comes from replacement of the COOH in the last steps of the synthesis.

388. (A) $D \xrightleftharpoons{OH^-} HOH +$

$$\left[CH_2\!=\!CH\ddot{C}HCH\!=\!\ddot{O}\!: \longleftrightarrow\ ^-\!:CH_2CH\!=\!CHCH\!=\!\ddot{O}\!: \longleftrightarrow\right.$$

$$\left.CH_2\!=\!CHCH\!=\!CH\ddot{O}\!:^-\right]$$

Each site with a − charge can abstract an H^+ from H_2O to give three products: CH_2=$CHCH$=$CHOH$ (enol tautomer) of **D**, **D** (vinylacetaldehyde), and CH_3CH=$CHCH$=O (crotonaldehyde).

(B) Crotonaldehyde, the conjugated keto isomer

389. (A) (I) The addition of the nucleophilic carbanion-enolate, usually of an aldehyde, to the C=O of its parent compound is called an *aldol* addition. (II) In a *mixed aldol addition* the carbanion-enolate adds to the C=O of a molecule other than its parent.

(B) The bases used are typically aqueous NaOH and NaOR in the corresponding ROH. Room temperature suffices.

(C) β-Hydroxycarbonyl compounds; hence the name *ald* for aldehyde and *ol* for alcohol.

(D) A C—C bond forms because the C, not the O, is the more reactive site in the carbanion-enolate. In fact, the enolate contributing structure is usually omitted when writing equations even though it makes the greater contribution.

(E)

Carbanion-enolate   Carbonyl   Alkoxide of   β-Hydroxcarbonyl
                       acceptor   β-hydroxcarbonyl compound   compound

(F) The alcohol can lose H_2O, even in base, giving an α,β-unsaturated carbonyl compound. If more extensive conjugation is engendered, dehydration occurs on formation of the alcohol; otherwise the reaction mixture must be warmed. The reaction leading directly to the unsaturated carbonyl compound is called an *aldol condensation.*

(G) Formation of the β-hydroxy carbonyl compound is reversible, but dehydration is irreversible under basic conditions. Formation of the alkene draws the overall reaction to completion.

(H) When the carbanion is generated from a substrate other than a carbonyl compound (see Table A18-1), an *aldol-type* reaction occurs. Except for this fact, there are no other differences.

390. (A) I.

Propanal   2-Methyl-3-hydroxypentanal

II.

Acetone   Diacetone alcohol
                          (4-Hydroxy-4-methyl-2-pentanone)

(B) Both reactions are reversible. However, reaction (I) from an aldehyde favors the product and reaction (II) from a ketone favors the reactant.

(C) As the product forms, continuously remove it from the basic catalyst.

Table A18-1

	Stable Carbanions	Reason for Stability
(a)	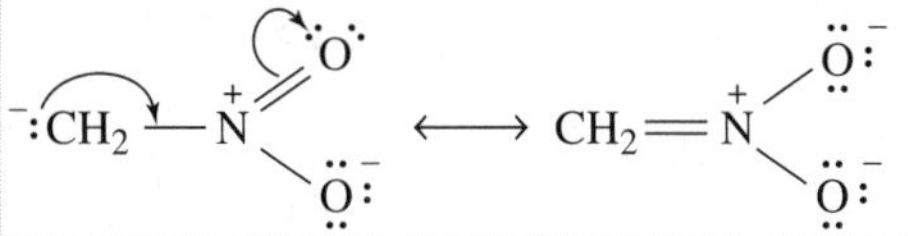 $^-$:CH$_2$—N$^+$(=O̤)(Ö$^-$) ⟷ CH$_2$=N$^+$(Ö$^-$)(Ö$^-$)	p-p π bond
(b)	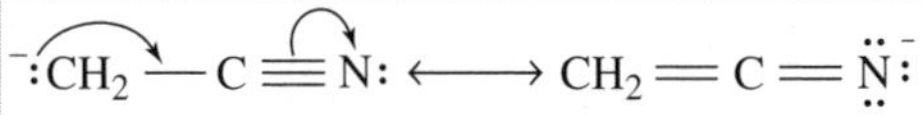 $^-$:CH$_2$—C≡N: ⟷ CH$_2$=C=N̈:$^-$	p-p π bond
(c)	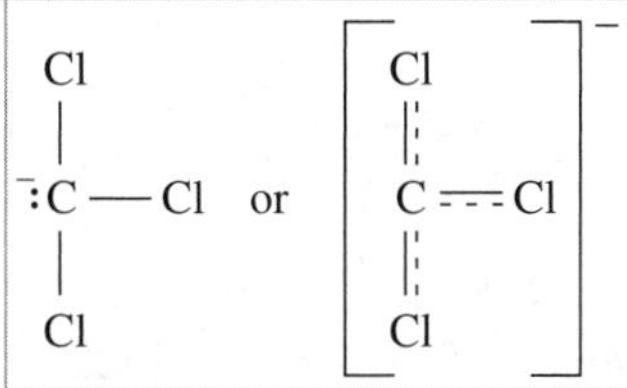 :C(Cl)(Cl)—Cl or [C(Cl)(Cl)=̇=Cl]$^-$	p-d π bond
(d)	CH$_3$C≡C:$^-$	sp hybrid
(e)	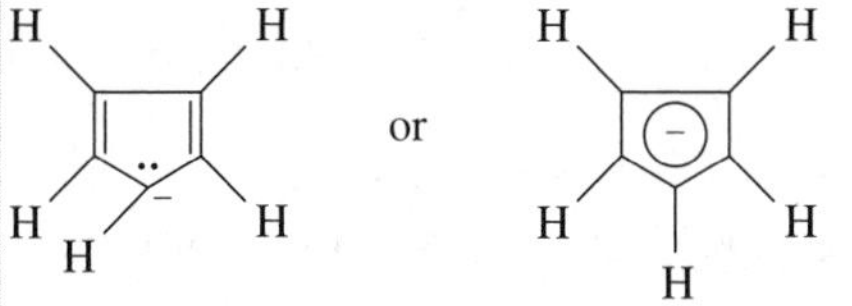 cyclopentadienyl anion (two resonance depictions)	Aromaticity
(f)	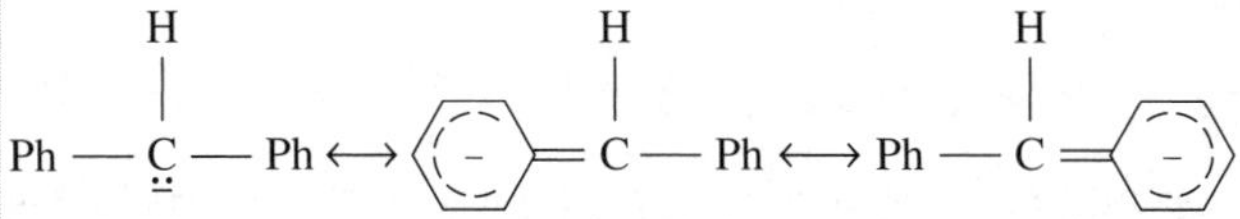 Ph—C̈$^-$—Ph ⟷ (benzyl resonance forms) ⟷ Ph—C=	p-p π bond
(g)	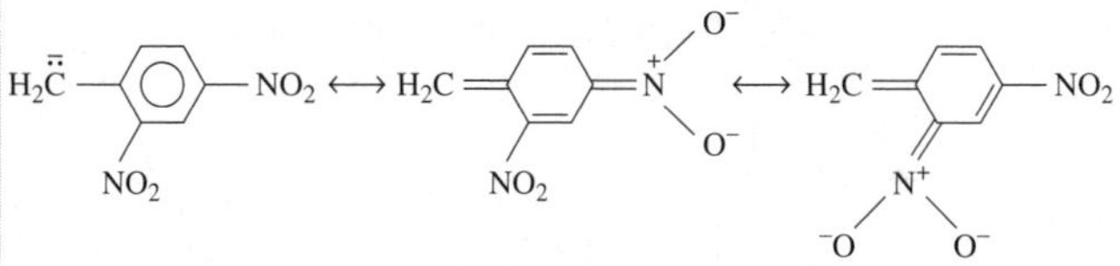 H$_2$C̈$^-$—C$_6$H$_3$(NO$_2$)—NO$_2$ ⟷ H$_2$C=C$_6$H$_3$(NO$_2$)—N$^+$(O$^-$)(O$^-$) ⟷ H$_2$C=C$_6$H$_3$(=N$^+$(O$^-$)(O$^-$))—NO$_2$	p-p π bond
(h)	RS—C̈H—SR or (RS=CH=SR)$^-$	p-p π bond
(i)	Me$_2$S$^+$—C̈H$_2$ or Me$_2$S=CH$_2$	Electrostatic attraction and p-d π bond
(j)	Ph$_3$P$^+$—C̈H$_2$ or Ph$_3$P=CH$_2$	Electrostatic attraction and p-d π bond
(k)	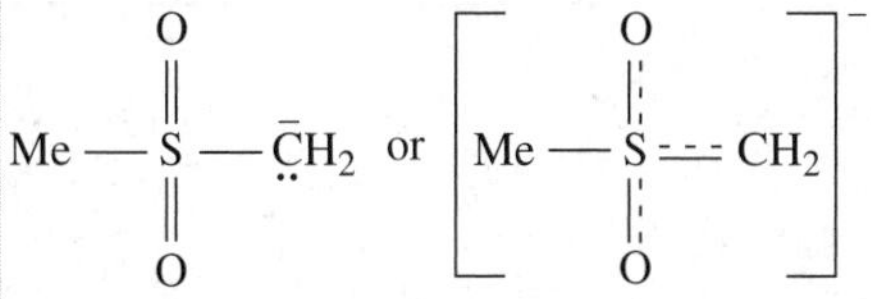 Me—S(=O)(=O)—C̈H$_2$ or [Me—S(=O)(=O)=̇=CH$_2$]$^-$	Electrostatic attraction and p-d π bond

391. In these *Claisen-Schmidt reactions*, where ArCHO must be the acceptor, the first formed β-hydroxy carbonyl compound undergoes rapid dehydration to give the stable α,β-unsaturated carbonyl grouping, now further conjugated with the Ph.

(A) $\left[\begin{array}{c} \text{H} \\ | \\ \text{PhC} - \text{CH}_2\text{C} - \text{H} \\ | \quad\quad || \\ \text{OH} \quad\quad \text{O} \end{array}\right] \longrightarrow \text{PhCH} = \text{CHCHO}$ *trans*

(B) $\left[\begin{array}{c} \text{H} \\ | \\ \text{PhC} - \text{CH}_2 - \text{C} - \text{CH}_3 \\ | \quad\quad\quad || \\ \text{OH} \quad\quad\quad \text{O} \end{array}\right] \longrightarrow \text{PhCH} = \text{CHCCH}_3$ *trans* $\overset{||}{\text{O}}$

392. Each product has six Cs, which is twice the number of Cs in CH_3CH_2CHO. This suggests an aldol addition as the first step.

(A) $CH_3CH_2CHO \xrightarrow{OH^-} CH_3CH_2CH(OH)CH(CH_3)CHO \xrightarrow[\Delta]{H^+} (A) + H_2O$

(B) The $C{=}C$ of **A** is reduced with Li, liq. NH_3, and EtOH, leaving CHO untouched.

(C) The CHO of **A** is selectively reduced by $NaBH_4$ in EtOH.

(D) Both $C{=}O$ and $C{=}C$ are reduced by catalytic (i.e., Pt) hydrogenation;

or $B \xrightarrow[EtOH]{NaBH_4} D.$

(E) $A \xrightarrow[OH^-, \Delta]{H_2NNH_2} CH_3CH_2CH{=}C(CH_3)_2 \xrightarrow{H_2/pd} E;$ or $B \xrightarrow[OH^-]{H_2NNH_2} E$

(F) Tollens' reagent, $Ag(NH_3)_2^+$, is a specific oxidant for $CHO \longrightarrow COOH.$

$$CH_3CH_2CH(OH)CH(CH_3)CHO \xrightarrow[2.H^+]{1.Ag(NH_3)_2^+} F$$

393. (A) This is a *Perkin condensation*.

$$\begin{array}{c} \text{H} \quad\quad \text{H} \quad \text{O} \quad\quad\quad \text{O} \\ | \quad\quad | \quad\; || \quad\quad\quad || \\ p\text{-CH}_3\text{C}_6\text{H}_4\text{C} + \text{(H)} - \text{C} - \text{C} - \text{O} - \text{CCH}_2\text{CH}_3 \longrightarrow \\ || \quad\quad\quad | \\ \text{O} \quad\quad\quad \text{CH}_3 \end{array}$$

$$\left[\begin{array}{c} \text{H} \quad \text{H} \quad \text{O} \quad\quad\quad \text{O} \\ | \quad\; | \quad\; || \quad\quad\quad || \\ p\text{-CH}_3\text{C}_6\text{H}_4\text{C} - \text{C} - \text{C} - \text{O} - \text{CCH}_2\text{CH}_3 \\ | \quad\; | \\ \text{HO} \quad \text{CH}_3 \end{array}\right] \xrightarrow{-\text{CH}_3\text{CH}_2\text{COOH}} p\text{-CH}_3\text{C}_6\text{H}_4\text{CH} = \overset{\overset{\displaystyle \text{CH}_3}{\displaystyle |}}{\text{C}}\text{COOH} \;(E)$$

(B)

$$\bigcirc{=}\text{O} + \text{(H)} - \overset{\overset{\displaystyle \text{H}}{\displaystyle |}}{\underset{\underset{\displaystyle \text{CH}_3}{\displaystyle |}}{\text{C}}} - \text{NO}_2 \longrightarrow \left[\begin{array}{c} \text{OH} \\ \diagup \\ \bigcirc \!\! \diagdown \\ \text{CHNO}_2 \\ | \\ \text{CH}_3 \end{array}\right] \xrightarrow{-\text{H}_2\text{O}} \bigcirc{=}\overset{\overset{\displaystyle \text{CNO}_2}{}}{\underset{\underset{\displaystyle \text{CH}_3}{}}{}}$$

(C)

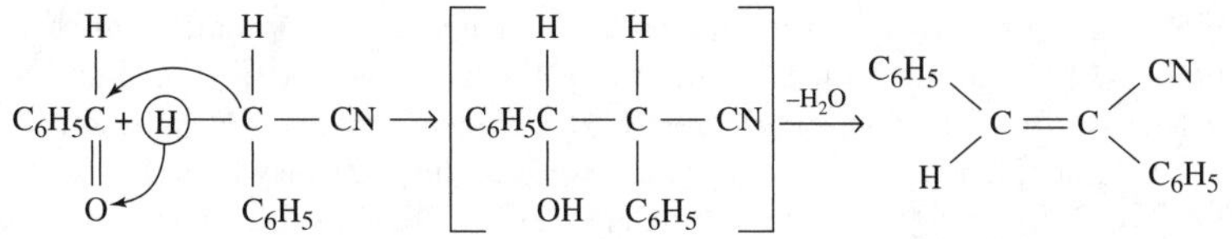

(Bulky C_6H_5's are *trans*.)

(D)

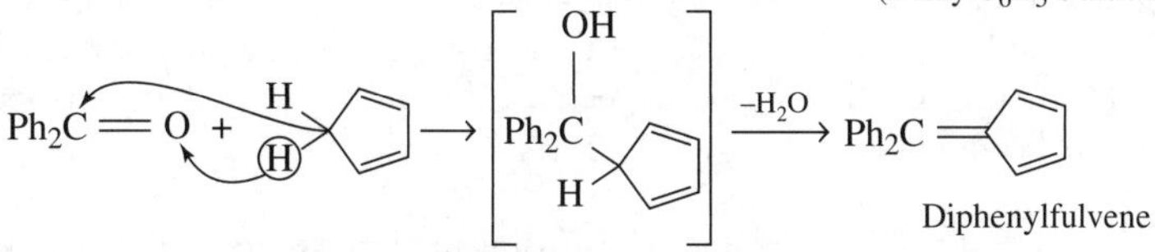

Diphenylfulvene

(E) Each CH_3 of $(CH_3)_2CO$ reacts with one PhCHO.

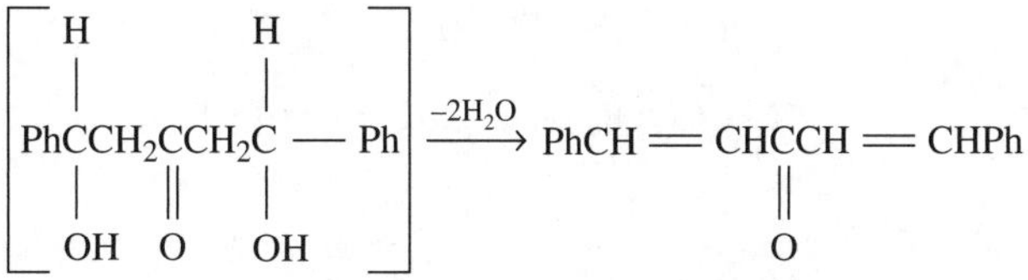

(F) This is the *Cope reaction*.

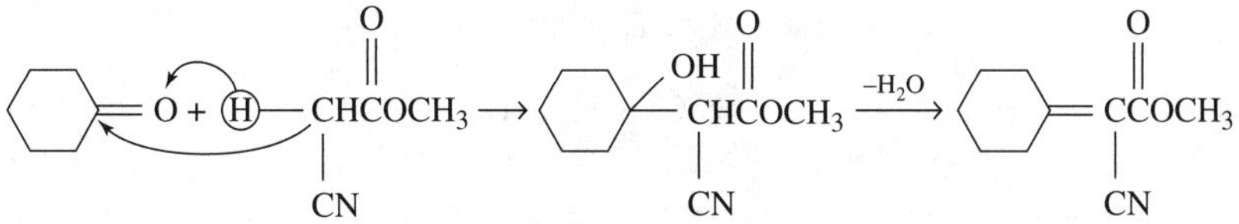

394. The first step is the formation of the α-carbanion, stabilized through extended π bonding with the C=O of —COOR.

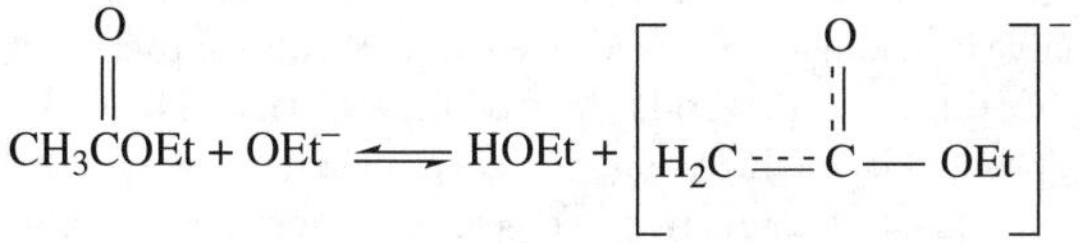

In the second step, the carbanion adds to the C=O of another molecule of ester, displacing OEt–.

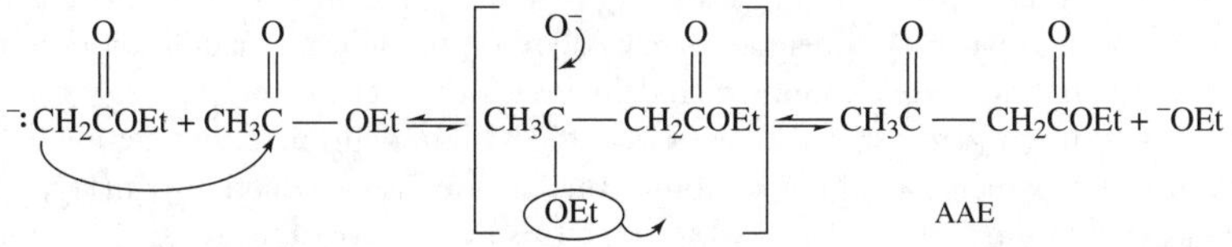

The equilibria for the two steps are unfavorable for product formation. However, 1,3-dicarbonyl compounds have fairly acidic protons between the two C=O's (for AAE, $pK_a \cong 11$, while for EtOH, $pK_a \cong 16$), and ⁻OEt converts AAE to its conjugate base, driving the reaction to completion.

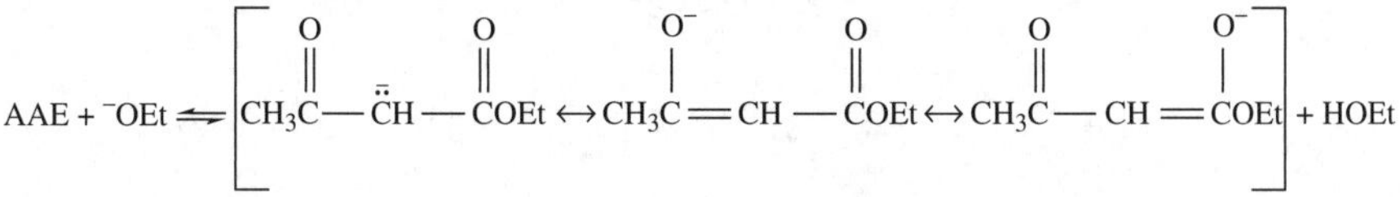

395. They both involve formation of an intermediate α-carbanion which then adds to the C=O of another molecule, generating a − charge on the O. The aldol O⁻ accepts H⁺ to give an OH. The Claisen O⁻ ejects ⁻OR from C, reforming the resonance-stabilized C=O group. The aldol O⁻ would have to eject the extremely basic H:⁻ or R:⁻ to reform the C=O. It is easier to eject the much less basic carbanion addendum, which is the reason the aldol addition is reversible. Both functional groups of the Claisen product, C=O and COOR, are at higher oxidation states than the corresponding groups of the aldol product, C—OH and C=O. This is expected because the ester is at a higher oxidation state than the carbonyl compound.

396. Since $CH_3COCH(C_2H_5)CH_2CH_3$ (**A**) is a methyl ketone, AAE, made as shown, is a likely intermediate.

$$CH_3COOH \xrightarrow{\text{LiAlH}_4} CH_3CH_2OH$$

Then

$$CH_3COOH + CH_3CH_2OH \xrightarrow{\text{H}_2\text{SO}_4} CH_3COOCH_2CH_3 \xrightarrow[\text{NaOEt*}]{}$$

$$CH_3COCH_2COOCH_2CH_3 \text{ (AAE)} \xrightarrow[\text{2CH}_3\text{CH}_2\text{Br**}]{\text{2NaOEt}}$$

$$CH_3COC(CH_2CH_3)_2COOCH_2CH_3 \xrightarrow[\text{2.H}^+]{\text{1.OH}^-} \textbf{A}$$

*from HOEt + Na.

**from CH_3CH_2OH + HBr.

397. A has 3° of unsaturation and since ozonolysis introduces two O atoms, 1° is a C=C. Since naphthalene is obtained on dehydrogenation of **A**, the other 2° of unsaturation are two fused six-member rings with no R side chains. Likewise, **B**, **C**, **D**, and **E** have no R side chains. Since the same product is obtained on reductive or oxidative ozonolysis of **A**, the 3° of unsaturation of **B** are two C=Os and a ring. To get a diketone, the C=C in **A** is tetrasubstituted and must be at the fusion position of the two rings. **B** is 1,6-cyclodecanedione. **E** has the same ring system as azulene, a fused seven- and five-member ring, and so must **C** and **D**, its precursors. The uv absorption of **C** at $\lambda_{\text{max}} = 300$ nm means that it is an α,β-unsaturated ketone, formed when **B** undergoes base-catalyzed intramolecular aldolization with NaOH to give the intermediate alcohol which dehydrates. The fact that only a single aldol product is formed substantiates that the two C=Os of **B** are equivalent and symmetrical and it is immaterial which acts as the acceptor. The Clemmenson reduction (Zn/Hg, HCl) of **C** reduces C=O to CH_2 to give **D** whose C=C is hydrogenated to give **E**. The structures are

| **A** | **B** | **C** | **D** | **E** |

Chapter 19: Amines

398. *Amines* are alkyl or aryl derivatives of NH_3. Replacement of one H of NH_3 by R or Ar results in a 1° amine (RNH_2); and if two or three Hs are replaced, the result is a 2° (R_2NH) or 3° (R_3N), respectively. **(A)** and **(C)** 1°; **(D)** and **(F)** 2°; **(B)** and **(E)** 3°.

399. (A) Isobutylisopropylamine
   (B) 1,4-tetramethylenediamine or 1,4-diaminobutane (also called *putrescine* because it is one of the putrid compounds in decaying animal matter)
   (C) l, 1′-dichlorotriethylamine
   (D) 3-aminopropanol (alcohol has priority over amine)
   (E) N,N-dimethyl-2-aminobutane or *sec*-butyldimethylamine

400. (A) Aniline
   (B) *o*-toluidine
   (C) *o*-aminobenzoic acid or anthranilic acid
   (D) N-methyl-2-naphthylamine
   (E) N,N-diethyl-*p*-anisidine
   (F) *m*-phenylenediamine
   (G) 2-amino-4′-nitrobenzophenone

401. The amino N is assigned the lowest number on the longest chain, and an N is placed before each substituent group on the nitrogen.
   (A) Ethanamine
   (B) N-methyl-1-butanamine
   (C) 1,2-ethanediamine
   (D) benzenamine
   (E) N-methyl-N-ethylcyclohexanamine
   (F) N,N-bis (1-chloroethyl)ethanamine

402. (A)

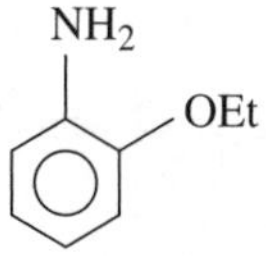

   (B)

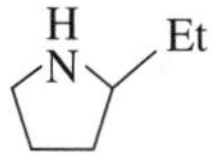

   (C)

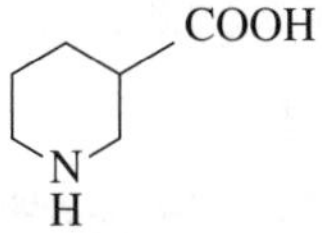

   (D)

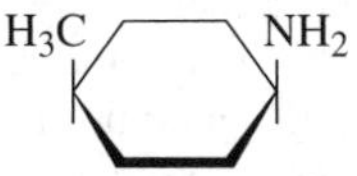

(E)   H
     N
     △

(F)   H
     N
     (morpholine-like ring with O)

403. (A) Water solubility depends on the H-bonding between the amine and H_2O, provided the R group is not too large. Either the N—H bonds with the O of H_2O or the O—H bonds with the N of the amine, or both. 3° Amines can only H-bond through their unshared electron pair with the H of H_2O. The amines with lower MW are water-soluble.

(B) Since all amines form H-bonds with hydroxylic solvents, they are very soluble in alcohols.

404. (A)   I. $MeNH_2 + H_2O \rightleftharpoons MeNH_3^+ + OH^-$
              Methylammonium ion

   II. $MeNH_2 + HCl(g) \longrightarrow MeNH_3^+Cl^-(s)$

              H
              \
   III. $MeN: + BNe_3 \longrightarrow MeH_2 \overset{+}{N} - \overset{-}{B}Me_3$ (The + and − are formal charges.)
              /
              H

(B) (I) and (II) Brönsted base. (III) Nucleophile. The product is called a *complex*.

405. (A) $K_b = \dfrac{[MeNH_3^+][OH^-]}{[MeNH_2]}$

(B) $pK_b = -\log K_b = -\log(4.3 \times 10^{-4}) = 3.4$

(C) $pK_a + pK_b = 14$ form which $pK_a = 14 - 3.4 = 10.6$

406. (A) The chemical equation for dissociation is $MeH_2 \overset{+}{N} - \overset{-}{B} Me_3 \rightleftharpoons MeH_2N: + BNE_2$

and
$$K_{diss} = \frac{[MeH_2N:][BMe_3]}{\left[MeH_2 \overset{+}{N} - \overset{-}{B}Me_3 \right]}$$

(B) The larger is K_{diss}, the more the complex dissociates and the less nucleophilic is the amine.

407. The N of amines is regarded as using sp^3 HOs with the unshared electron pair occupying one tetrahedrally directed HO. As the Rs get bulkier, the additional crowding can be somewhat alleviated if the bonding orbitals acquire less p character (while the lone pair HO assumes more p character). They tend to become hybridized somewhere between sp^3 and sp^2, with a concomitant increase in the bond angles. This modification is possible only when one of the HOs houses an unshared pair of electrons. Acceptance of an H^+ by the amine forces the orbitals toward the tetrahedral sp^3 configuration with a reduction of bond angles and increased steric crowding among the Rs. The ammonium ion suffers a kind of strain, called *B-strain* (back strain), present in "back" of the amine and away from the entering H^+. Another contributing factor to the declining basicity is the increasing steric hindrance to the solvation of the cation. The bulkier the Rs, the more B-strain there is and the weaker is the basicity.

408. (A) Electron delocalization through extended π bonding (resonance)
    (B) induction
    (C) solvation
    (D) steric effects toward solvation or by inhibition of resonance
    (E) s character
    (F) field effect

409. $-\overset{|}{\underset{..}{N}}:^-$ is called an *amide ion.* For example, $Me\overset{H}{\underset{..}{N}}:^-$ is the methylamide ion.

410. (A) The acidic phthalimide ($pK_a \cong 8.3$) is first converted into its anion by OH^-.

Phthalimide anion

    (B) Halides unreactive in S_N2 displacements cannot be used. (I) Me_3CBr is 3°. (II) Me_3CCH_2Cl is neopentyl. (III) 2° Amines give poor yields due to elimination. (IV) The Br in $p\text{-MeC}_6H_4Br$ is not activated by an electron-withdrawing group.

411. $\underset{A}{PhSO_2NHEt} \rightarrow \underset{B}{PhSO_2\overset{..}{N}Et} \rightarrow \underset{C}{PhSO_2NET_2} \rightarrow \underset{D}{PhSO_2OH} + \underset{E}{Et_2NH_2^+}$

412. The product is (*S*) *sec*-butylamine. :R migrates with its electron pair to the electron-deficient :$\overset{..}{N}$, and configuration is retained because C—C is being broken at the same time that C—N is being formed in the transition state.

413. Many nitrosamines are carcinogenic. They are found in beer and in tobacco smoke. They are also formed during tanning of leather, "corning" beef, and frying bacon that has been cured with $NaNO_2$. In addition, HONO is formed in the human body by the action of gastric HCl on nitrites ingested in foods. It reacts with 2° amino groups, converting them to nitrosamines (see Problem 489).

414. (A) The amine undergoes exhaustive methylation, forming $RCH_2CH_2NMe_3^+I^-$, **A**, which is converted to **B**, the quaternary ammonium hydroxide, $RCH_2CH_2NMe_3^+OH^-$. When heated, a *Hofmann elimination* (also called *Hofmann degradation)* occurs:

$$RCH_2CH_2NMe_3^+OH^- (\textbf{B}) \longrightarrow RCH{=}CH_2(\textbf{C}) + H_2O + Me_3N$$

(B) E2
(C) NMe_3
(D) NH_2^- is a very poor leaving group

415. The NH_2 group is an extremely powerful ring activator in electrophilic substitution, and it is difficult to get just monosubstitution. To diminish its activation, it is converted to the moderately activating amide:

(A) $PhNH_2 \xrightarrow[\text{base}]{\text{ac.anhydride}} PhNHCOCH_3 \xrightarrow{Br_2} p\text{-}BrC_6H_4NHCOCH_4 \xrightarrow[\Delta]{OH^-}$
$p\text{-}BrC_6H_4NH_2$

(B) $PhNHCOCH_3 \xrightarrow[H_2SO_4]{HNO_3} p\text{-}O_2NC_6H_4NHCOCH_3 \xrightarrow[\Delta]{OH^-} p\text{-}O_2NC_6H_4NH_2$

416. (A)

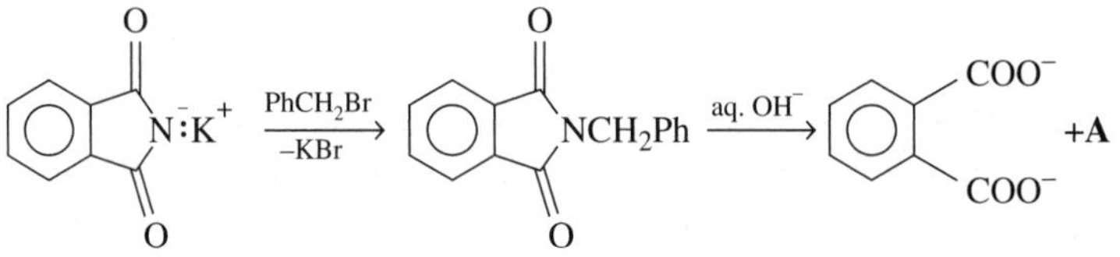

(B) $PhCH_2Br \xrightarrow{\text{excess } NH_3} A$

(C) $PhC{\equiv}N \xrightarrow[2.\,H_2O]{1.\,LiAlH_4} A$

(D) $PhCH{=}O \xrightarrow[H_2/Ni]{NH_3} A$

(E) $PhCH_2CONH_2 \xrightarrow[2.\,NH_3]{1.\,Br_2,\,KOH} A$

417. (A) $p\text{-}NO_2C_6H_4CH_3 \xrightarrow[H^+]{KMnO_4} p\text{-}NO_2C_6H_4COOH \xrightarrow[H^+]{C_2H_5OH}$
$p\text{-}NO_2C_6H_4COOC_2H_5 \xrightarrow{Zn/HCl}$

$$[p\text{-}\overset{+}{N}H_3C_6H_4COOC_2H_5]Cl^-$$
Hydrochloride salt of benzocaine

The free base can be generated by neutralizing the acidic $ArNH_3^+$ with OH^-.

(B) $PhNH_2 \xrightarrow{(CH_3CO)_2O} PhNHCOCH_3 \xrightarrow{HOSO_2Cl^*}$

$p\text{-}ClSO_2C_6H_4NHCOCH_3 \xrightarrow{NH_3^{**}}$

$p\text{-}H_2NSO_2C_6H_4NHCOCH_3 \xrightarrow[2.\ OH^-]{1.\ H_3O^+} p\text{-}H_2NSO_2C_6H_4NH_2$

Note that the sulfonamide is much more stable than the amide and withstands hydrolysis under these conditions.

*Chlorosulfonic acid.

**This reaction can be violent, and NH_3 must be added cautiously!

418. (A) By pointing the carbonyl groups toward each other as given, the alkene is shown to be $H_2C{=}CHCH_2CH_2CH_3$. The amine is 1° because 3 eq of MeI were required to give the 4° ammonium ion. Since the amine is resolvable, NH_2 is bonded to a chiral C; the compound is $CH_3CH(NH_2)CH_2CH_2CH_3$. The other amine, $NH_2CH_2CH_2CH_2CH_2CH_3$, which would give the same alkene, is achiral.

(B) **(B)** is a 3° amine because it reacts with only 1 eq of MeI. Since $H_2C{=}CHCH_3$ is the alkene, there is a three-carbon chain attached to N, either as *n*- or *i*-Pr along with two Mes to account for the two additional Cs. **B** is $C_3H_7NMe_2$; the structure of C_3H_7 is uncertain.

(C) **C** reacts with 2 eq of MeI; it is a 2° amine. Stepwise formation of $H_2C{=}CH_2$ and $H_2C{=}CHCH_3$ shows **C** is $C_3H_7NHCH_2CH_3$ with the same uncertainty about the structure of C_3H_7 as in **(B)**.

419. Basicity and the absence of N—H stretching bands indicate a 3° amino group, —$N(CH_3)_2$; the equivalent CH_3s account for the quartet. The positive Tollens' test, the bands at 1695 and 2720 cm^{-1}, and the very downfield doublet reveal a CHO. The 5° of unsaturation means the presence of a benzene ring along with a HC$=$O, and the two singlets indicate the ring is disubstituted. Since the two more upfield doublets must arise from the four unsubstituted ring Cs, they must come from two equivalent pairs; the substituents are *para*. The compound is $p\text{-}(CH_3)_2NC_6H_4CHO$.

Chapter 20: Phenols and Their Derivatives

420. Alcohols have an OH attached to an sp^3 hybridized carbon ($-\overset{|}{\underset{|}{C}}-OH$). Enols have an OH attached to a vinyl group. ($-\overset{|}{C}{=}\overset{|}{C}-OH$). *Phenols* are a general group with an OH attached to a carbocyclic aromatic ring (ArOH). Specifically, Ar is a phenyl ring for phenols. The compound with the specific name *phenol* is C_6H_5OH. (In medicine, its old name *carbolic acid* is still sometimes used.) Naphthols are phenolic-type compounds where Ar is a naphthyl ring (NapOH).

421. (A) Both compounds can be considered as tautomers of a keto structure. The large resonance energy of C=O usually causes the keto tautomer to be much more stable than the enol.

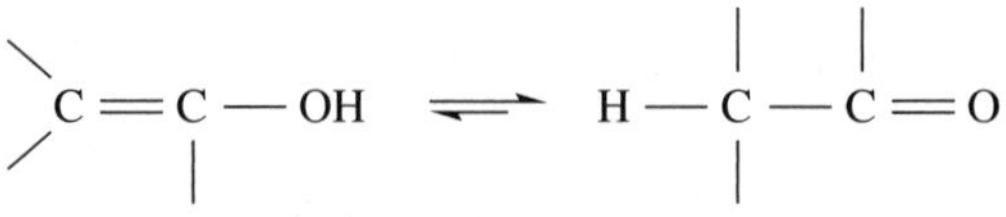

However, the keto form of phenol can be attained only with loss of the stable aromatic ring making it very much less stable than phenol.

(B)

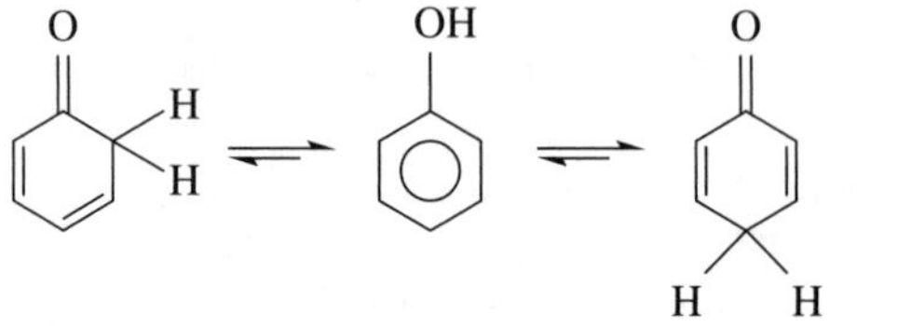

2,4-Cyclohexadienone   Phenol   2,5-Cyclohexadienone
ortho-keto form   "enol" form   *para*-keto form

422.

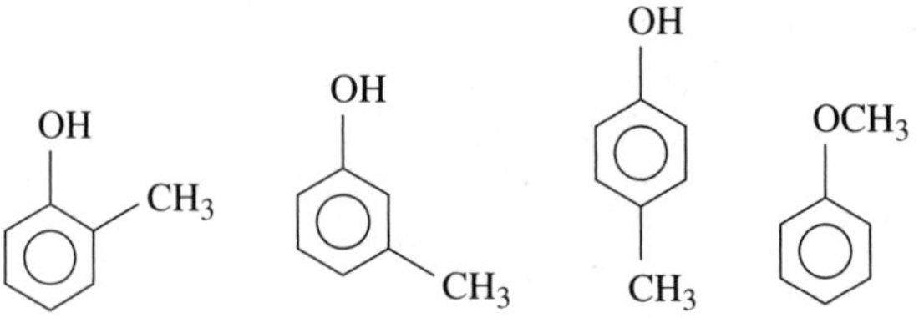

(A) *o*-Methylphenol   *m*-Methylphenol   *p*-Melhylphenol   Methoxybenzene
(B) *o*-Cresol   *m*-Cresol   *p*-Cresol   Anisole
(C) 2-Methylbenzenol   3-Methylbenzenol   4-Methylbenzenol   Methoxybenzene

Although the CA name for C_6H_5OH is *phenol*, substituted phenols are abstracted as derivatives of *benzenol*.

423. COOH, CHO, SO_3H have priority over OH [see **(D)**, **(E)**, and **(F)**].
  (A) When OH has priority, it is given number 1; 2-Chloro-4-methylphenol.
  (B) 4-Aminophenol or 4-hydroxyaniline. The latter name is especially used for aniline derivatives.
  (C) *p*-Hydroxyacetanilide
  (D) *o*-Hydroxybenzoic acid or salicylic acid
  (E) *m*-Hydroxybenzaldehyde
  (F) 2,4-Dihydroxybenzenesulfonic acid
  (G) 2,4,6-Trinitrophenol or picric acid
  (H) 1,2-Dihydroxy-4-methylbenzene or 4-methylcatechol

424. (A)

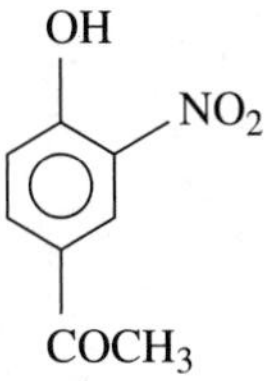

OH
NO$_2$
COCH$_3$

(4-hydroxy-3-nitrophenyl with COCH$_3$ para)

(B)

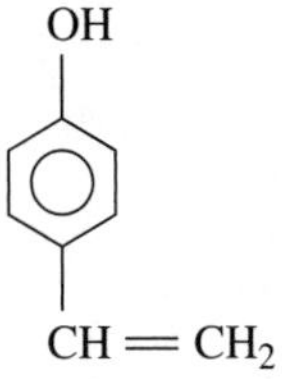

OH
CH $=$ CH$_2$

(C)

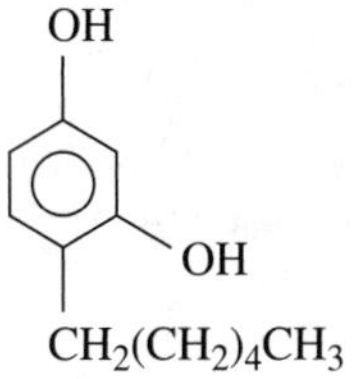

OH
OH
CH$_2$(CH$_2$)$_4$CH$_3$

(D)

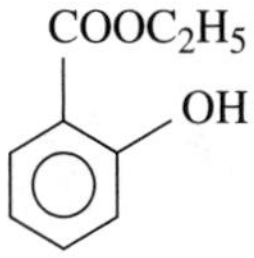

COOC$_2$H$_5$
OH

(E)

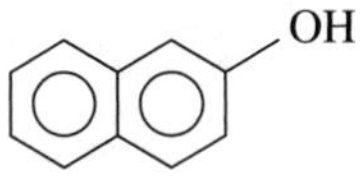

OH

(F)

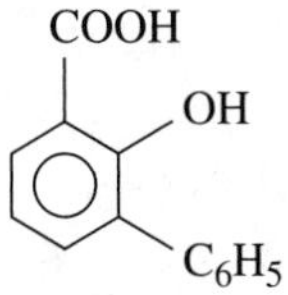

COOH
OH
C$_6$H$_5$

(G)

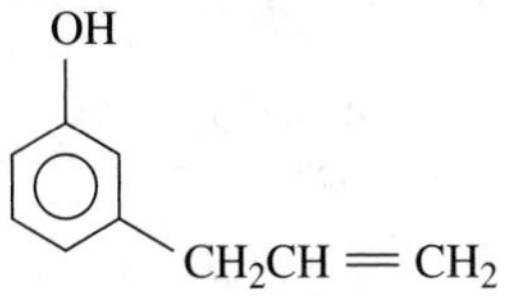

OH
CH$_2$CH $=$ CH$_2$

(H)

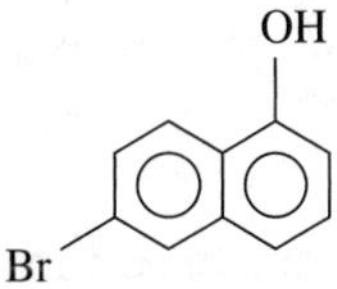

OH
Br

425. Hydrolysis of the diazonium salt.

$$\text{PhH} \xrightarrow[\text{}]{\text{HNO}_3/\text{H}_2\text{SO}_4} \text{PhNO}_2 \xrightarrow[\text{2. NaOH}]{\text{1. Sn/HCl}} \text{PhNH}_2 \xrightarrow[\text{0°C}]{\text{NaNO}_2/\text{aq. HCl}} \text{PhN}_2^+\text{Cl}^- \xrightarrow[\Delta]{\text{H}_2\text{O}} \text{PhOH}$$

426. (A) Since naphthalene is easily nitrated at the α position, this synthesis is best achieved through the diazonium salt.

$$\text{NapH} \xrightarrow[\text{}]{\text{HNO}_3/\text{H}_2\text{SO}_4} \alpha\text{-NapNO}_2 \xrightarrow[\text{2. NaOH}]{\text{1. Sn/HCl}} \alpha\text{-NapNH}_2 \xrightarrow[\text{0°C}]{\text{NaNO}_2/\text{H}^+} \alpha\text{-NapN}_2^+\text{Cl}^-$$

$$\xrightarrow[\Delta]{\text{H}_2\text{O}} \alpha\text{-NapOH}$$

   (B) NapH is not nitrated at the β position, but is sulfonated there.

$$\text{NapH} \xrightarrow[\text{180 °C}]{\text{H}_2\text{S}_2\text{O}_7} \beta\text{-NapSO}_3\text{H} \xrightarrow[\text{2. H}^+]{\text{1. NaOH, 330°C}} \beta\text{-NapOH}$$

427. The – charge on the alkoxide anion, RO^-, is completely localized, but the – charge on PhO^- is delocalized by extended π bonding to the *ortho* and *para* ring positions, as indicated by the starred sites in the resonance hybrid.

PhO^- is therefore a weaker base than EtO^- (RO^-), and PhOH (ArOH) is a stronger acid than ROH.

428. (A) *p*-Nitrophenol is stronger because

with a + charge on N has a greater electron-withdrawing inductive effect than has Cl. Even more significantly it has an effective electron-withdrawing resonance effect.

   (B) 2,4,6-Trinitrophenol (picric acid), a moderate acid, is more acidic because it has one more properly situated NO_2.

   (C) In the *ortho* and *para* positions, NH_2 is electron-donating by resonance and is acid-weakening. In the *meta* position it is electron-withdrawing and acid-strengthening by induction. *m*-Aminophenol is the stronger acid.

429. Charge delocalization in the nitrophenolate ion is much more effective because of the direct interaction between O^- and NO_2, which interaction is not possible in the *p*-nitrobenzoate anion.

Direct extended π bonding   No direct extended π bonding

430. Phenols are esterified and undergo Williamson syntheses like alcohols.

(A) No reaction.

(B)

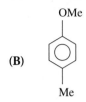

p-Methylanisole

(C)

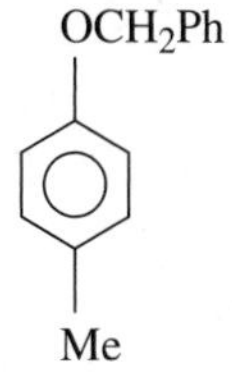

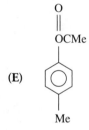

Benzyl *p*-tolyl ether

(D) No reaction. Unless activated, aryl halides are inert toward nucleophilic displacements.

(E)

$$\begin{array}{c} \text{O} \\ \| \\ \text{OCMe} \end{array}$$

p-Tolyl acetate

(F)

$$\begin{array}{c} \text{O} \\ \| \\ \text{OCPh} \end{array}$$

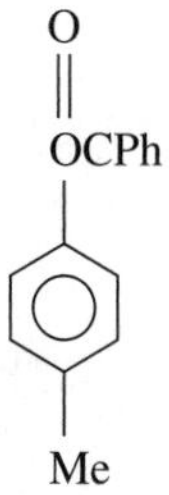

p-Tolyl benzoate

(G)

p-Tolyl acetate

(H)

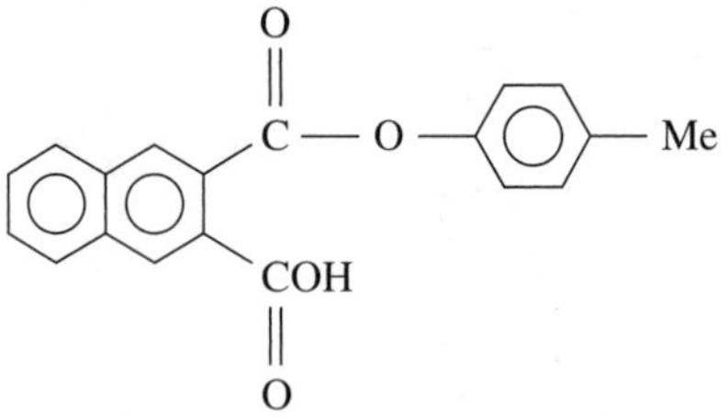

p-Tolyl hydrogenphthalate

(I)

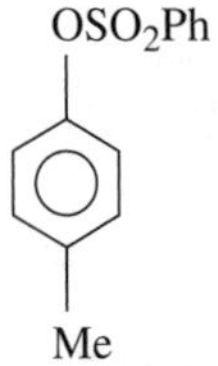

p-Tolyl benzenesulfonate

(J) No reaction.

(K) 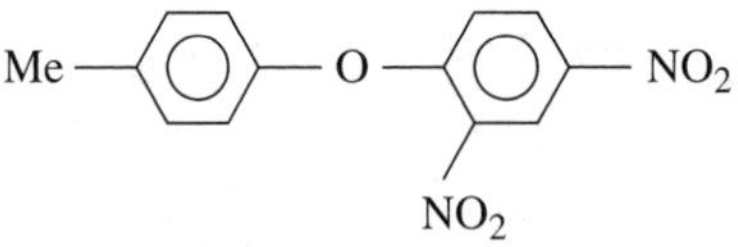 Me—⬡—O—⬡—NO_2
with NO_2

2,4-Dinitrophenyl p-tolyl ether

431. (A) $PhO^-Na^+ + O=C=O \xrightarrow[\text{6 atm}]{125°C} o\text{-}HOC_6H_4COO^-Na^+ \xrightarrow{H^+} o\text{-}HOC_6H_4COOH$

Sodium salicylate   Salicylic acid

(B) Acelylation of salicylic acid with acetic anhydride gives aspirin, acetylsalicylic acid, the most consumed and one of the most beneficial drugs.

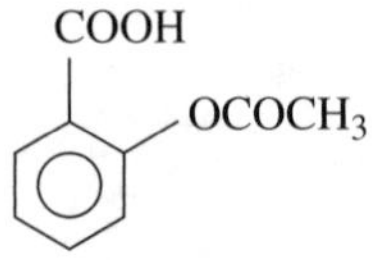

Aspirin

(C) CO_2 is a weak electrophile. Nevertheless, it is able to substitute on the strongly activated ring of PhO^- because there is some $+$ charge on C.

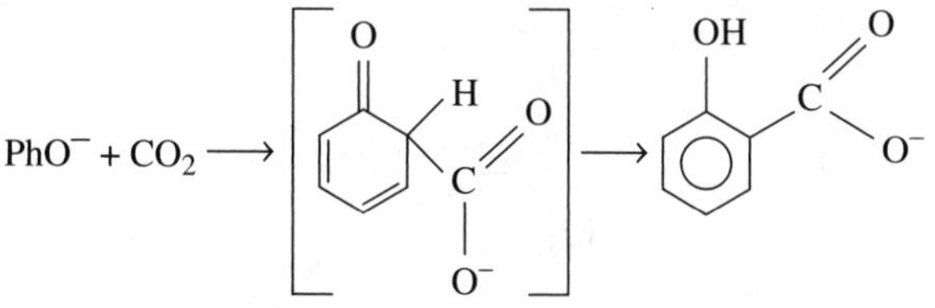

PhO$^-$ + CO$_2$ →

Intermediate   Salicylate anion

432. The allyl group migrates from O to the ring, preferably *ortho* but *para* if the *ortho* positions are blocked.

(A)

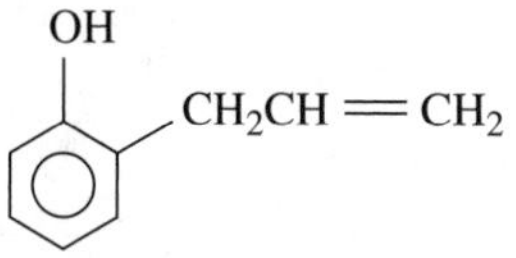

OH

CH$_2$CH $=$ CH$_2$

o-Allylphenol

(B)

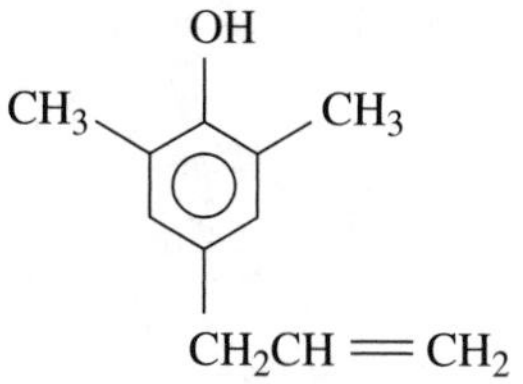

OH

CH$_3$ CH$_3$

CH$_2$CH $=$ CH$_2$

4-Allyl-2,6-dimethylphenol

433. (A)

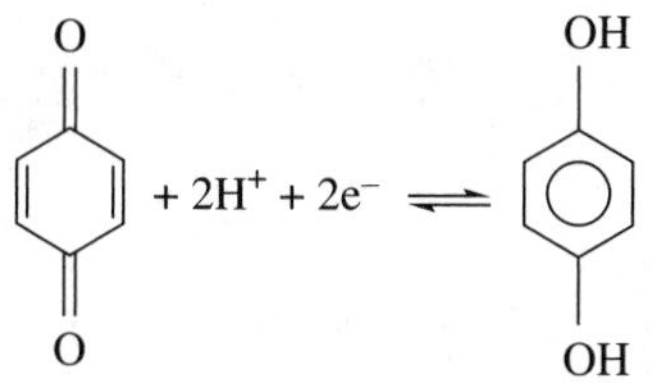

$+ 2H^+ + 2e^- \rightleftharpoons$

p-Quinone   Hydroquinone

This type of equilibrium is involved in several biochemical redox systems.

(B) $E°$ is the *voltage* of an electrochemical cell in which one compartment contains a 1 M solution of *p*-quinone, and the other an aqueous ethanolic solution of 1 M H$^+$, with a strip of platinum immersed in each solution as electrodes.

(C) The more positive the $E°$, the more the equilibrium shifts to the right, the more easily the quinone is reduced, and the less stable it is. Also the more positive the $E°$, the stronger the quinone is as an oxidizing agent.

(D) Hydroquinones are used in the film-developing step when they reduce the light-activated AgBr to Ag and Br⁻.

434. (A) PhH $\xrightarrow{2H_2SO_4}$

SO₃H

SO₃H

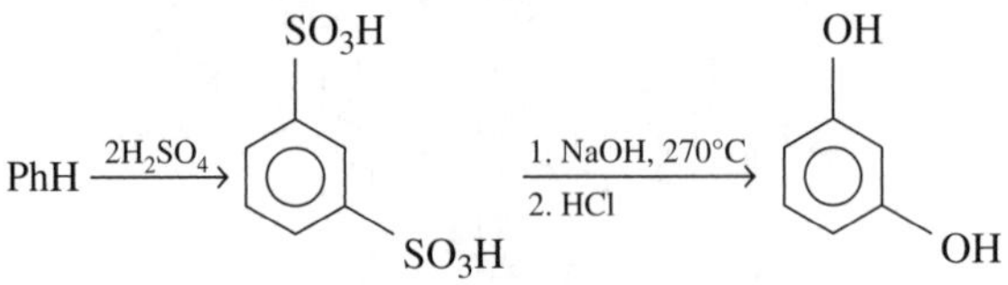

1,3-Benzenedisulfonic acid

$\xrightarrow[\text{2. HCl}]{\text{1. NaOH, 270°C}}$

OH

OH

Resorcinol

(B) C_6H_6 $\xrightarrow{HNO_3/H_2SO_4}$ $C_6H_5NO_2$ $\xrightarrow[\text{2. NaOH}]{\text{1. Sn/HCl}}$ $C_6H_5NH_2$ $\xrightarrow[\text{H}_2\text{SO}_4,\,10°\text{C}]{Na_2Cr_2O_7}$

O

O

p-Quinone

$\xrightarrow[\text{H}_2\text{O}]{SO_2}$

OH

OH

Hydroquinone

435. (A)

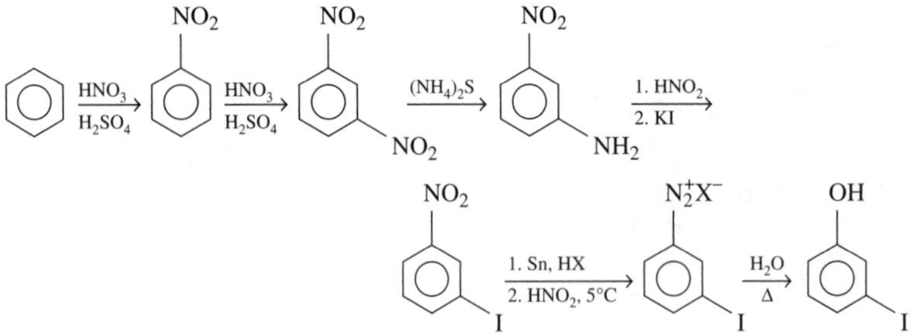

NO₂

$\xrightarrow[\text{H}_2\text{SO}_4]{HNO_3}$

NO₂

$\xrightarrow[\text{H}_2\text{SO}_4]{HNO_3}$

NO₂

NO₂

$\xrightarrow{(NH_4)_2S}$

NO₂

NH₂

$\xrightarrow[\text{2. KI}]{\text{1. HNO}_2}$

NO₂

I

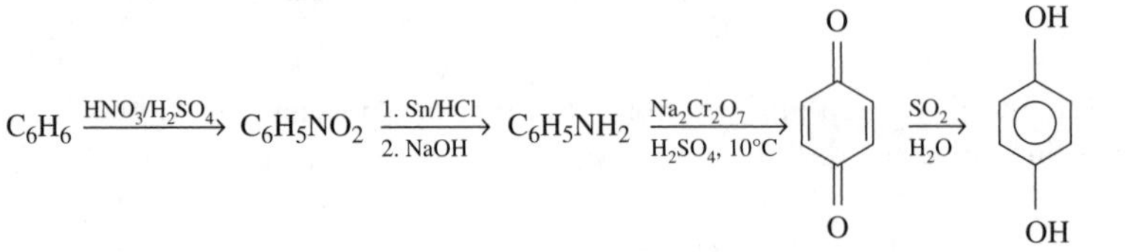

$\xrightarrow[\text{2. HNO}_2,\,5°\text{C}]{\text{1. Sn, HX}}$

N₂⁺X⁻

I

$\xrightarrow[\Delta]{\text{H}_2\text{O}}$

OH

I

m-Iodophenol

(B)

Me

$\xrightarrow[\text{H}_2\text{SO}_4]{HNO_3}$

Me

NO₂

$\xrightarrow[\text{Fe}]{Br_2}$

Me

Br

NO₂

$\xrightarrow[\text{2. HNO}_2,\,5°\text{C}]{\text{1. Sn, HX}}$

Me

Br

N₂⁺X⁻

$\xrightarrow[\Delta]{\text{H}_2\text{O}}$

Me

Br

OH

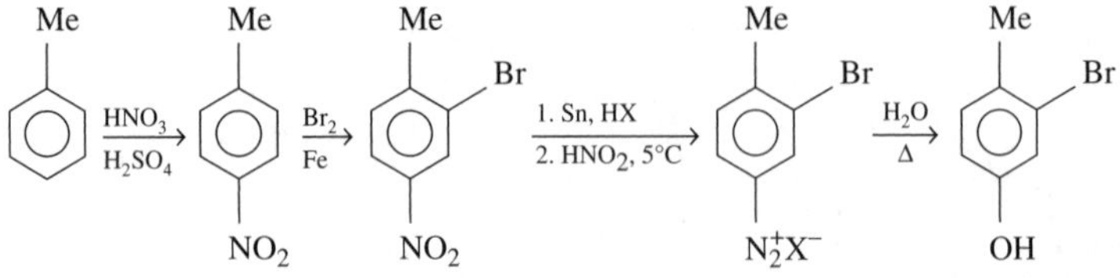

3-Bromo-4-methylphenol

(C)

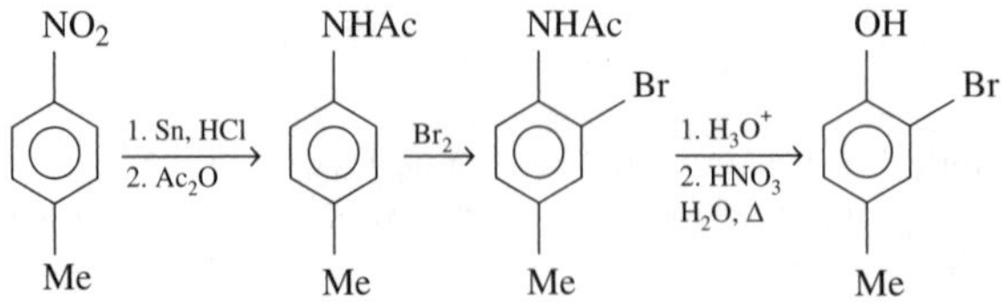

NO₂

Me

$\xrightarrow[\text{2. Ac}_2\text{O}]{\text{1. Sn, HCl}}$

NHAc

Me

$\xrightarrow{Br_2}$

NHAc

Br

Me

$\xrightarrow[\text{H}_2\text{O},\,\Delta]{\substack{\text{1. H}_3\text{O}^+ \\ \text{2. HNO}_3}}$

OH

Br

Me

2-Bromo-4-methylphenol

436. (A) I.

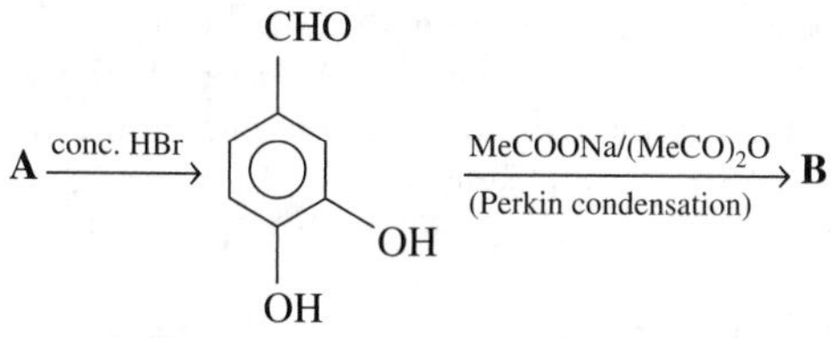

A $\xrightarrow{\text{conc. HBr}}$ [CHO, OH, OH benzene] $\xrightarrow[\text{(Perkin condensation)}]{\text{MeCOONa/(MeCO)}_2\text{O}}$ **B**

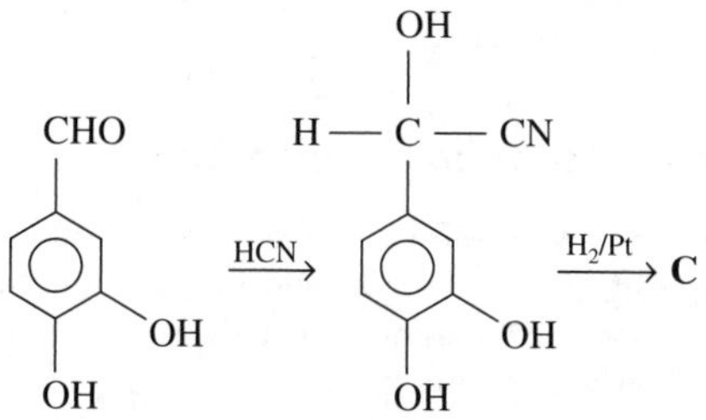

II.

[CHO, OH, OH benzene] $\xrightarrow{\text{HCN}}$ [benzene with CHO→H—C(OH)—CN, OH, OH] $\xrightarrow{\text{H}_2/\text{Pt}}$ **C**

(B) **D** $\xrightarrow[\text{2. HOAc}]{\text{1. O}_3,\ \text{Zn}}$ [CHO, OMe benzene] $\xrightarrow[\text{OH}^-]{\text{CH}_3\text{NO}_2}$ [CH=CHNO$_2$, OMe] $\xrightarrow{\text{H}_2/\text{Ni}}$ [CH$_2$CH$_2$NH$_2$, OMe] $\xrightarrow[\text{2. neutralize}]{\text{1. HI, }\Delta}$ **E**

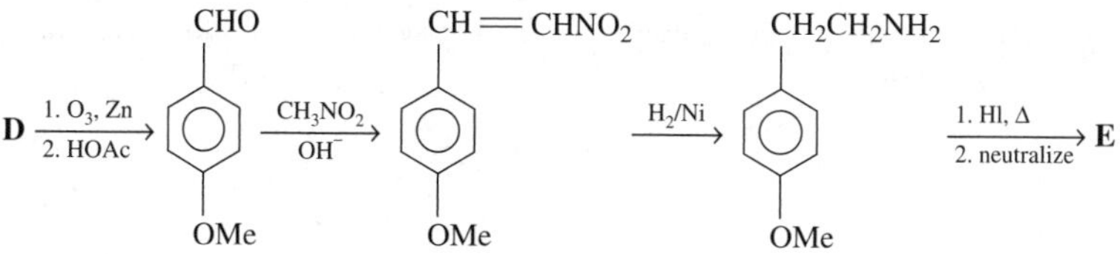

437. (A) $p\text{-NO}_2\text{C}_6\text{H}_4\text{OEt}$, A; $p\text{-EtOC}_6\text{H}_4\text{NH}_3^+\text{Cl}^-$, B; $p\text{-EtOC}_6\text{H}_4\text{N}_2^+\text{Cl}^-$, C; $p\text{-EtOC}_6\text{H}_4\text{—N=N—C}_6\text{H}_4\text{OH-}p$, D; $p\text{-EtOC}_6\text{H}_4\text{NH}_2$ (**E**) + $p\text{-H}_2\text{NC}_6\text{H}_4\text{OH}$ (**F**).

438. There are 6° of unsaturation, four of which are due to a benzene ring. Since **C** does not dissolve in NaOH or give a color with FeCl$_3$, it is not a phenol. Formation of H$_2$C=O on ozonolysis means that **C** has a chain with a terminal=CH$_2$ grouping, and since **D** is an aldehyde (positive Tollens' test), the grouping is —CH=CH$_2$. The double bond accounts for the fifth degree of unsaturation. **E** is a monocarboxylic acid formed by complete oxidation of the alkenyl side chain, and its molecular weight is 166. No other C can be directly attached to the ring because it would have oxidized, giving a dicarboxylic acid. The two remaining Os must be present as ether linkages probably present as a ring, the sixth degree of unsaturation, fused to the benzene ring. This is confirmed by isolating H$_2$C=O and 3,4-dihydroxybenzoic acid on cleavage with HI. This fused ring is actually a stable acetal. The molecular formula of **E** is C$_8$H$_6$O$_4$. The acetal ring and the benzene ring account for seven Cs, leaving three Cs for the alkenyl side chain. The structures for **C**, **D**, and **E** are:

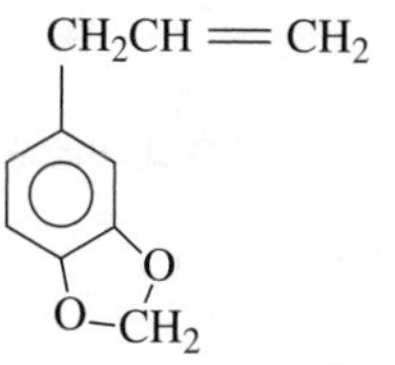

C 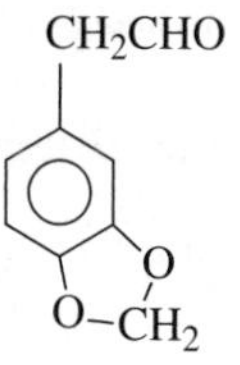   **D** 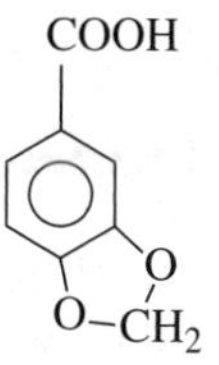   **E**

439. The level of acidity, the facile reaction with Br_2, the broad band at 3250 cm^{-1}, and the broad singlet at $\delta = 4.9$ ppm suggest a phenolic compound. The 4-H multiplet al 7.0 ppm, the dibromination (not tribromination), and the strong ir band at 750 cm^{-1} indicate an *ortho*-substituted phenol. The nine-H singlet at $\delta = 1.3$ ppm is typical of a *t*-butyl group, which accounts for the additional four Cs. **F** is *o*-HOC$_6$H$_4$C(CH$_3$)$_3$.

440. The strong electron-donating effect of OH makes the ring of PhOH very electron-rich, enabling it to readily donate electrons to oxidizing agents.

Chapter 21: Aromatic Heterocyclic Compounds

441. The struclural features are the same as for a carbocyclic compound: coplanarity of ring, each ring atom must have a *p* AO for cyclic overlap, and a Hückel number of electrons. There is one distinction from a carbocyclic compound: not all the electrons need come from π bonds, some may come from the unshared pair on the heteroatom.

442. The numbering system and use of Greek letters are shown for a general five-member ring and for pyridine:

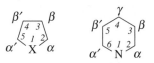

(I) 2,4-Dimethylfuran, α,β'-dimethylfuran. (II) 1-Ethyl-5-bromopyrrole-2-carboxylic acid, N-ethyl- α'-bromo-α-pyrrolecarboxylic acid. (III) 4-Methyl or -γ-methylpyridine. The methylpyridines are also commonly called *picolines* with Greek letters to indicate position of the Me—this one is γ-picoline. (IV) 3-Pyridinecarboxyamide, pyridine-β-carboxamide. The common name is nicotinamide, and the acid, commonly called *nicotinic acid*, is vitamin B$_3$, or niacin. (B) The suffix for six-member N-containing heterocycles is *-ine*. The name is 4-methylazine.

443. **(A)** This ring system is called benzofuran, and O is numbered 1. 3,4-Dimethylbenzofuran.
  (B) This is the quinoline ring system, with N numbered 1. 3,7-Dibromoquinoline.
  (C) In this isoquinoline ring system, N is numbered 2. 1,4-DimethylisoquinoIine.
  (D) The fused ring is an indole, and the N is number 1. Indole-2-carboxylic acid.

444. The heteroatom with no double bond is named first and assigned the number 1 position. The numbering proceeds so that other heteroatoms get the lowest possible numbers. Ring index nomenclature is given with common names in parentheses.
  (A) 4-Methyl-1,2-oxazole (4-methyloxazole since this ring is commonly called oxazole).
  (B) 4-Methyl-1,3-oxazole (4-methylisoxazole since this ring is commonly called isoxazole).
  (C) 2-Phenyl-1,3-diazole (2-phenylimidazole from the common name of this ring).
  (D) 1,2,4-Triazole.
  (E) 2,4-Dibromo-1,3-thiazole.

445. Ring index nomenclature is used with common names given in parentheses.

   (A) 1,4-Diazine (pyrazine).

   (B) 4H-1,4-Thiazine, where the 4H indicates that N with number 4 has an attached H.

   (C) 2,4-Dihydroxy-5-methyl-1,3-diazine . This name is seldom used. This is a *pyrimidine* ring, and the compound is 2,4-dihydroxy-5-methylpyrimidine, commonly called *thymine* in biochemistry.

   (D) 4-Amino-2-hydroxypyrimidine (called *cytosine* in biochemistry).

   (E) 2,4-Dihydroxypyrimidine (*uracil* to biochemists).

   (F) For eight-member rings the suffix *-ocine* is used: 1-thia-4-oxa-6-azocine. Note the numbering sequence of the three heteroatoms.

446. (A) Heat with sulfur at 560°C.

   (B) React the two compounds with Cu_2C_2 to get $HOH_2CC\equiv CCH_2OH$ which is then heated with NH_3 under pressure.

   (C) Corncobs (and other grain hulls) contain the polypentoside pentosan, $(C_5H_8O_4)_n$, which on being heated with HCl gives pentoses. These products then are dehydrated and cyclized to form furfural (2-furancarboxaldehyde). Furfural loses CO (decarbonylation) when heated with steam and metal oxide catalysts at 400°C and produces furan.

447. The carbonyl Cs become the α Cs in the heterocyclic compound.

(A) 2,3-Dimethylbutanedial → A dienediol → 3,4-Dimethylfuran

(B) Acetonylacetone → 2,5-Dimethylthiophene

(C) 3-Methyl-4-oxopentanal → 2,3-Dimethylpyrrole

448. This *Hantzsch pyridine synthesis* occurs as follows:

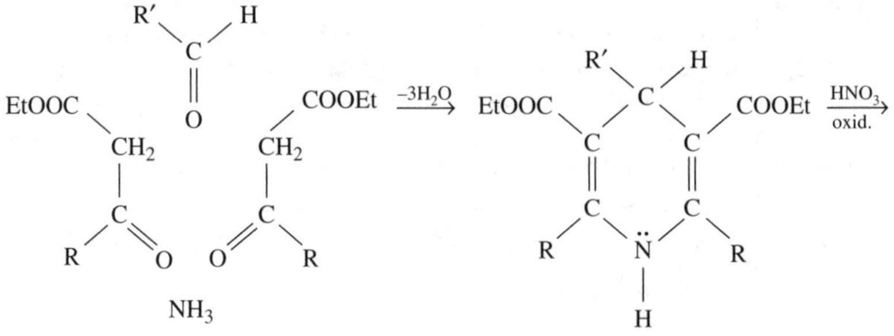

A 1,4-dihydropyridine

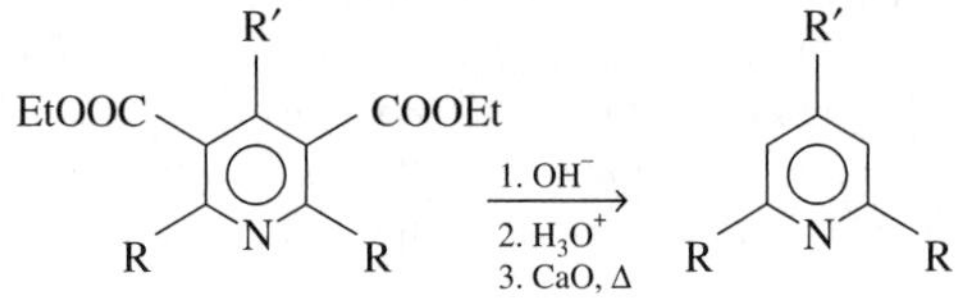

The product must have the same R groups at C^2 and C^6, and it may also have an R at C^4 that comes from the aldehyde.

449. We might expect $PhNH_2$ to be more basic because its N has sp^3 HOs while the N of pyridine has sp^2 HOs. However, in $PhNH_2$ there is considerable electron delocalization from N to the ring, providing much delocalization energy. This delocalization is destroyed when H^+ adds to the N, thereby decreasing the basicity of aniline.

450. (A) PyH, a Brönsted base, gives the salt pyridinium chloride, .

    (B) PyH, a nucleophile, reacts with BMe_3, a Lewis acid, to give C_5H_5N—BMe_3.
    (C) N-Methylpyridinium iodide, $C_5H_5NMe^+ I^-$, is formed by an S_N2 reaction.
    (D) $C_5H_5NH^+Cl^- + H_2C$=CMe_2. 3° Halides undergo E2 reactions instead of S_N2 reactions.

451. (A) (I) 2-Nitrofuran, (II) 2-acetylfuran.
    (B) (I) 2-Pyrrolesulfonic acid, (II) 2-pyrrolecarboxaldehyde (Reimer-Tiemann reaction), and (III) 2-phenylazopyrrole, — N = N — Ph.

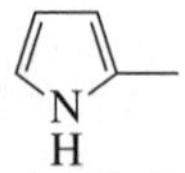

    (C) (I) Thiophene-2-sulfonic acid, (II) 2,5-dibromothiophene, and (III) 2-chlormethylthiophene.

Note that milder reagents suffice for electrophilic substitution of these heterocycles than for PhH.

452. E^+ attacks the more reactive benzene ring preferably at the α positions, giving about an equal mixture of 5- and 8-bromoquinoline.

453. The more reactive benzene ring is oxidized to quinolinic acid (2,3-pyridinedicarboxylic acid).

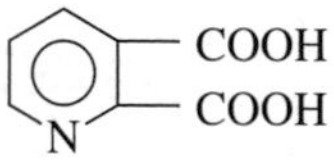

Quinolinic acid

454. The first step is an acylation of thiophene to give **A**, which undergoes a second acylation on the thiophene ring to give **B**.

(A)

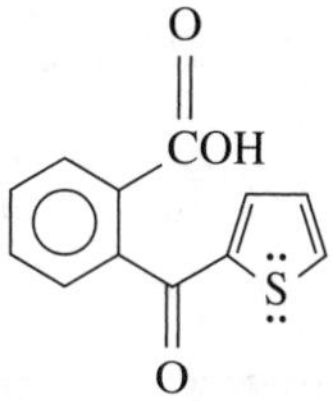

(B)

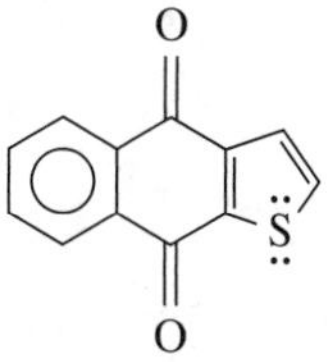

455. (A) Cannizzaro:

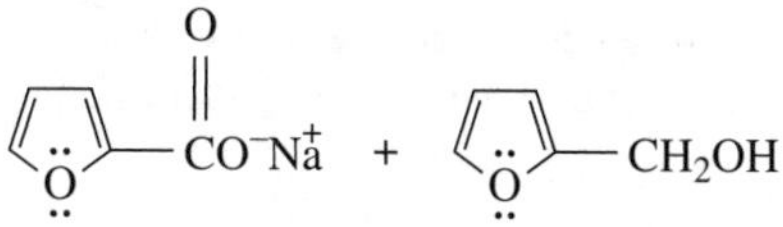

Sodium furoate   Furfuryl alcohol

(B) Crossed aldol:

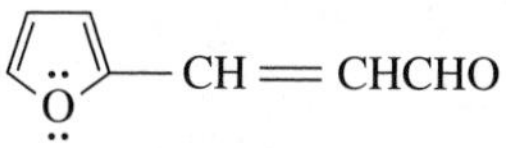

3-(2-Furyl)-propenal

(C) Perkin condensation:

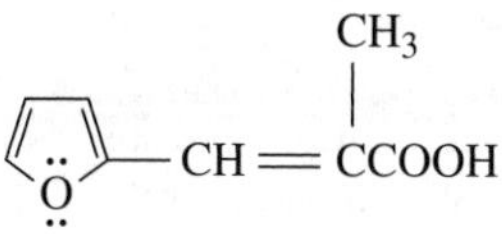

3-(2-Furyl)-2-methylpropenoic acid

(D) Crossed-aldol type:

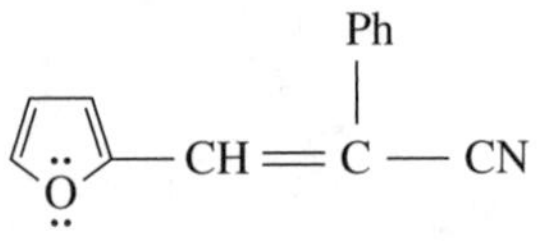

$$\text{(Furyl)}—CH\!=\!\underset{\underset{\displaystyle Ph}{|}}{C}—CN$$

3-(2-Furyl)-2-phenylpropenonitrile

(E) Crossed-aldol type:

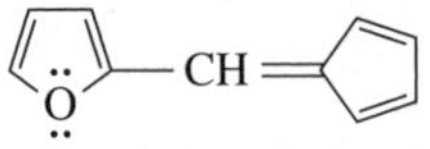

(Furyl)—CH=(cyclopentadiene)

2-Furylfulvene

456. Direct bromination of pyridine affords the 3-isomer, but bromination of pyridine-N-oxide gives the 4-isomer. The oxide is then reduced.

PyH $\xrightarrow{\text{PhCO}_3\text{H}}$ Py-N-oxide $\xrightarrow{\text{Br}_2}$ 4-bromopyridine-N-oxide $\xrightarrow[\text{2. OH}^-]{\text{1. Zn/HCl}}$ 4-Br-Py

457. (A)

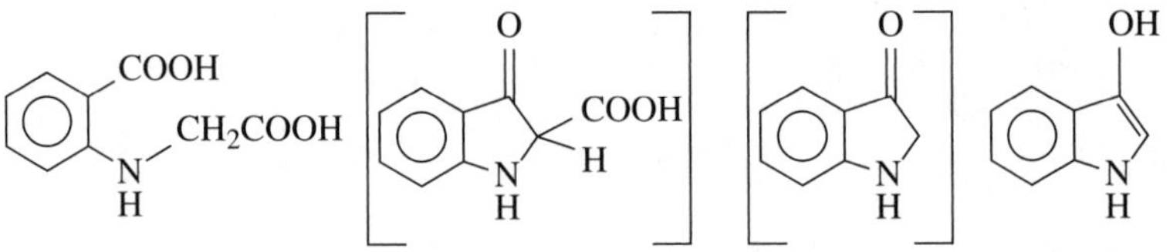

E   F   G   H

F is formed by a Dieckmann-type ring closure with carboxylic acids rather than esters.

(B) **I** is formed by a transamination, and **J** is formed by an intramolecular Claisen condensation.

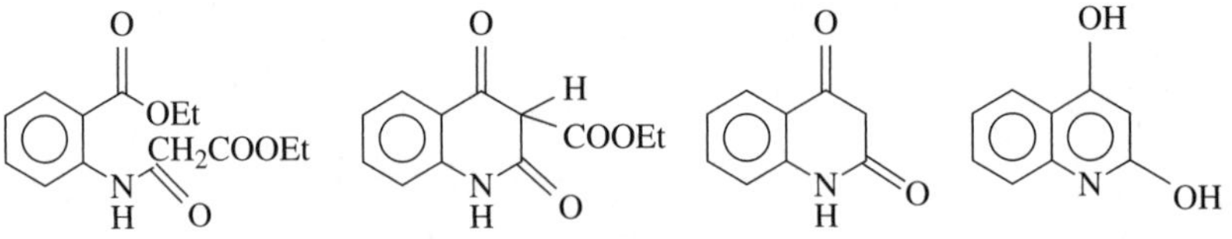

I   J   K   L

458. Piperidine and pyrrole have an N—H bond, absorbing at ≈3500 cm⁻¹, that pyridine lacks. They can be distinguished by the fact that the H—C$_{sp^3}$ stretch in piperidine appears below 3000 cm⁻¹ while in pyrrole the H—C$_{sp^2}$ stretch appears above 3000 cm⁻¹.

459. Compound **A** has 3° of unsaturation, and since it is acid-insoluble and possesses an N and no O, it is likely to be a substituted pyrrole. The additional two Cs are present as either two Mes or an Et. Compound **B** is the corresponding pyrrolidine which must be a 3° amine because it reacts with only 1 eq of MeI. Therefore, **A** is an N—Me or N—Et substituted pyrrole. Compound **D** is an unsaturated amine, which confirms the supposition that **B** is a cyclic amine. The butadiene portion of the final product comes from the four Cs of the pyrrole ring, and the presence of Me at C^2 of the chain means there is an Me on the β position of the pyrrole ring. Now we know A is an N—Me pyrrole. The structural formulas are:

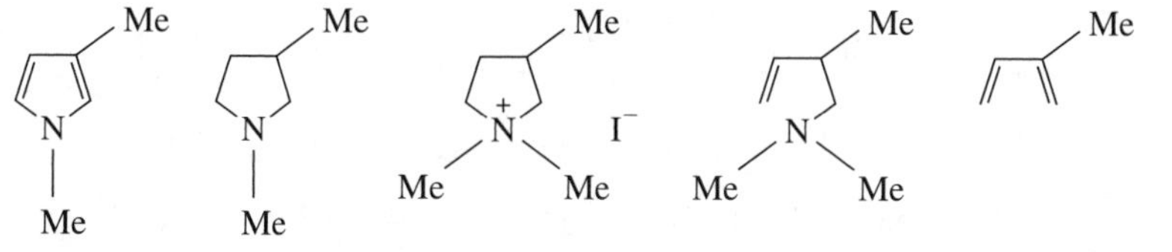

A   B   C   D   E

460. (A)

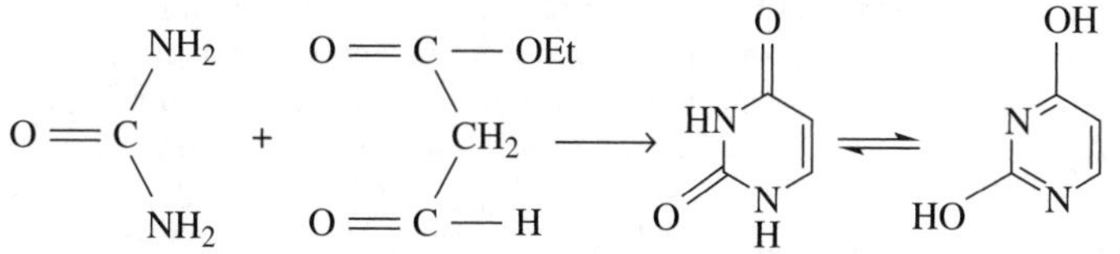

A, uracil

(B)

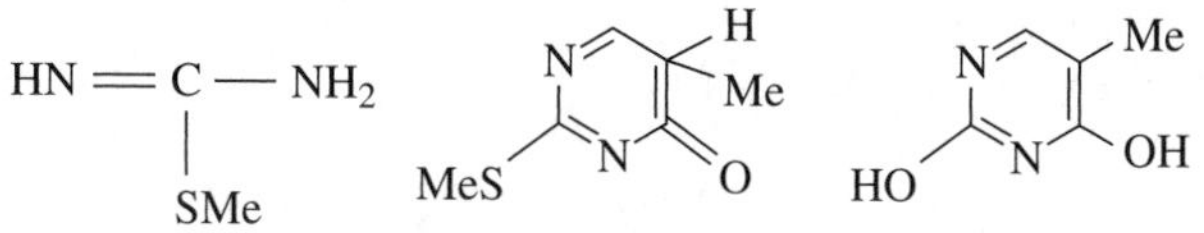

B   C   **D, thymine**

Chapter 22: Amino Acids, Peptides, and Proteins

461. (A) $RCH(\overset{+}{N}H_3)COO^-$. *α-Amino acids* are the units that comprise all *proteins*.

(B) Ten amino acids are *essential* in the diet because they cannot be synthesized in the body. *Nonessential* amino acids are synthesized by body cells from metabolites of ingested food.

462. (A) Glycine, $H_3\overset{+}{N}CH_2COO^-$

(B)

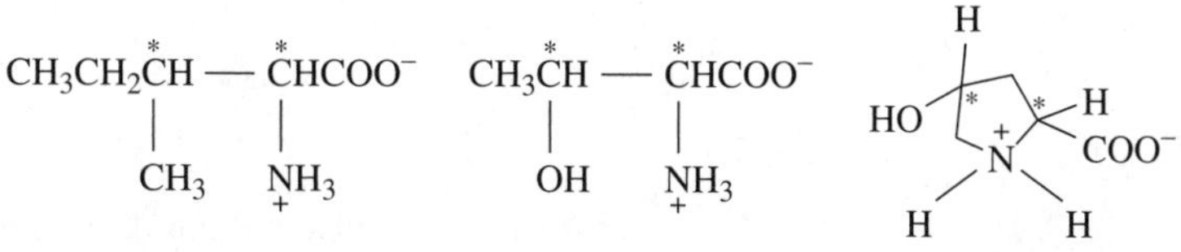

Isoleucine   Threonine   4-Hydroxyproline

Acting as a base   Acting as an acid

463. $OH^- + H_3\overset{+}{N}CHRCOOH \rightleftharpoons \boxed{H_3\overset{+}{N}CHRCOO^- + H_2O} \rightleftharpoons H_2NCHRCOO^- + H_2O^+$

Cation, A   Ampholyte, B   Anion, C

Net charge   (+1)   (0)   (−1)

464.

$$\underset{\text{Net charge }(+2)}{\overset{\text{COOH}}{\underset{\displaystyle (CH_2)_3}{\overset{\displaystyle CHNH_3^+}{\big|}}}} \underset{H^+}{\overset{OH^-}{\rightleftharpoons}} \underset{(+1)}{\overset{\text{COO}^-}{\underset{\displaystyle (CH_2)_3}{\overset{\displaystyle CHNH_3^+}{\big|}}}} \underset{H^+}{\overset{OH^-}{\rightleftharpoons}} \underset{(0)}{\overset{\text{COO}^-}{\underset{\displaystyle (CH_2)_3}{\overset{\displaystyle CHNH_2}{\big|}}}} \underset{H^+}{\overset{OH^-}{\rightleftharpoons}} \underset{(-1)}{\overset{\text{COO}^-}{\underset{\displaystyle (CH_2)_3}{\overset{\displaystyle CHNH_2}{\big|}}}}$$

With lower groups $CH_2NH_3^+$, $CH_2NH_3^+$, $CH_2NH_3^+$, CH_2NH_2.

465. If a filter paper-strip moistened with a solution of a mixture of AAs is placed between two electrodes, the charged molecule will migrate to one electrode or the other at a rate that depends on its net charge and the applied voltage. The net charge depends on the pH. The strip is then stained with a reagent that reacts with the AA, thereby forming a color whose position on the strip is compared for identification with that of a known sample.

466. (A) $Me_2CHCH_2COOH \xrightarrow{Br_2/P} Me_2CHCHBrCOOH \xrightarrow[NH_3]{\text{excess}} Val$

(B) $Me_2CH\overset{\displaystyle O}{\overset{\|}{C}}COOH \xrightarrow[H_2/Pt]{NH_3} Val$

(C)

$Me_2CHCH_2COOEt + Br_2/P$

467. Treatment of an aldehyde with NH_3 and CN^- produces an α-aminonitrile that is hydrolyzed to the α-amino acid.

$PhCH_2CHO \xrightarrow[NH_3]{CN^-} PhCH_2CH(NH_2)CN \xrightarrow[2.\,H_3O^+]{1.\,OH^-,\,\Delta} PhCH_2CH(\overset{+}{N}H_3)COO^- \text{ (Phe)}$

468. (A) $-\overset{\displaystyle O}{\overset{\|}{C}}-\overset{\displaystyle H}{\overset{|}{N}}-$, amide linkage

(B) A *peptide* is an amide formed by intermolecular reaction of the amino group of one AA and the carboxyl group of a second AA. Dipeptides are made from two AAs, tripeptides from three AAs, etc., which may be the same or different. If there are four to ten AA residues, the peptide is called an *oligopeptide*. A *polypeptide* is a chain made up of many AAs. The terms *peptide* and *polypeptide* are often used interchangeably. A *protein* consists of one or more polypeptide chains, and each chain can contain as much as several hundred AAs. The total number of residues may vary from 50 to over 1000.

(C) By convention, the amino acid with the free amino group (N-terminus) is written at the left end and the one with the unreacted carboxyl group (C-terminus) at the right end. The suffix -*ine* is replaced by -*yl* for each AA in the chain reading from left to right, followed by the full name of the C-terminal AA.

   (D) Tyrosylthreonyltryptophan. (Note that tryptophan is the only AA without a second COOH whose name does not end in "ine".)

469. (A) There are four dipeptides: Ala.Ala, alanylalanine; Ala.Gly, alanylglycine; Gly.Ala, glycylalanine; and Gly.Gly, glycylglycine.

   (B) $3 \times 3 \times 3 = 3^3 = 27$ tripeptides.

   (C) $3 \times 2 \times 1 = 3! = 6$ tripeptides.

   (D) $3^4 = 81$ tetrapeptides.

470. (A)

$$\overset{+}{N}H_3 \qquad O \qquad\qquad CHMe_2$$
$$Me - CH - C - NH - CH - COO^-$$
$$\text{N-terminal} \qquad \text{C-terminal}$$

   (B)

$$^{+}NH_3 \qquad O \qquad\qquad Me$$
$$Me_2CH - CH - C - NH - CH - COO^-$$
$$\text{N-terminal} \qquad\qquad \text{C-terminal}$$

471. First, the amino and carboxyl groups that are not to be linked in peptide bonds must be blocked so as to be unreactive. Then all other reactive functional groups in the Rs must also be protected, to prevent their participating in the coupling procedure. The coupling must be effected by a method that does not cause racemization or chemical alteration of the side chains. Finally, all protecting groups must be removed quantitatively by mild methods that do not cause rearrangements, racemization, or cleavage of the peptide bonds.

472. Peptides contain only one free α-NH_3^+ and one free α-COO^- at their termini. In addition, the R groups of some of the AA residues in the chain have substituents that contribute to the total acid-base behavior of the peptide. Thus, each peptide has a characteristic titration curve and an isoelectric pH. Peptides are separable by ion-exchange chromatography, electrophoresis, or a combination of both.

473. The AA sequence is Glu.Glu.Ala because carboxypeptidase liberates the C-terminal Ala. The N-terminal amino group is tied up with the adjacent Glu's carboxyl group in a lactam, making it unavailable for reaction with the Sanger reagent, and the other carboxyl group is part of an amide. The required structure is

$$CH_2CONH_2$$

474. The formation of **E** indicates that the N-terminus in **D** is Gly. Write the dipeptides with Gly first so that they overlap in a continuous way, Gly.Lys; L̶y̶s̶.Ala; A̶l̶a̶ . Val, giving the structure of **D** as Gly.Lys.Ala.Val. The terminal carboxyl is present as the amide (no reaction with carboxypeptidase). The formation of Arg.Try by cleavage of the carboxyl peptide bond of Try with chymotrypsin means that Try is bonded to Gly of **D**. **C** is Arg. Try.Gly.Lys.Ala.Val-amide.

475. (A) $RS—SR + 2HSCH_2CH_2OH(excess) \rightleftharpoons$

$2RSH + HOCH_2CH_2S—SCH_2CH_2OH$

(B) Any disulfide bonds in the protein are cleaved prior to determining the AA sequence. The large excess of mercaptoethanol is used to drive the equilibrium to the right.

476. (A) *Globular*, somewhat spherical, and *fibrous*, long fibers or planar sheets.
(B) Enzyme, transport, contractile, structural, hormones, antibodies, etc.

477. The *primary* structure is simply the AA sequence of the peptide chain. The *secondary* structure is a result of the different conformations that the chain can take. The *tertiary* structure is determined by any folding of the chain in on itself. A *quaternary* structure results when two or more peptide chains in some proteins are linked together by weak forces of attraction of their surface groups. Such proteins are called *oligomers* (dimers, trimers, etc.).

478. (A) The H-bonding between an N—H of one AA residue and the O=C of another properly situated AA residue.
(B) (I) The peptide sequence is coiled into a right-hand spiral in the α-*helix*, with the R groups positioned on the outside of the spiral. Each amide H—N bonds to the O=C on the next turn of the coil, four residues away by H-bonds, stabilizing this arrangement. (II) In the *pleated sheet* or β-structure, the peptide chains lie side by side in an open structure, with interchain amide H-bonding holding the chains together. *Parallel* pleated sheets have chains running in the same direction, all with their N-terminal residues starting at the same end. *Antiparallel* pleated sheets have their chains running in opposite directions. The α Cs rotate slightly out of the plane of the sheet to minimize repulsions between their bulky R groups, giving rise to the crimps or pleats. In both cases, the R groups alternate positions above and below the sheet. (III) The *random* coil structure has no repeating geometric pattern; encompassed within it are sequences in a helical conformation, a pleated sheet conformation, and regions that appear to have no discernable repeating structure, but are actually not random conformations.

479. The unique three-dimensional shape of a protein is the result of the intramolecular forces of attraction that cause bending and coiling in the helical coil. These forces are a function of the nature of the AA side chains within the molecule. *Globular* proteins have their nonpolar R groups pointing to the interior (the hydrophobic or nonaqueous region) and their polar side chains projecting toward the aqueous environment, somewhat like a micelle. They are somewhat water soluble. *Fibrous* proteins are insoluble in water.

Their polypeptide chains are held together by interchain H-bonds. The following are the attractive forces responsible for the tertiary structure:

(A) Ionic: bonding between COO^- and NN_3^+ at different sites

(B) H-bonding: mainly between side-chain NH_2 and COOH, also involving OHs (of serine, e.g.) and the N—H of tryptophane

(C) Weakly hydrophobic van der Waals attractive forces engendered by side-chain R groups

(D) Disulfide cross linkages between loops of the polypeptide chain

480. The same kind of attractive and repulsive forces responsible for the tertiary structure operate to hold together and stabilize the subunits of the quaternary structure.

Chapter 23: Carbohydrates

481. The general formula for a carbohydrate is $C_n(H_2O)_m$. This formula, with *carbo* for carbon and *hydrate* for H_2O, accounts for the name *carbohydrate*. For simple carbohydrates, $n = m$.

482. (A) Sugars.

(B) The suffix *-ose*. Ketonic sugars sometimes have the suffix *-ulose*.

483. (A) *Saccharide* is another name for carbohydrates and is used for their classification. It comes from the Latin name *saccharum* for sugar.

(B) A *monosaccharide* is a single simple sugar.

(C) A *dissacharide* is composed of two monosaccharide units.

(D) *Oligosaccharides* are composed of 3–10 monosaccharide units.

(E) Polysaccharides have more than 10 monosaccharide units.

484. The number of Cs in a chain is indicated by their prefixes, such as *-di-*, *-tri-*, etc.:

(A) Ketotetrose

(B) aldohexose

(C) deoxyaldopentose. *Deoxy* indicates the absence of an OH. More specifically, this is a 2-deoxyaldopintose where the number shows which C is devoid of OH

485. The relative number of atoms of C, H, and O in 100 g of glucose would be $40.0/12 = 3.33$, $6.7/1 = 6.7$, and $53.3/16 = 3.33$, respectively. Thus, C:H:O = 1:2:1; the empirical formula is CH_2O, and the empirical weight (ew) = 30. The molecular weight is determined from the freezing point depression data. Thus, 9.0 g of glucose in 100 g of H_2O is equivalent to 90 g in 1 kg of water. The molality and molecular weight of the solution are, respectively,

$$m = \frac{0.93°C}{1.86°C/mol} = 0.50 \text{ mol} \quad \text{and} \quad MW = \frac{90 \text{ g}}{0.50 \text{ mol}} = 180 \text{ g/mol}$$

The molecular formula is $(CH_2O)_n$, where $n = 180$ (MW)$/30$ (ew) = 6, or $(CH_2O)_6$. Glucose is $C_6H_{12}O_6$; it is a hexose.

486. (A) Since sugars are *polyhydroxy* compounds, the minimum number of OHs is two. Hence the simplest aldosugar is the triose, glyceraldehyde.

(B) Fischer arbitrarily wrote the D structure for the dextrorotatory enantiomer. Therefore D is (+), L is (−).

(C) D is R and L is S.

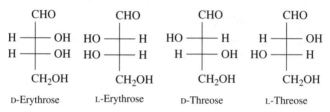

D (OH on right)   L (OH on left)

487. (A) Two chiral Cs: $HOCH_2C^*HOHC^*HOHCHO$.

 (B) The D sugar is arbitrarily written with the OH on the highest number stereocenter on the right side; the L sugar has this OH on the left side.

D-Erythrose L-Erythrose D-Threose L-Threose

488. Diastercoisomers with more than one stereocenter that differ in the configuration about only one stereocenter are called *epimers*. D-Threose and D-erythrose are epimers because their configuration about C^2 differs.

489. (A) These reagents all oxidize CHO to COOH or its salt in basic solutions.

 I. Both give a positive test, the formation of a shiny silver mirror, with $Ag(NH_3)_2^{2+}$. The ketosugar reacts because it rearranges to an aldosugar under the basic conditions.

 II. The reagent is the Cu^{2+} tartrate complex in NaOH. The discharge of the blue color of *Fehling*'s solution and the formation of a red precipitate of Cu_2O denote a positive test, given by both sugars.

 III. *Benedict*'s reagent is the Cu^{2+} citrate complex in NaOH, and a positive test is indicated by the same changes as with Fehling's solution. Again both sugars react.

 IV. Only the aldosugar reacts—a positive test is indicated by loss of the orange color of the aqueous Br_2 solution.

 (B) The product from both sugars, $HOCH_2CHOHCHOHCHOHCHOH$-COOH, is an example of an *aldonic (glyconic) acid*.

490. (A)

  D-Therose C^2 epimeric cyanohydrins

 (B) The C chain is increased by 1; this is a step-up reaction.

491. (A) **E** is an aldonic acid; **F** is its calcium salt, [HOCH$_2$CHOHCHOHCHO-HCHOHCOO$^-$]$_2$Ca^{2+}; **G** is an aldopentose, HOCH$_2$CHOHCHOHCHOHCHO.

    (B) A shortening of the carbon chain by one C.

    (C) This oxidative decarboxylation is called the *Ruff degradation.*

    (D) The α-CHOH is oxidized to —CH=O without any configuration changes of the other chiral Cs. No epimers are formed.

492. L-Gulose and D-glucose were oxidized to aldaric acid. Fischer concluded that D-glucose, written with CHO on top, and L-gulose, written with CHO on the bottom, have the same configuration about the chiral Cs. Since the structure of L-gulose was known, the structure of D-glucose was established, as well as its C^2 epimer, D-mannose.

493. No. Only enantiomers have this characteristic property, and anomers are not enantiomers.

494. α-L-(−)-Glucose. By definition, the α-anomer has the OH on the same side as the OH on the C that establishes the family designation.

495. For the ring to be stable and readily formed, it must have five or six atoms, one of which is an O. Hemiacetals with five-member rings are called *furanoses,* named after furan. Those with six-member rings are called *pyranoses,* named after pyran.

496. (A) The Haworth structure has a flat ring perpendicular to the plane of the paper. Twist C^6 of the Fischer projection [Figure A23-1(A)] behind the plane of the paper, and rotate the C^4—C^5 bond so that the C^{5}OH is close enough to the C=O to form a ring [Figure A23-1(B)]. This operation points the terminal CH$_2$OH *upward* for all D-sugars. Invariably the ring O projects away from the viewer, and the anomeric C is on the far right. As the result of this manipulation all groups on the left in a Fischer structure are up in [Figure A23-1(C)], and those on the right are down. See Figure A23-1. In the β-anomer, the anomeric OH is up.

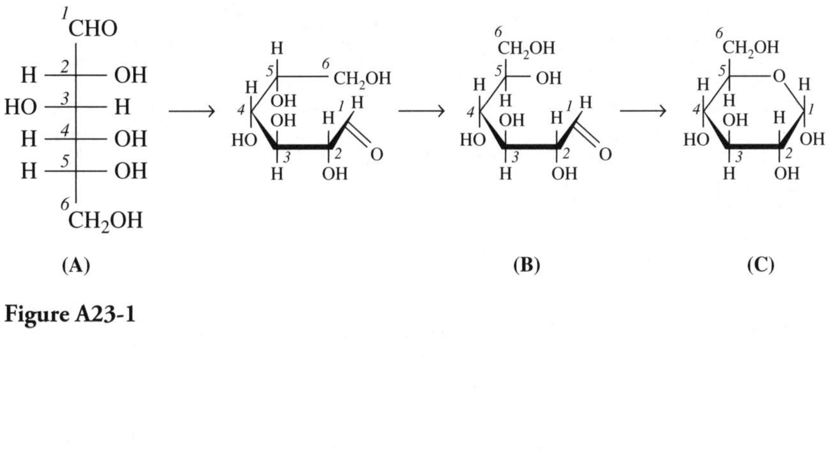

(A)   (B)   (C)

Figure A23-1

242 > Answers

497. Draw the C^6H_2OH group and the β-anomeric OH up, and work out the *cis-trans* relationships of the remaining groups as shown in Figure A23-2. The numbers are those in the keto form.

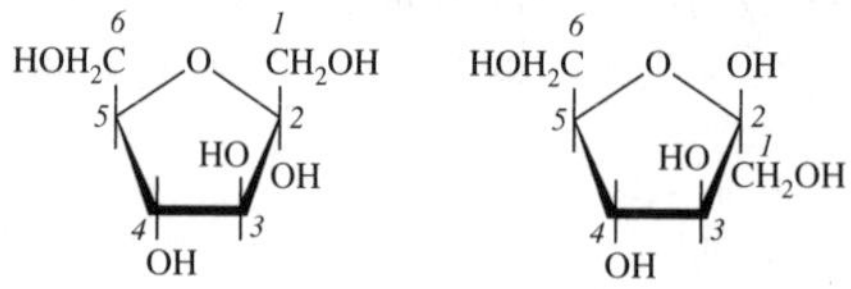

α-D-Fructofuranose   β-D-Fructofuranose

Figure A23-2

498. (A) A *disaccharide* is a glycoside in which the anomeric OH of one monosaccharide is bonded by an acetal linkage to an OH of a second monosaccharide, called the *aglycone*. The aglycone has a typical ether linkage.

(B) The aglycone is the end monosaccharide on the right.

499. (A) *Glycogen* is the reserve polysaccharide of animals whereas starch is the reserve for plants. Glycogen has a structure similar to amylopectin, except it has more cross-linking.

(B) *Cellulose*, the most abundant naturally occurring organic compound on earth, is the chief component of wood and plant fibers; cotton is nearly pure cellulose. Cellulose differs from starch in having β-1,4-glucosidic linkages and not α. The chains are mainly linear with little branching. Cellulose also has more glucose units, giving it a higher molecular weight.

500. (A) $\Pi = MRT$, where M is the molarity, R is the gas constant (0.082 L·atm/mol·K), and T is the absolute temperature.

$$M = \frac{\Pi}{RT} = \frac{5.0 \times 10^{-3}\ \text{atm}}{(0.082\ \text{L}\cdot\text{atm/mol}\cdot\text{K})(298\ \text{K})} = 2.0 \times 10^{-4}\ \text{mol/L}$$

and
$$MW = \frac{10.0\text{g/L}}{2.0 \times 10^{-4}\ \text{mol/L}} = 5.0 \times 10^4\ \text{g/mol}$$

(B) Each glucose unit (MW = 180 g/mol) bonds to the starch chain with loss of one H_2O unit (18 g/mol), giving an MW of 180 − 18 = 162 g/mol per unit. Thus, in this sample we have 5.0×10^4 g mol^{-1}/162 g mol^{-1} unit^{-1} = 309 units, or an approximate average of 300 glucose units.